ANECDOTES OF ENLIGHTENMENT

ANECDOTES OF ENLIGHTENMENT
Human Nature from Locke to Wordsworth

JAMES ROBERT WOOD

University of Virginia Press
Charlottesville and London

University of Virginia Press
© 2019 by the Rector and Visitors of the University of Virginia
All rights reserved
Printed in the United States of America on acid-free paper

First published 2019

1 3 5 7 9 8 6 4 2

Library of Congress Cataloging-in-Publication Data

Names: Wood, James Robert, 1980– author.
Title: Anecdotes of Enlightenment : human nature from
Locke to Wordsworth / James Robert Wood.
Other titles: Anecdote and enlightenment, 1700–1800
Description: Charlottesville : University of Virginia Press, 2019. |
Includes bibliographical references and index.
Identifiers: LCCN 2019004599 | ISBN 9780813942209 (cloth : alk. paper) |
ISBN 9780813942216 (ebk.)
Subjects: LCSH: Anecdotes—History and criticism. | European literature—
18th century—History and criticism. | Enlightenment. | Europe—Intellectual life—
18th century. | Europe—Civilization—18th century.
Classification: LCC PN165 .W66 2019 | DDC 809/.982—dc23
LC record available at https://lccn.loc.gov/2019004599

Cover art: Unknown artist, silhouette of David Garrick and William Hogarth from
Samuel Ireland's *Graphic Illustrations of Hogarth* (1794–99).

To Ema

For look where e're the glittering Sun-beams come,
Thro a small chink into a darkned room,
A thousand little *bodies* strait appear
In the small beam of light, and wander there;
For ever fight, reject all shews of peace;
Now meet, now part again, and never cease.
Whence we may estimate how *Atoms* strove
Thro the vast *empty Space,* and how they move:
Such knowledge from mean Images we get,
And easily from small things rise to great.

—Lucretius, *Of the Nature of Things,*
translated by Thomas Creech (1682)

Contents

Acknowledgments

Many people have made their mark on this book. When this book was a Stanford dissertation, John Bender helped me keep the core arguments of the project in view whenever my pursuit of eighteenth-century anecdotes threatened to take me too far into the undergrowth. Terry Castle has been an enthusiastic supporter from the beginning and imbued the project with her sense of intellectual fun. Denise Gigante was a close and canny reader of the dissertation from which this book emerged, and the ideas behind the book first took shape in her graduate seminars. Dan Edelstein, Roland Greene, Annette Keogh, Saikat Majumdar, Sianne Ngai, Jessica Riskin, Blakey Vermeule, and Alex Woloch were all important mentors at this time. Fellow grad students Andrew Bricker, Christopher Donaldson, Steffi Dippold, Heidi Hayoung Lee, Jillian Hess, Hannah Hudson, Stephen Osadetz, Natalie M. Phillips, Jenna Sutton, and Claude Willan helped shape the book in its early stages. Matthew Garrett, Jesse Molesworth, Brad Pasanek, Miruna Stanica, and Robin Valenza were important interlocutors and inspirations. The Stanford Humanities Center supported me with a Geballe Fellowship. I was fortunate to discuss my ideas there with Harris Feinsod, Lori Flores, Heather Love, Giorgio Riello, and Karen Sanchez-Eppler.

I've since benefited from conversations with many people in the wider community of eighteenth-century studies, including Rebecca Anne Barr, Jennie Batchelor, Michael Brown, Daniel Carey, Daniel Cook, Eugenia Zuroski Jenkins, Jonathan Kramnick, Jonathan Lamb, Ramesh Mallipeddi, David Mazella, Clíona Ó Gallchoir, David O'Shaughnessy, Adam Potkay, Manushag N. Powell, Amy Prendergast, David Simpson, Sarah Tindal Kareem, Kate E. Tunstall, and James Ward. Special thanks go to Aileen Douglas for supervising my postdoctoral work at Trinity College Dublin. Thanks also to Katherine Baxter and Amit Yahav for their invitations to present work in progress and to April London for including me on a panel on the anecdote at ASECS.

At the University of East Anglia, Alexander Freer, Peter Kitson, Claire Jowitt, Thomas Karshan, Thomas Roebuck, and Matthew Taunton took time from their busy schedules to read and comment on work in progress. Peter Womack and Alison Donnell supported me as an early career researcher, and Rebecca Pinner and Bharat Tandon kept me going with their friendship.

Linda Hardy started me on the road to researching and teaching literature for a living at Victoria University of Wellington, New Zealand. Dougal McNeill and Philip Steer, now both fellow academics, remain friends from that time. Another Kiwi friend, Rowan McCaffery, generously gave me a crash course in set theory.

Jenny Davidson and the University of Virginia Press's anonymous reader were generous in their assessment of the book and incisive in pointing out how it could be better. Angie Hogan at the University of Virginia Press saw something in the book, even when it was a very wooly manuscript, and expertly shepherded it through to publication. Thanks also to Jane Curran for her careful copyediting of the manuscript.

Parts of chapter 1 appeared in very early form in "Mr. Spectator's Anecdotes and the Science of Human Nature" in *Eighteenth-Century Life*, 38, no. 1 (2014), 63–92. Parts of chapter 3 also appeared in "Four Ways of Telling Anecdotes about the *Endeavour*," in *Scénographie du voyage et imaginaire viatique,* edited by Isabelle Bour and Line Cottegnies (Paris: Hermann, 2018), 151–68. My thanks to the editors for allowing me to draw on this previously published material here. I would also like to acknowledge the assistance of the special collections librarians at the Beineke Library, the British Library, the Houghton Library, and the Royal Irish Academy for their help with manuscripts in their collections. Special thanks go to Justine Mann at the University of East Anglia and Kim Downie at the University of Aberdeen, who took photographs of rare books in their collections and gave me permission to use them in this book.

My family in New Zealand have kept me grounded in my travels around the world. Grimalkin and Tikka provided much feline affection during the writing of this book. I give my deepest thanks and love to Ema Vyroubalová, my partner in life and letters. This book is dedicated to her.

Abbreviations

B   Joseph Banks, *The Endeavour Journal of Joseph Banks, 1768–1771,* edited by J. C. Beaglehole, 2nd ed., 2 vols. (Sydney: Angus & Robertson, 1963); cited by volume and page number

BL   Samuel Taylor Coleridge, *Biographia Literaria,* edited by James Engell and W. Jackson Bate (Princeton: Princeton University Press, 1983); cited by volume and page number

C   James Cook, *Journal of the Voyage of the* Endeavour, *1768–71,* edited by J. C. Beaglehole (Cambridge: Hakluyt Society and Cambridge University Press, 1955); cited by page number

CPM   Thomas Beddoes, *Contributions to Physical and Medical Knowledge, Principally from the West of England* (Bristol, 1799); cited by page number. Because the pagination for this book restarts from "1" after the introduction, I have identified all references to the introduction using the abbreviation "Intro."

EH   Eliza Haywood, *Selected Works of Eliza Haywood,* edited by Alexander Pettit et al., 6 vols. (London: Pickering & Chatto, 2000); cited by set, volume, and page number

EHU   David Hume, *An Enquiry Concerning Human Understanding: A Critical Edition,* edited by Tom L. Beauchamp (Oxford: Oxford University Press, 2000); cited by page number

EMPL   David Hume, *Essays Moral, Political, and Literary,* edited by Eugene F. Miller, rev. ed. (Indianapolis: Liberty Classics, 1994); cited by page number

EPM   David Hume, *An Enquiry Concerning the Principles of Morals,* edited by Tom L. Beauchamp (Oxford: Oxford University Press, 2006); cited by page number

H	John Hawkesworth, *An Account of the Voyages Undertaken by the Order of his Present Majesty for making Discoveries in the Southern Hemisphere, and successively performed by Commodore Byron, Captain Wallis, Captain Cartertet, and Captain Cook, in the Dolphin, the Swallow, and the Endeavour,* 3 vols. (London, 1773); cited by volume and page number
HE	David Hume, *The History of England from the Invasion of Julius Caesar to the Revolution in 1688,* edited by William B. Todd, 6 vols. (Indianapolis: Liberty Classics, 1983); cited by volume and page number
J	James Boswell, *Boswell's Journal of a Tour to the Hebrides with Samuel Johnson, LL.D., 1773,* edited by Frederick A. Pottle and Charles H. Bennett (Melbourne: William Heinemann, 1963); cited by page number
L	John Locke, *An Essay Concerning Human Understanding,* edited by Peter H. Nidditch (Oxford: Clarendon Press, 1975); cited by page number
LB	William Wordsworth, *Lyrical Ballads, and Other Poems, 1797–1800,* edited by James Butler and Karen Green (Ithaca, NY: Cornell University Press, 1992); cited by line number or page number as specified in the parenthetical reference
LDH	David Hume, *The Letters of David Hume,* edited by J. Y. T. Greig, 2 vols. (Oxford: Clarendon Press, 1932); cited by volume and page number
LS	Laurence Sterne, *The Florida Edition of the Works of Laurence Sterne,* edited by W. G. Day, Joan New, Melvyn New, and Peter de Voogd, 8 vols. (Gainesville: University Press of Florida, 1978–2008); cited by volume and page number
M	Charles de Secondat Montesquieu, *The Spirit of the Laws,* edited by Anne M. Cohler, Basia, Carolyn Miller, and Harold Samuel Stone (Cambridge: Cambridge University Press, 1989); cited by page number
NHR	David Hume, *A Dissertation on the Passions; The Natural History of Religion,* edited by Tom L. Beauchamp (Oxford: Oxford University Press, 2007); cited by page number
PW	William Wordsworth, *The Prose Works of William Wordsworth,* edited by W. J. B. Owen and Jane Worthington Smyser, 2nd ed., 3 vols. (Oxford: Clarendon Press, 1974); cited by volume and page number

S   Joseph Addison and Richard Steele, *The Spectator*, edited by Donald F. Bond, 5 vols. (Oxford: Oxford University Press, 1965); cited by volume and page number

T   David Hume, *A Treatise of Human Nature*, edited by David Fate Norton and Mary J. Norton, 2 vols. (Oxford: Oxford University Press, 2007); citations are to the first volume and given by page number

V   Voltaire, François-Marie Arouet de. *Œuvres complètes de Voltaire*, edited by Theodore Besterman et al. (Oxford: Voltaire Foundation, 1968–); cited by volume and page number

Z   Erasmus Darwin, *Zoonomia; or, the Laws of Organic Life*, 2 vols. (London, 1794–96); citations are given by volume and page number.

ANECDOTES OF ENLIGHTENMENT

Introduction

On Wednesday April 15, 1747, an anecdote appeared in London's *General Advertiser* concerning a New England woman by the name of Polly Baker. As the story went, Baker had been brought before a court of law "at *Connecticut* near *Boston*" and accused of having given birth to a child out of wedlock.[1] She had already been punished four times for this offence, twice with fines and twice with whippings. At this particular arraignment, however, Baker not only convinced the court not to impose any penalty on her, she also persuaded one of her judges to marry her the following day. She accomplished all this with a speech in which she argued that she had served the colony's interests by increasing its population, pointed out the injustice of making women shoulder all the legal consequences for giving birth to bastard children, and declared that, in conceiving her children and bringing them into the world, she had simply been observing "the Duty of the first and great Command of Nature, and of Nature's God, *Encrease and Multiply.*"[2] Baker concluded her speech by announcing that instead of being given yet another whipping, she ought to have a statue erected to memorialize her name for posterity. Although the article makes no mention of any monument being made, Baker would achieve a kind of immortality through the anecdotes about her that soon began to increase and multiply on both sides of the Atlantic.[3] Within days of its first publication, the Polly Baker anecdote began to appear in newspapers in the English provinces and, after a week, in Ireland and Scotland as well. A few months later, news of Polly Baker had reached British America, where one of several newspapers to print the story of her speech was the *Boston Weekly Post-Boy*, which featured the anecdote as its lead article for Monday, July 20, 1747.[4] Polly Baker had come full circle.[5]

The Polly Baker story subsequently became one of eighteenth century's most widely circulated anecdotes. An anonymous "A. Z." contributed the anecdote to the April 1774 number of the *Covent-Garden Magazine; or, Amorous Repository*, where it appeared among the journal's other titillating stories.[6] Polly Baker is included in the *Eccentric Biography; or, Memoirs of Remarkable Female Characters, Ancient and Modern* (1803), a compendium of women "remarkable for some extraordinary deviation from the generality of the sex."[7] The tale of Polly Baker was told in more elevated contexts as well. The English deist Peter Annet (under the pseudonym "Gideon Archer") footnoted the anecdote with his own remarks in his serious-minded *Social Bliss Considered: In Marriage and Divorce; Cohabiting Unmarried, and Public Whoring* (1749), using Polly Baker's speech to bolster his own arguments for the morality of unmarried couples living under the same roof. In the first footnote, Annet acknowledges that the truth of the story may well be suspect, but contends that Baker's reasoning is sound whether or not the anecdote concerning her is true, remarking further that there are many people who "cannot credit the truth of a story that has nothing improbable in it; but can credit stories reported by a credulous people to be done in distant ages, and in a strange country, which are impossible to nature."[8] Annet implies that believing in the story of Polly Baker's speech is much more reasonable than believing in the biblical stories of miracles. By contrast to Annet, Guillaume-Thomas-François Raynal presented the anecdote as an established fact in his *Histoire philosophique et politique des établissements et du commerce des Européens dans les deux Indes* (1770–74), where it serves to illustrate the harshness of Puritan New England's laws governing sexual mores.[9] The anecdote is used more playfully in one of the manuscript versions of Denis Diderot's *Supplément au voyage de Bougainville* (first drafted in 1772), in which the story is told by a figure designated as "B," in the midst of a discussion with "A," on the question of whether sexual modesty is learned or innate. The first response "A" has, on hearing the story, is to question its veracity, asking "B," "Isn't this a tale you've just fabricated?"[10]

One piece of evidence that the anecdote of Polly Baker was indeed a fabrication, contrived by none other than Benjamin Franklin, is another anecdote told by Thomas Jefferson in an 1818 letter to Robert Walsh. According to Jefferson, Franklin was at his estate at Passy near Paris in the midst of a conversation on the "numerous errors" in Raynal's *Histoire philosophique et politique* with the American diplomat Silas Deane, when Raynal himself unexpectedly walked in. After Deane had informed Raynal what he and Franklin had just been talking about, Raynal declared that he had taken care not to "insert a single fact" into his history "for which I had not the most unquestionable authority." When Deane brought up the story of Polly Baker, Raynal claimed the story was indeed true, although he admitted that he could not remember where he had found it. At this point, Jefferson writes, "Doctor Franklin who had been for some time shaking with restrained laughter at the Abbe's confidence in his authority for that tale, said, 'I will tell you, Abbe, the origin of that story. When I was a printer and editor of a newspaper, we were sometimes slack of news, and to amuse our customers, I used to fill up our vacant columns with anecdotes, and fables, and fancies of my own, and this of Polly Baker is a story of my making, on one of those occasions.'" To which Raynal replied, "Oh, very well Doctor, I had rather relate your stories than other men's truths."[11] Whether or not Jefferson's anecdote about the Polly Baker anecdote is itself to be believed, what is not in doubt is Polly Baker's ability to adapt herself to wildly different contexts: a book criticizing conventional sexual mores, an anthology of eccentric women, a history of European colonialism, and a racy periodical. The Polly Baker anecdote was not unique in either its viral communicability or its capacity to spark off debate on what or was not natural to human beings. Countless anecdotes animated the Enlightenment. This is a book about them.

Anecdotes of Enlightenment centers on the British Enlightenment, tracing a tradition of thinking with anecdotes from the late seventeenth century up to the early nineteenth century. The Enlightenment culture of the anecdote was not, of course, unique to Britain.[12] Other books could easily be written exploring anecdotes in other national contexts. I have chosen to focus on the British Enlightenment simply because it is the one that I know best. But even to concentrate on the British Enlightenment is to encounter many peripatetic stories that traversed linguistic and national boundaries and helped connect the British Enlightenment to the Enlightenment as a whole. Whether they came from near or afar, anecdotes prompted philosophers, essayists, travel writers, and poets to rethink what they believed they knew about human nature. Writers were drawn to anecdotes of people (and occasionally animals) who seemed to differ markedly from themselves: tales of hunchbacks and housekeepers, polytheists and parrots, savages and slaves. Anecdotes opened paths leading out to the perceived peripheries of the human world. But anecdotes also tended to unsettle conventional notions of what was central and what was peripheral in human life, frequently pointing thinkers toward the conclusion that both the norm and the exception obey the very same set of laws.

The Polly Baker story illustrates how anecdotes in general could allow the abstract laws of human nature to acquire narrative form. Indeed, the story's true protagonist might be said to be what Baker calls "the first and great Command of Nature, and of Nature's God, *Encrease and Multiply*"— a phrase that equates God's injunction to Adam and Eve (and later to Noah) in Genesis to fill the world with people with the law of nature directing all living things to propagate themselves. In the anecdote, the "first and great Command of Nature, and of Nature's God" ends up triumphing over the New England law forbidding sex out of marriage.[13] One reason that writers kept coming back to the anecdote of Polly Baker was that her singular story lent itself to thinking about the nature of sexual desire in general. The anecdotes that entered into Enlightenment writings on the human similarly identified and dramatized larger problems for the study of human nature. They told of isolated instances of human (or human-like) behavior that deviated from tacit norms. For many Enlightenment writers, the process of reconciling anecdotal anomalies promised to illuminate much more fundamental laws than those on the law books: the laws of human nature itself.

In practice, however, anecdotes signally failed to establish clear and uncontestable laws behind the diversity of human experience, for the tendency of anecdotes was to provoke debate on the nature of human nature rather than to close it down. Commentators on the Polly Baker anecdote, for example, did not agree on exactly what it was that the anecdote implied about the nature of sexual desire and its relation to existing social arrangements. Annet used the story to argue that many of the legal restrictions placed on sexual behavior on both sides of the Atlantic were unjust. But the anonymous writer of the "Interesting Reflections on the Life of Miss Polly Baker" (1794), while conceding that "To instruct mankind in the art of extirpating those passions planted in us for the wisest and most benevolent purposes, would be like teaching them to arrest the circulation of the blood," nevertheless recommended that "proper channels, and legal gratification" ought to be provided to contain and direct the "torrent, to which we owe the most the blissful moments of our life."[14] These interpreters of the Polly Baker anecdote made Baker, the harlot who claims the right to judge her own case, subject once again to judgment. Annet uses the Polly Baker story to argue that many laws and conventions governing the expression of human sexuality are unjustified impositions on natural desires. But the anonymous author of "Interesting Reflections on the Life of Miss Polly Baker" gives the same laws a necessary part to play in channeling these desires. Where Annet sees the Polly Baker anecdote as a clarion call to rethink conventional morality, the writer of the "Interesting Reflections" sees it as a comic fable showing up the absurdity of allowing women to pursue their desires without regard for law or convention. Neither writer can have the final word. What André Jolles says in *Simple Forms* (1929) about the genre of the "case"— a narrative that poses a problem for deciding how some law or other is to be applied—could also be said of the anecdote's function in Enlightenment writing on the human. In these writings, the anecdote "asks the question, but cannot give the answer." In the anecdote, as in the "case," it is the "swaying and swinging of the mental disposition of weighing and judging" that "becomes manifest in the form" and not the law itself.[15] This is why different commentators could discover very different principles of human nature at work in the same anecdote. Anecdotes like the story of Polly Baker did not serve to establish universal laws of human nature. To borrow a phrase from Jacques Derrida, the anecdote obeys "a law of singularity which must come into contact with the general or universal essence of the law without ever being able to do so."[16] Instead of fixing laws of human nature for once and for all, anecdotes provided Enlightenment writers points of departure from which to embark on the quest to discover these laws. They did so by posing the problem of how singular occurrences might be accounted for in universal terms.

Anecdotes are characterized by *singleness* and *singularity*. The *Oxford English Dictionary* captures these two essential features of the anecdote in its definition of the genre as "The narrative of a detached incident, or of a single event, told as being in itself interesting or striking."[17] Anecdotes are short narratives of events singled out as worthy to be told because they are singular, swerving in one way or another from the usual order of things.[18] As Novalis wrote in one of his notebooks in the final years of the eighteenth century, "A large class of anecdotes are those which show a human trait in a strange, striking way, for example, cunning, magnanimity, bravery, inconstancy, bizarrerie, cruelty, wit, imagination, benevolence, morality, love, friendship, wisdom, narrow-mindedness etc." Anecdotes furnish what Novalis describes as "a gallery of many kinds of human actions, an anatomy of humanity," which supplies "the study of man" with cases on which to work.[19] As he was writing down these thoughts on the anecdote as a genre, Novalis could look back on the eighteenth century as an age in which anecdotes had served as indispensable aids to the study of humankind.

Anecdotes served as touchstones in Enlightenment writing on human nature despite their known unreliability as accounts of actual happenings. The anecdote's tenuous and yet tenacious claim to historical reference is one quality that distinguishes it from the novel, which began to display a more manifest and open fictionality as its generic outlines became more defined over the eighteenth century.[20] Indeed, the emergence of the anecdote as a distinct and identifiable genre closely tracks that of the novel—at least in the English language, in which the novel came to be distinguished from the romance.[21] The anecdote and the novel may even be regarded as mirror genres, for where the novel appears to make fiction conform to the rules of reality, the anecdote seems to make reality conform to the rules of fiction. Unlike the novel, however, the anecdote was a small narrative of human life that could be incorporated into longer works that aimed to identify the general laws governing human thought and behavior.

Far from than treating anecdotes as readily intelligible stories that pointed to clear conclusions about human nature, Enlightenment writers valued anecdotes precisely for their unassimilable oddness: a quality that seemed essential to their ability to jolt the mind into reflecting on the wellsprings of human nature. In his short remarks on the anecdote, Novalis draws attention to this ability of the anecdote to "produce an effect" and "engage our imagination in a pleasing way"—although he also attempts to distinguish anecdotes that generate this elusive "effect" from the kind that illustrate specific human traits and are of clear value to "the study of man." I would argue, however, that all anecdotes (or at least all successful ones) create an "effect" that is inextricable from their singularity of content and shortness of form. Anecdotes are more than mere representations of preceding events. They are also textual, social, and cognitive events in themselves.[22] Beyond the initial "effect" they produce, anecdotes can engender endless versions and variants of themselves, multiplying in mouths and minds. And more than simply illustrating what is already known, anecdotes can galvanize the work of thought.

A few qualifications should be added here to this definition of the anecdote as the story of a single and singular event. Firstly, some anecdotes might better be described as narrating circumstances rather than events, for the happenings that anecdotes narrate are not always presented as occurring within clear temporal or spatial limits.[23] Secondly, the happening narrated in an anecdote can be represented as happening once or many times over. The latter kind of anecdote is, to use Gérard Genette's term, "iterative," in the sense that in it "a single narrative utterance takes upon itself several occurrences together of the same event."[24] An anecdote that is "iterative" in this sense might tell of a repeated habit or compulsion characteristic of a particular person, as when the fictional character Tristram Shandy divulges a "small anecdote known only in our own family" that his father "had made it a rule for many years of his life,—on the first *Sunday night* of every month throughout the whole year,—as certain as ever the *Sunday night* came,—to wind up a large house-clock which we had standing upon the back-stairs head, with his own hands" (*LS* 1:6), adding that the day of the month that Walter allocated to winding the clock was also the one on which he fulfilled his marital duties to his wife. However, even "singular" anecdotes (anecdotes of happenstances presented as happening only once) are potentially "iterative" in the sense that they invite themselves to be told again and again.[25] In fact, a tendency to transform singularity into repetition is characteristic of anecdotes in general, whether the happenings of which they tell are represented as happening once or many times over.

Anecdotes can be told in a variety of ways. The original anecdote of Polly Baker was, for example, mostly taken up with a transcription of the speech that Baker had purportedly given in the Connecticut courthouse, with the speech's framing context supplied in a short headnote. Anecdotes can also be told in verse, as in William Wordsworth's poem "Anecdote for Fathers." Within the indistinct limits that distinguish anecdotes from more extended historical or fictional narratives, anecdotes can vary in length. At one extreme, there are anecdotes that are told within the confines of a single sentence, as when Carl Linnaeus records in *Nemesis Divina*, the manuscript of theological case studies that he compiled between 1750 and 1765, "On the day when my mother died in Småland and I was in Uppsala, I was more melancholy than I have ever been, although I knew nothing of her death."[26] Anecdotes can, of course, be longer than this. Even anecdotes that are relatively short in some versions may be longer in others. The version of the Polly Baker anecdote that was printed in the *Edinburgh Magazine*, for example, gave Baker a detailed backstory that she had lacked in the version that appeared in the *General Advertiser*, expanding her tale to nearly double its original length. Too much elaboration, however, and an anecdote ceases to be an anecdote and begins to be something else—potentially, a novel.[27] The anecdote's protean adaptability—its ability to be told in different ways, to signify differently in different contexts, and even to be transformed into other genres—was key to the catalyzing function the genre served in the intellectual culture of the Enlightenment. The anecdote's mutual entwinement with the Enlightenment is the subject to which I now turn.

ANECDOTES AND ENLIGHTENMENT

What do anecdotes have to do with the Enlightenment? Probably the simplest way of connecting the anecdote to the Enlightenment is through the metaphor of light. Anecdotes are little enlightenments, little stories shining light on human life. Many writers have associated the genre with illumination.[28] The miscellanist Isaac D'Israeli observes in his *Dissertation on Anecdotes* (1793) that anecdotes can reveal facets of human beings that more extended descriptions might miss. "A well-chosen anecdote frequently reveals a character, more happily than an elaborate delineation," D'Israeli observes, "as a glance of lightening will sometimes discover what escapes us in a full light."[29] Benedetto Croce, in his *History as the Story of Liberty* (1938), remarks that anecdotes provide "information upon particular, separate, unconnected events, which therefore stand in no relation to any superior event: lights which blaze and fade out one after the other and do not light up the landscape, but are fitful fires."[30] The individual anecdote's "enlightenment effect" may be small and transient. But Croce's metaphor implies that many anecdotes, taken together, may just have the power to light up the landscape of human knowledge.

To place the anecdote at the heart of the Enlightenment is to move the English term "the Enlightenment" closer to its French equivalent "*les lumières,*" which for Tzvetan Todorov better captures the Enlightenment's self-conscious effort to find illumination outside the authority of scripture. "Having cast off the shackles of the past," Todorov writes, "people set out to formulate new laws and norms using purely human means, without recourse this time to magic or revelation. The certainty of a unique source of light [*la lumière*] descended from above gave way to the idea of a plurality of light sources [*les lumières*] spreading from one person to another."[31] The French plural noun *les lumières* also sorts better with present models of the Enlightenment as a constellation of "Enlightenments" rather than a single unified movement. J. G. A. Pocock envisages, for example, a loosely affiliated "family of Enlightenments, displaying both family resemblances and family quarrels (some of them bitter and even bloody)."[32] Much research has been concerned with identifying the distinctive forms that the Enlightenment took in particular national and regional contexts.[33] In addition, distinctively religious Enlightenments have been identified, including Protestant, Catholic, and Jewish Enlightenments.[34] Many historians have nevertheless found a considerable area of overlap between the various Enlightenments in the shared premise that "the human being and not God was the starting point for meaningful philosophical reflection," as Michael Brown puts it in his recent study of the Irish Enlightenment.[35] Anecdotes supplied useful "starting points" for naturalistic inquiries into human nature because they framed human beings as creatures whose thoughts, passions, morals, and beliefs could be studied in much the same way as any phenomenon in the natural world might be. Students of human nature used anecdotes to ground their inquiries in narratives that could be credited as at least possible representations of actual incidents in human life. As isolated narratives of odd and singular occurrences, anecdotes were crucial to the Enlightenment's effort toward reestablishing knowledge not on the authority of the ancients, nor on God's word as revealed in the Bible, but on the close observation of human beings in the world, seen both as individuals and as components of larger social wholes.[36]

The Enlightenment was more, however, than a particular intellectual tendency or a set of ideas. It lived in the literary and social interactions made possible by the proliferation of coffeehouses and clubs, the expansion of postal networks and print markets, and the invention of new genres such as the periodical essay. These developments, according to Jürgen Habermas's influential account of them, gave birth to an Enlightenment public sphere: a space for open discussion on matters of public concern outside the authority of the state.[37] More recently, Clifford Siskin and William Warner have looked to institutional and social developments as keys to understanding the Enlightenment. Siskin and Warner depart from Habermas, however, in viewing the qualitative increase in the possibilities for communicating not as making the Enlightenment possible but rather as constituting it. For them, the explosion in various modes of "mediation" in the period *was* the Enlightenment.[38] They thus offer a neat solution to the definitional dilemma that has vexed many historians of the Enlightenment, though at the cost of downplaying the importance of the specific content of the mediations themselves.[39]

To view the Enlightenment through the lens of the anecdote is to combine what we might call the "intellectual" and "institutional" approaches. The careers of eighteenth-century anecdotes can tell us a great deal about how ideas emerged from social and textual interactions and were shaped by them. Anecdotes could circulate between such diverse forms of communication as coffeehouse conversations, letters, and essays. They were adaptable, capable of being told in different situations and of acquiring different kinds of significance according to how, where, by whom, and to whom they were told. Anecdotes thus operated at the intersections between the proliferating pathways for oral and written communication that crisscrossed the Enlightenment. As Monika Fludernik observes, the anecdote is situated "on the borderline between the written and oral genres."[40] Because the anecdote straddled the worlds of speech and writing, the genre helped to imbue written texts with the ambience of face-to-face interaction and to bring stories gleaned from manuscripts, periodicals, and books into oral conversation. Anecdotes fostered the social and textual interactions in which new ideas about human nature were being articulated. But anecdotes also tended to exceed the parameters of Habermas's "rational-critical public debate."[41] They frequently appear as irruptions of irrationality in the texts that contain them, bizarre stories that cannot be easily accounted for or explained away. Often, the initial effect of anecdotes was not to make human nature immediately comprehensible but, on the contrary, to make it strange.[42] Anecdotes are concerned at the level of content with happenings that register as anomalous, aberrant, or eccentric. In terms of form, anecdotes often jut into the texts in which they are contained, waylaying, diverting, and interrupting them.

We often find Enlightenment writers acknowledging the superfluity and frequent silliness of the anecdotes they tell, even as they admit their own inability to resist sharing them. In the fourth edition of the *Essay Concerning Human Understanding* (first edition 1690, fourth edition 1700), for example, John Locke gives a number of examples of the mind's penchant for associating ideas that have no natural connection to one another, before half-apologetically telling his readers:

> Instances of this kind are so plentiful every where, that if I add one more, it is only for the pleasant oddness of it. It is of a young Gentleman, who having learnt to Dance, and that to great Perfection, there happened to stand an old Trunk in the Room where he learnt. The *Idea* of this remarkable piece of Houshold-stuff, had so mixed it self with the turns and steps of all his Dances, that though in that Chamber he could Dance excellently well, yet it was only whilst that Trunk was there, nor could he perform well in any other place, unless that, or some such other Trunk had its due position in the Room. (*L* 399)

The young gentleman's arrangement of the room illustrates the arrangement of his mind.[43] It also illustrates the disarrangement of his mind. The anecdote produces a sense of disarrangement in Locke's *Essay* itself, causing Locke to struggle to justify the story's inclusion in its pages. Locke's apprehension that his reader might very well be skeptical that the dancer ever actually existed prompts him to add a brief explanation and defense of his decision to tell the anecdote at all: "If this Story shall be suspected to be dressed up with some comical Circumstances, a little beyond precise Nature; I answer for my self, that I had it some Years since from a very sober and worthy Man, upon his own knowledge, as I report it; and I dare say, there are very few inquisitive Persons, who read this, and who have not met with Accounts, if not Examples of this Nature, that may parallel, or at least justify this" (*L* 399–400). Here Locke moves between two grounds on which to claim the anecdote's value as evidence for the study of the human mind. He first tries to convince his reader that the story is at least true, appealing to the character and virtue of the "very sober and worthy Man" who first told it to him. In doing so, Locke relies on same codes of gentlemanly conduct that helped foster belief in the truthfulness of scientific reports in the period.[44] Locke then justifies the story's inclusion in the *Essay* by suggesting that the story can stand in for a very large set of incidents that will have been observed firsthand by the reader. The anecdote takes on an odd kind of universality in Locke's interpretation of it, illuminating a form of madness to which all human beings are susceptible by nature.

The characteristic apologies and disclaimers that so often preface the telling of anecdotes suggest that to tell one is to run some risk of embarrassment. Indeed, in his *Lectures on Rhetoric and Belles Lettres* (1783), Hugh Blair advised the prospective historian that "on occasions where a light or ludicrous anecdote is proper to be recorded, it is generally better to throw it into a note, than to hazard becoming too familiar, by introducing it into the body of the work."[45] Philosophical tellers of anecdotes nevertheless took the chance of seeming "too familiar," or even ridiculous, in order to exploit the anecdote's ability to reorder existing ideas about what it means to be human. Anecdotes drew attention to human phenomena that seemed to lie beyond the ken of systematic reasoners on human nature. And yet, by the same token, anecdotes allowed philosophers to advertise their own intellectual powers, demonstrating their ability to make sense of even the most anomalous story. Anecdotes thus maintained a close, though often fractious, relationship with intellectual systems in the Enlightenment. Perhaps not coincidentally, two of the most famous anecdotes of the long eighteenth century are stories that bring philosophical systems and impactful events into close conjunction with one another: Isaac Newton watching an apple fall to the ground (or having it land on his head in later versions) and Samuel Johnson kicking a stone to refute George Berkeley's idealism.[46] In these stories, anecdotes seem to be capable of either building or destroying systems.

The first anecdote appears to lay down the foundation for one system, and the second seems to demolish another at a stroke.[47]

Anecdotes can set trains of thought into motion as well as shunt them onto new tracks. D'Israeli remarks in his *Dissertation on Anecdotes* that "when anecdotes are not merely transcribed, but animated by judicious reflections, they recal others of a kindred nature: one suggests another; and the whole series is made to illustrate some topic that gratifies curiosity, or impresses on the mind some interesting conclusion in the affairs of human life."[48] This mental leaping from one anecdote to another can occur within the self-dialogue of a single mind or in the course of conversation with others, whether the conversation is conducted face-to-face or through the medium of writing. D'Israeli implies that any "interesting conclusion" that presses itself on the mind through this intellectual encounter with anecdotes remains a provisional one, for anecdotes can never restrict in advance what might be made of them, and there are always more anecdotes to be found and told.[49]

More recently, in an essay sketching out a never-completed history of the anecdote from Herodotus to the New Historicism, the literary critic Joel Fineman also describes the anecdote as a narrative form that engenders a distinctively recursive and self-revising type of thinking. Fineman presents the anecdote as a story that punctures the historical grand narrative or *grand récit*, revealing the limits of its explanatory powers. The "hole" created by the anecdote in the historical "whole" may, in turn, be filled in by a new grand narrative that seeks to account for the anomaly to which the anecdote has drawn attention. This grand narrative may in turn be punctured by another anecdote, thus beginning the process all over again.[50] Fineman envisions the anecdote as a genre that works both to break apart and to build up grand narratives of history in a potentially endless cycle. Like D'Israeli before him, Fineman stresses the anecdote's capacity to enable open-ended modes of thinking that shuttle back and forth between the particular and the universal.

Unlike the history of the anecdote that Fineman envisaged, which would tell the genre's story over the *longue durée*, my book is focused on the long eighteenth century. This was an especially significant period in the longer history of the anecdote, in part because it is in this century that the word "anecdote" acquires the primary sense it presently holds in English. But the stories that were referred to as "anecdotes" in the long eighteenth century did not always correspond to the kind of stories that are typically referred to by that name nowadays. Indeed, the meanings attached to the word "anecdote" changed over the period from the late seventeenth to the early nineteenth century. In this book, I focus on the anecdote primarily in its "modern" sense as a self-contained narrative of a single event or circumstance in human life. To allow the various meanings that attached to the word "anecdote" in the eighteenth century to frame my project would have meant abandoning the aim of investigating the workings of the anecdote as a coherent narrative genre from Locke to Wordsworth. However, the different meanings that the word "anecdote" possessed over the long eighteenth century are relevant to the understanding of the genre now signified by the word, especially because the term "anecdote" has retained many of its early associations. The following section accordingly surveys the changing meanings of the word "anecdote" from antiquity up to the early nineteenth century.[51]

"ANECDOTE": A BRIEF SEMANTIC HISTORY

The word "anecdote" goes back to the Ancient Greek noun ἀνέκδοτος, which might be literally translated as "something not given out." The *Greek-English Lexicon* identifies three meanings of the word: an unmarried girl, an unpublished text, or a secret remedy for a disease.[52] These very different significations are linked by the basic idea of people or things hovering just on the threshold of being "given out." The girl may be given in marriage, the text may be published, and the remedy may be one day made known. This sense of anecdotes as stories whose "givenness" is somehow precarious persists in the contemporary sense of the word "anecdote," for historical anecdotes often appear to us as stray stories from the past that have survived but could just have easily been lost, that may or may not give us information on actual events, and whose wider significance remains enigmatic. A different meaning, however, attached to the word "anecdote" when it was introduced into English and other European languages in the seventeenth century through the discovery and publication of a work by the sixth-century historian Procopius, whose Greek text was printed with a Latin translation under the double title of the *Anekdota* and the *Arcana Historia* in 1623. This was the unpublished and scandalous counterpart to Procopius's official histories of the Byzantine emperor Justinian, *Of the Buildings of Justinian* and the *Wars of Justinian*, both of which appeared during the course of Justinian's reign. The belated publication of the *Anekdota* established the genre of the secret history as the story of the shadowy goings-on behind the public facades of powerful figures and institutions. The Greek title *Anekdota* gave rise to the word "anecdote" in English, while the translated Latin title *Arcana Historia* produced the term "secret history."[53]

The "anecdote" and the "secret history" were closely associated genres in the seventeenth and early eighteenth centuries, although they were never exactly synonymous. Even on the title page of the 1623 folio of Procopius's secret history of Justinian, the plural noun "*Anekdota*" is already implicitly contrasted with "*Arcana Historia*" in the singular. The word "anecdote" usually signified a specific disclosure of a secret history. Ephraim Chambers in his *Cyclopedia* of 1728 defined "Anecdotes" as "a Term used by some Authors, for the Titles of *Secret Histories;* that is of such as relate the secret Affairs and Transactions of Princes; speaking with too much Freedom, or too much Sincerity, of the Manner and Conduct of Persons in Authority, to allow of being made publick."[54] Only when brought together in a single work did anecdotes of the "Affairs and Transactions of Princes" comprise a secret history. This is the meaning of the word "anecdote" that Lemuel Gulliver intends when, in the third book of *Gulliver's Travels* (1726), he censures what he calls "the Roguery and Ignorance of those who pretend to write *Anecdotes,* or secret History; who send so many Kings to their Graves with a Cup of Poison; will repeat the Discourse between a Prince and chief Minister, where no Witness was by; unlock the Thoughts and Cabinets of Embassadors and Secretaries of State; and have the perpetual Misfortune to be mistaken."[55] Gulliver dismisses the anecdotes to be found in contemporary secret histories because he is able to compare them to the firsthand accounts he garners from the spirits of historical figures on the island of Glubbdubdrib. These accounts are, however, very much in the vein of secret history, exposing the low and venal motivations of those in power.

In the middle decades of the eighteenth century, the word "anecdote" underwent a semantic shift that brought it closer to its present signification as a narrative of an interesting but incidental event. The anecdote could now be described as "a minute passage of private life," which is how Johnson defines it in the fourth edition of his *Dictionary of the English Language* in 1773.[56] A parallel shift took place in the meaning of the word "anecdote" in French. The first edition of the *Dictionnaire de l'Académie française*, published in 1694, defines "anecdotes" in the plural as "memoirs in which are written the secrets of the policy and behavior of Princes."[57] In the fourth edition of 1740, however, the link between the anecdote and the secret history is beginning to weaken. The *Dictionnaire* now defines "Anecdote" as "some distinctive or specific secret of the past that was omitted or suppressed by preceding historians." It goes on to offer "*anecdote curieuse*" ("curious anecdote"), "*Les Anecdotes de Procope*" ("the anecdotes of Procopius"), and "*Les Anecdotes sont ordinairement satyriques*" ("anecdotes are normally satirical") as examples of the word in use.[58] Although the meaning of the word as a portion of secret history is still present in this entry, "*anecdote curieuse*" anticipates the direction that the word "anecdote" would take in both French and in English. In the 1740 *Dictionnaire* the anecdote is still defined by contrast to received history although, in its new sense, previous historians might have excluded an anecdote not because they were afraid of telling it but simply because it seemed too insignificant to report. Anecdotes are now coming to be regarded as pieces of information that appear, at least at first sight, to lack historical consequence but are nevertheless "*curieuse.*" The shift in meaning indicates that from the mid-eighteenth century, anecdotes were no longer associated exclusively with secret history. Rather, anecdotes are beginning to refer to the inconsequential pieces of information that accumulate on the historical peripheries.

David Hume, a writer who will figure prominently in this book, lived over the period in which the meaning of the word "anecdote" was changing. His own shifting uses of the word help illustrate the logic underlying the anecdote's semantic turn from a revelation of "secret history" to a "minute passage of private life." The word "anecdote" appears in Hume's early essay "Of the Study of History" (1741), in which Hume takes it upon himself to criticize women for neglecting serious historical literature. The one exception that Hume makes for women's general disinterest in historical works are works of secret history, which Hume says women will read if they contain "some memorable transaction proper to excite their curiosity." But Hume denies that secret history qualifies as real history: "as I do not find that truth, which is the basis of history, is at all regarded in these anecdotes, I cannot admit of this as a proof of their passion for that study."[59] Although the intended object of Hume's attack is the anecdote as a building block of secret history, his use of the word in this essay nevertheless helps us see how the sense of the anecdote slid from its "old" sense as a component of secret history to its "new" sense as a disconnected narrative of a historical or pseudohistorical event.

Hume prefaces his critical remarks on the anecdotes of secret history by telling exactly the kind of story that we would now call an anecdote. He recalls that "I was once desired by a young beauty, for whom I had some passion, to send her some novels and romances for her amusement in the country." Hume explains that he gallantly decided to avoid taking any unfair "advantage" from such inflaming reading material, sending her Plutarch's *Parallel Lives* instead, "assuring her, at the same time, that there was not a word of truth in them from beginning to end." Hume claims that the woman was taken in by the deception, at least until "she came to the lives of ALEXANDER and CÆSAR, whose names she had heard of by accident; and then returned me the book, with many reproaches for deceiving her" (*EMPL* 564). As Rebecca Tierney-Hynes remarks, the reader of "Of the Study of History" is encouraged to read Hume's admission that he "was desired by a young beauty, for whom I had some passion" to assume that Hume himself was the object of desire, until it is revealed that what the woman desired was simply that Hume would send her his collection of "novels and romances."[60] Just as Hume misleads the young lady into thinking that she is reading a romance, he uses the word "desired" to mislead readers of "Of the Study of History" into momentarily thinking they are about to be reading something akin to an amatory secret history. Hume's little story is marshaled in an essay that is highly attuned to distinctions of genre. Jerome Christensen remarks that "the mighty arms of Alexander and Caesar summon a historical reality (a world where actions have consequences) which is not the domain of novels and romances."[61] What falls between these two generic stools, however, is Hume's anecdote in "Of the Study of History" itself—a story Hume presents as if it were true but of little or no consequence. Hume's tale is not part of history proper, nor a novel or a romance, nor even a secret history. Rather, it sits at the intersection of history, secret history, and the fictions Hume calls "novels and romances," occupying the interstitial generic space that the anecdote would soon come to inhabit.[62]

Only a decade after "Of the Study of History" appeared, we find Hume using the word in the "modern" sense in a letter of July 2, 1757, in which he informs Gilbert Elliot that a new epic, the *Epigoniad,* had been published earlier the same year by the Scottish poet William Wilkie. Hume uses the occasion as an excuse to share with Elliot "some Anecdotes with regard to the Author" (*LDH* 1:253). One of these anecdotes concerns a "very pleasant Trick" played by the Edinburgh surgeon James Russell on the English physician John Roebuck. Russell had introduced Roebuck to Wilkie when the poet was out sowing corn on his farm, being "all besmear'd with Dirt & Sweat, with a Coat & Visage entirely proportion'd to his occupation." Roebuck was apparently taken aback when he discovered the extent of Wilkie's learning when the farmer began to talk of the poets of antiquity in Ancient Greek:

> Dr. Roebuck, who had scarce understood his rustic English, or rather his broad Scotch, immediatly comprehended him, for his Greek was

admirable: And on leaving him, he coud not forbear expressing the highest Admiration to Russel, that a Clown, a Rustic, a mere Hind, such as he saw this Fellow was, shou'd be possest of so much Erudition. *Is it usual,* says he, *for your Peasants in Scotland to read the Greek Poets? O yes,* replies Russel, very coolly, *we have long Winter Evenings; and in what can they then employ themselves better, than in reading the Greek Poets?* Roebuck left the Country in a full Perswasion that there are at least a dozen Farmers in every Parish who read Homer, Hesiod, & Sophocles, every Winter Evening, to their Families; and, if ever he writes an Account of his Travels, it is likely he will not omit so curious a Circumstance. (*LDH* 1:254)

Hume's anecdote is similar in theme to the one he inserted into "Of the Study of History." Both anecdotes are stories of people being deceived. Roebuck is tricked into mistaking a Scottish farmer's singular erudition as an example of a general phenomenon, while Hume's female acquaintance is misled into reading history as fiction. The deceptions told in the anecdotes mirror their anecdotes' own possible deceptions of their readers. Hume's story of how legitimate history was falsely presented as fiction may well be a fiction falsely presented as history, and Hume's story of how an Englishman was deceived may itself be an act of deception. J. Y. T. Greig, the editor of Hume's letters, writes in a footnote to the anecdote, "It is a pity to spoil a good story, but Roebuck was far from being what Hume suggests—a casual visitor to Scotland. He knew Scotland well, and lived a great part of his life in it" (*LDH* 254n3). The unreliability of the Wilkie story reflects the anecdote's congenital unreliability as a genre: anecdotes present themselves as records of actual events, though it is rare to find an anecdote whose historicity can be established beyond reasonable doubt.

A common concern with apocryphal incidents typically left out of standard works of history connects the anecdote in its old sense, as a component of secret history, to the anecdote in its emergent sense, as a disconnected narrative of human life. The anecdotes of secret history told of supposed facts that historians had deliberately excluded from their histories. But the "new" anecdotes could now be about ordinary people as well as the powerful or the famous. The underlying connection between the "old" anecdote and the "new" was that both brought the margins of history to the center of attention. This helps explain why anecdotes in both senses of the word have been associated with the practice of gleaning. In his *Anecdotes de Florence* (1685), one of the early secret histories modeled on Procopius's *Anekdota,* the French historian Antoine Varillas wrote, "*l'écrivain d'Anecdotes fait scru-pule de se charger des matieres pompeuses, & comme il tend principalement à connoître ce qu'il y a de particulier dans les inclinations, il s'arréte quelquefois à remasser les choses que l'Historien aura rebutées*," which the 1686 English translation renders as "The Writer of *Anecdota* makes a scruple of charging himself with pompous matters, and as he principally aims at knowing what is peculiar in the Inclinations, he stops sometimes, to glean up such matters as were neglected and flung aside by the Historian."[63] Writing at a time when the anecdote was beginning to lose its exclusive association with se cret history, Voltaire observes in *Le Siècle de Louis XIV* (1739) that "Anec-dotes are a circumscribed field on which we glean after the great harvest of history."[64] In both metaphors, anecdotes are understood as the things left behind after "the great harvest of history": items in the historical record that have been discarded by previous historians as either too risky or too trivial to report.

The fact that the word "anecdote" began to signify what it now does in English over the long eighteenth century does not, of course, mean that anecdotes only appeared from this period onward. The anecdote has long existed both as a form of oral storytelling and as a subgenre of written texts. We should remember, moreover, that even in the latter half of the eighteenth century, the word "anecdote" does not always refer to a small narrative of a self-contained event. A wide range of writings were described as "anecdotes" in this period. Horace Walpole's *Anecdotes of Painting* (1762–80), for exam-ple, does include some narratives that we would now recognize as anecdotes, although, as Karen Junod notes, its title serves primarily to signal the book's modest ambitions as a history of art.[65] The fifth edition of Ephraim Cham-bers's *Cyclopedia* (1778–1788), indicates that "anecdotes" in the latter half of the eighteenth century were not necessarily even narratives per se. The entry on "Anecdotes" recycles the first edition's definition of the anecdote as a "term used by some authors, for the title of *Secret Histories*" but goes on to note that the term "more properly denotes a relation of detached and in-teresting particulars."[66] Even in the early nineteenth century, an "anecdote" could refer broadly to a disconnected piece of historical information. This sense of the anecdote is predominant in the title of John Nichols's *Literary Anecdotes of the Eighteenth Century* (1812–15), a series of volumes compiling miscellaneous information on writers and printers. In addition, residual as-sociations with secret history continued to attach to the word "anecdote." Maria Edgeworth's *Castle Rackrent* (1800) begins, for example, with a mock defense of "secret memoirs" and "private anecdotes," such as those on which her own history of the Rackrent family is allegedly based, wherein the link between the anecdote and the genre of secret history is still apparent.[67]

The sense of the anecdote as a small narrative genre concerned with singular circumstances on the fringes of history, then, was one of several meanings that were attached to the word "anecdote" in the second half of the eighteenth century. Only gradually did this sense emerge as the primary meaning of the word. This semantic winnowing was, however, well underway at the end of the eighteenth century. Even though D'Israeli in his *Dissertation on Anecdotes* argues for a broad definition of the genre, quoting approvingly the *Cyclopedia*'s definition of the "anecdote" as "a relation of detached and interesting particulars," he nevertheless attests to the tendency to understand the anecdote as a specifically narrative genre when he observes: "To most one anecdote resembles another; a little unconnected story that is heard, that pleases, and is forgotten."[68] From now on, when I quote eighteenth-century uses of the word "anecdote" I do so with the claim that the writer is using the word in a sense close to its present meaning. With the history of the word "anecdote" sketched out, it is time to examine the even trickier semantics of the phrase "human nature."

ANECDOTES AND HUMAN NATURE

Invocations of "human nature" are ubiquitous in Enlightenment writing. As Roger Smith quips, to quote examples of the phrase in the eighteenth century "is a bit like quoting references to God in the Bible."[69] Yet Enlightenment writers were well aware of the complexities involved in both the word "human" and in the word "nature." Hume remarks in the *Treatise of Human Nature* (1739–40), for example, that there is no word "more ambiguous and equivocal" than the word "nature." He observes that the word "nature" is sometimes used in opposition to miraculous happenings, in which case everything that is not a miracle belongs to nature. Then again, "nature" can also be defined against things that are simply "rare and unusual," though not miraculous (*T* 304). Hume points out, finally, that "nature" can be contrasted with "artifice," an opposition that gives rise to the philosophical problem of deciding whether ideas of virtue have their origin in nature or not (*T* 305). The meaning of the word "nature" is shown to constantly shift depending on the contexts in which it is used.

The compound noun "human nature" posed even more difficulties, for the boundaries of the human itself were by no means self-evident across the long eighteenth century. Locke, for example, argued that the distinction between the human and the nonhuman could only be a nominal one.

He suggests in the *Essay Concerning Human Understanding* that we define the human using arbitrary yardsticks, leaving us with no way of deciding between competing definitions of what being human entails: "He that annexes the name *Man,* to a complex *Idea,* made up of Sense and spontaneous Motion, join'd to a Body of such a shape has thereby one Essence of the *Species Man;* And he that, upon farther examination, adds rationality, has another Essence of the *Species* he calls *Man:* By which means, the same individual will be a true *Man* to the one, which is not so to the other" (*L* 453). Locke goes on to quote an anecdote in order to show that even the person who would define humanness as an individual's exhibition of human shape has not made it clear what "a body of such a shape" actually means. The anecdote suggests that, even on its own terms, an appeal to human shape is no reliable way of establishing who is human and who (or what) is not.

Locke tells the anecdote on the authority of the French writer Gilles Ménage in the second expanded edition of the *Menagiana, ou bons mots, rencontres agreables, pensées judicieuses, et observations curieuses* (first edition 1684, second edition 1695): "*When the Abbot of St. Martin, says he, was born, he had so little of the Figure of a Man, that it bespake him rather a Monster. 'Twas for some time under Deliberation, whether he should be baptized or no. However, he was baptized and declared a Man provisionally* [till time should shew what he would prove.] *Nature had moulded him so untowardly, that he was called all his Life the Abbot Malotru,* i.e. Ill shaped."[70] This anecdote, hinging on the authorities' hesitation between seeing the future Abbot of St. Martin as a human being and a monster, is a microcosm of the much larger problem of determining where to set the line between the human and the nonhuman. As Locke observes shortly after quoting the anecdote of the Abbot of St. Martin, "if several Men were to be asked, concerning some odly-shaped *Fœtus,* as soon as born, whether it were a *Man,* or no, 'tis past doubt, one should meet with different Answers" (*L* 454). Locke uses the "real" dispute over the baby who would become the Abbot of St. Martin and the hypothetical one of the "odly-shaped *Fœtus*" to suggest that there is no definition of the human upon which all human beings (however defined) might agree. The paradox is that the labor of investigating the nature of human understanding does not actually bring Locke closer to answering the question of what makes human beings human. On the contrary, Locke finds that his inquiries into human understanding only make his own understanding of the human recede further from his grasp. Just as the word "nature" in the title *A Treatise of Human Nature* is hopelessly ambiguous, the word "human" in the title *An Essay Concerning Human Understanding* is revealed in the book itself to be impossible to pin down. Both Locke and Hume are acutely aware of the extent to which their own object of study—human nature—is to no small extent a creation of human language. Studying human nature entails for them a close attention to how language functions (or notably fails to function), especially in those stories that we have come to know as anecdotes.

A compound noun composed of two equivocal words, "human nature" was an eel-like concept in the Enlightenment, sliding between description and proscription, identity and difference, inclusion and exclusion.[71] Enlightenment anecdotes also exhibit the slipperiness of the phrase "human nature," appearing precisely at those junctures at which the human becomes difficult to grasp. In the Enlightenment science of human nature, anecdotes could work to unsettle commonsense ideas of what is natural in human beings, or even to raise doubts about the very idea of the human itself. The anecdote's ability to make the idea of the human an active site of inquiry was the very quality that drew so many thinkers to the genre. The attraction to anecdotes was an expression of the wider empirical impulse that motivated so many intellectual projects in the Enlightenment. Croce draws attention to this affinity between the anecdote and empirical inquiries into the natural world when he writes that the genre is "born and bred out of a need to keep alive and increase the experience of the most diverse and varied manifestations of the human soul; collecting into a sort of herbal more and more new specimens from ever new places."[72] The difficulty of defining "human nature" did not stop writers from collecting anecdotal specimens of it. Anecdotes stood to human nature in much the same relation that the bodies of butterflies and the periods of pendulums stood to nature in general: manifestations of a universal category that did not have to be defined as a whole for its parts to be studied. Anecdotes in the Enlightenment allowed human nature to be investigated in the same empirical fashion as any event, object, or animal in the natural world.[73]

However, anecdotes also pull against what has often been seen as a necessary corollary of this naturalistic trend: the Enlightenment's propensity to transform distinctions between human beings into absolute differences grounded in an unalterable nature. Justin E. H. Smith, for example, argues that the growing tendency to view human beings as part of the natural world entailed "the collapse of a certain universalism about human nature" and its "gradual but steady replacement over the course of the early modern period by a conception of human beings as *natural* beings, and thus as no less susceptible to classification in terms of a naturalistic taxonomy than any other natural being, plant or animal or mineral."[74] The gradual shift toward more naturalistic understandings of human nature, for Smith, leads to the scientific racism of the nineteenth century. Dorinda Outram makes a similar argument that ideas about gender hardened in the Enlightenment, contending that "social and cultural differences between men and women" were increasingly presented in the Enlightenment "as 'natural' and therefore right and inevitable."[75] But the movement from treating human nature as a natural phenomenon to treating human differences as rooted in an unchangeable order of things was not so inevitable as Outram and Smith imply. To look closely at how anecdotes function in Enlightenment writing on the human is to see the extent to which Enlightenment writers experimented with very different understandings of human nature.

Anecdotes could, of course, be used to argue for a human nature divided against itself along axes of gender and race. In practice, however, the act of thinking through problems of human nature through anecdotes often framed human differences as different expressions of a universal human nature. We often find writers presenting anecdotes initially as wholly singular stories, subsequently treating them as typical of a particular society or nation, before finally considering them as revelations of a nature shared by all human beings. This tentative movement from anecdotal singularity to suppositional universality, a movement that characterizes the anecdote as a way of thinking, tended to render human nature itself a moving object of study in the Enlightenment. Hence while most investigators of human nature in the Enlightenment did presuppose some kind of underlying order beneath the observed diversity of the human world, their ideas of human nature were anything but fixed or settled. Indeed, many writers after Locke were well aware of human nature's status as a kind of mental fiction that allowed the work of reflecting on oneself and on others to proceed.

Philosophers and their readers were often conscious, too, of the ways that the discipline of philosophy tended to alienate the philosophers themselves from the human norm. In Hume's *Treatise,* for example, Hume's descent into the workings of the mind culminates in the discovery at the end of Book One that his findings have sundered him from the human race and rendered him a "strange uncouth monster" (*T* 172). Many of Hume's contemporaries might have been tempted to take this self-description at face value, in view of the many stories that circulated about Hume's odd behavior in public. In this book I follow Gilles Deleuze and Félix Guattari in taking seriously (or at least a little seriously) the apocryphal stories that attach themselves

barnacle-like to famous philosophers. Deleuze and Guattari call these stories "vital anecdotes" and argue that they can often be seen as narrative en-
capsulations of philosophical systems. Their own example of one such "vital
anecdote" is the story told by Thomas De Quincey that Immanuel Kant,
"for fear of obstructing the circulation of the blood," employed an elaborate
contraption in order to hold his stockings up, a device involving a "watch-
spring in a wheel" and an "elastic cord," to the two ends of which "were
attached hooks, which hooks were carried through a small aperture in the
pockets, and so passing down the inner and outer side of the thigh, caught
hold of two loops which were fixed on the off side and the near side of each
stocking."[76] Deleuze and Guattari playfully present the stocking contraption as the sartorial equivalent of Kant's self-supporting forms of thought
that sustain our experience, asking "is not Kant's stocking-suspender a vital
anecdote appropriate to the system of Reason?"[77] Anecdotes like these, they
argue, illuminate the "conceptual personae" that animate philosophers' writings: alternative selves that philosophers develop through the process of
doing philosophy. But these anecdotes not only embody philosophers' "conceptual personae"; they also inevitably reflect back on the actual flesh-and-
blood philosophers, turning them into figures of laugher and pity. "Vital
anecdotes," write Deleuze and Guattari, "recount a conceptual persona's relationship with animals, plants, or rocks, a relationship according to which
philosophers themselves become something unexpected and take on a tragic
and comic dimension that they could not have by themselves," and in them
"we philosophers become always something else and are reborn as public
garden or zoo."[78] In this book we often find Enlightenment explorers of
human nature themselves appearing in anecdotes, wherein they become eccentric examples of the very phenomenon that they claim to be explaining.

My book joins a body of critical work that has emphasized how apparent
deviations from human nature were central to the elaboration of Enlightenment ideas of the human. Felicity A. Nussbaum in *The Limits of the Human*
(2003), for example, has explored how mental and physical anomalies allowed new ideas of race and gender to be developed in Enlightenment writing.[79] Richard Nash in *Wild Enlightenment* (2003) has considered how the
figure of the "wild man," embodied in individuals such as Peter the Wild
Boy, became "a complex *alter ego* to the idealized abstraction of 'the Citizen
of Enlightenment,'" as well as a test case for theories of human nature.[80]
Finally, Jenny Davidson in *Breeding* (2008) has traced the nature-nurture
debate back to the long eighteenth century, taking as her starting point the
ambiguity of the word "breeding" itself, which can signify both the process

of procreation and the cultivation of manners. The ambiguity surrounding the word "breeding" neatly suggests the difficulty of deciding what is natural in human behavior and what represents a deviation from it.[81] These commentators all attend to how apparent departures from human nature (anomalies for Nussbaum, wildness for Nash, and nurture for Davidson) are closely bound up with the creation of new knowledge of the subject in the eighteenth century.

One contribution this book aims to make to this critical conversation is to show the usefulness of a formal approach for thinking about the Enlightenment concept of human nature.[82] I emphasize the formal character of the concept of human nature itself, which is often envisaged in Enlightenment as a set of abstract principles analogous to the mathematical laws that natural philosophers were discerning behind the physical world. One function of the anecdote was to breathe life into these lifeless laws of human nature. But the anecdote was also a genre that possessed specific formal properties that helped shape how Enlightenment writers thought about the human. The anecdote's brevity, for example, lent it analytical focus. Rather than describing the structure of human nature as a whole, the anecdote helped isolate particular phenomena in the human world for further investigation. In addition, the anecdote's formal deracination created a kind of negative space around it: a void in which the explorer of human nature could take imaginative leave from everyday life, all the while keeping a toehold within it.

The simple narrative structures of anecdotes also suggested the existence of similarly simple laws to be discerned behind the variety of human activity. Viktor Shklovsky draws attention to this schematic side to anecdotes when he notes that many anecdotes that appear to be new are, in fact, adaptations of previous anecdotes whose origins may lie very far back in time.[83] In addition, a quick survey of some of the anecdotes investigated in this book illustrates how anecdotes tend to cluster around a small number of what Shklovsky would describe as plot schemata: a human being acts or talks like an animal (Samuel Johnson's pantomime of the hopping of a kangaroo), an animal acts or talks like a human being (a Brazilian parrot's conversation with Prince Maurice of Nassau-Siegen), a trial is resolved in an unexpected way (the story of Polly Baker's speech and Sancho Panza's anecdote of the wine tasting event that ends with the discovery of a key with a leathern thong attached to it), someone is driven to act in a strange and stereotyped manner (John Locke's anecdote of the dancer and the trunk and Erasmus Darwin's anecdote of the farmer cursed with perpetual coldness), and someone says something at odds with the conversational situation in which they are involved (David Hume repeatedly exclaiming "there you are" while sitting on a sofa between two women, and Edward's apparently nonsensical answer to his father's repeated questions in William Wordsworth's "Anecdote for Fathers"). Explorers of human nature were aware of the comparatively small number of basic structures that underpinned a far larger number of anecdotes. They exploited these structures in order to find other anecdotes with which to respond to the anecdotes told by their predecessors. Just as the same anecdote could lend itself to divergent interpretations, one anecdote could lead to the telling of many other anecdotes, which could then work to modify the conclusions that had been reached on the basis of the first. A formal approach, then, can reveal how anecdotes shaped the contours of Enlightenment thought on human nature. At the same time, a focus on form also allows us to see how anecdotes themselves were shaped under the pressure of certain kinds of intellectual inquiry. As Eric Hayot observes in a critique of Stephen Greenblatt's anecdotal method, short, forceful, and apparently self-contained anecdotes can be made through the acts of textual excision and reduction.[84] By tracing the textual history of particular anecdotes, we can track how Enlightenment writers manufactured anecdotes in order to pose questions about the natures of men and women and propose particular answers to those questions.

A formal approach, lastly, helps draw attention to the internal tensions within the Enlightenment concept of human nature. Although the schematic nature of anecdotal form helped intimate the presence of an underlying order behind human affairs, there was an unavoidable disjunction between anecdotal narratives of human life and any laws of human nature that might be derived from them, a disjunction that becomes obvious whenever anecdotes are joined to general principles of human nature. An example of this procedure appears in the *Spectator* (1711–12, 1714), in which Addison has Mr. Spectator write that "Human nature is the same in all reasonable Creatures; and whatever falls in with it, will meet with Admirers amongst Readers of all Qualities and Conditions." This universalizing statement is immediately followed by an anecdote that Addison drew from an English translation of Boileau's "Critical Reflections on Longinus": "*Moliere*, as we are told by Monsieur *Boileau*, used to read all his Comedies to an old Woman who was his House-keeper, as she sat with him at her Work by the Chimney-Corner; and could fortell the Success of his Play in the Theatre, from the Reception it met at his Fire-Side: For he tells us the Audience always followed the old Woman, and never failed to laugh in the same

Place" (*S* 1:297). This anecdote tells of a repeated coincidence between the old woman's and the future audience's laughter. But no matter how many times the old woman laughs at the "right" place, the anecdote is still built on a single and singular set of interactions between one playwright and his housekeeper. The anecdote becomes notable and narratable only insofar that its readers expect the paying audience's laughter *not* to coincide exactly with the old woman's. The relationship between the anecdote and the affirmation of the uniformity of human nature is paradoxical: the anecdote gains its interest and exemplary status from its appearance of exceptionality, but then this exceptionality also makes it, so it would seem, a strange choice of story to illustrate the regularity of human nature. In this case, Addison leaves it up to the reader to square the contradiction between anomalous case and the presumptive universality of human taste.

This brings me to the core question the anecdote raises whenever it is used as a means of understanding human nature: how could the singular and anomalous anecdote possibly produce knowledge of the workings of a universal human nature? I have found Giorgio Agamben's description of the relationship between the "exception" and the "example" useful for answering this question. The exception, writes Agamben, "is situated in a symmetrical position with respect to the example, with which it forms a system."[85] The example is seen to be "excluded from the normal case not because it does not belong to it but, on the contrary, because it exhibits its own belonging to it." That is, examples are marked out as special cases because they are detached from the usual state of affairs so that they may stand as examples. To use Agamben's own example, if the phrase "I love you" is used as an example of a speech act, then it cannot, by this token, act as an actual declaration of love. Agamben describes the exception, by contrast, as "included in the normal case precisely because it does not belong to it." Exemplary examples of exceptions would be the hysterics and neurotics populating the writings of Sigmund Freud, whose strange symptoms turn out to illuminate the normal workings of the psyche. Agamben remarks that examples and exceptions tend to approach one another: they are, in his words, "correlative concepts that are ultimately indistinguishable."[86] Examples, on close analysis, turn out to be exceptional; exceptions, on reflection, begin to seem exemplary. These paradoxes regularly attend the telling of anecdotes in the science of human nature, stories that often work to blur the very distinction between the normal case and the exception.[87]

As well as providing a useful formal account of the underlying logic behind the practice of using strange and singular anecdotes to understand human nature, Agamben's description of the opposed and yet "correlative" and "ultimately indistinguishable" nature of the example and the exception points toward a solution to a problem with the definition of the anecdote that Fludernik identifies when she observes that previous critics have failed to provide grounds for distinguishing the anecdote from the *exemplum*.[88] Agamben's distinction between exemplarity and exceptionality, however, allows us to make a provisional distinction between the anecdote and the *exemplum*, while at the same time acknowledging that we can regard the *exemplum* as an anecdote if we emphasize its exceptionality, just as we can view an anecdote as an *exemplum* if we emphasize its exemplarity. In practice, narrative *exempla* can often be seen to depart from the arguments to which they are attached: works from Geoffrey Chaucer's *Canterbury Tales* (c. 1387–1400) to Michel de Montaigne's *Essais* (1580–95) play with the *exemplum*'s tendency to drift from the precept it is supposed to exemplify.[89] The anecdote, however, tends to register at least initially as an exception. By contrast to the *exemplum*, which often draws its authority from established tradition, the anecdote tends to draw its force from the initial unfamiliarity of its provenance. That said, the most familiar *exemplum* is capable of being revivified, just as the most striking anecdote is apt to fade into cliché. In the next chapter, I look at how the *Spectator* pitted the modern story of Inkle and Yarico against the familiar narrative *exemplum* of the Ephesian Matron. If *exempla* tend to move from exemplarity to exceptionality, anecdotes tend to move in the opposite direction, from exceptionality to exemplarity. The animating energy of the anecdotes I study in this book depends, however, on the way the anecdotes never quite reach the condition of exemplarity. They usually retain a stubborn exceptionality. For many Enlightenment thinkers, it was precisely the anecdote's resistance to intellectual assimilation that allowed it to challenge received wisdom on human nature.

I have written this book as a study of the uses of the anecdote in the Enlightenment science of human nature, although my approach to this topic has inevitably been influenced by my training in literary criticism, a discipline that has long made use of anecdotes, especially in its New Historicist mode.[90] One implication of this book is that there is no necessary relationship between the practice of thinking with anecdotes and a commitment to human particularity and difference: a relationship that tends to be assumed in discussions of New Historicism by detractors and exponents alike.[91] Indeed, anecdotes of human eccentricity in this period were valued because they presented stumbling blocks to the universalizing project of describing human nature. If these anecdotes could be accounted for, so it appeared, then all phenomena in human life might be explained in terms of general principles. Although the science of human nature presumed the universality of its object of study, anecdotes in Enlightenment writing on the human often come unexpectedly close to the uses of the anecdote in the New Historicism, in spite of its practitioners' declared preference for the particular over the universal.

Without pressing this correspondence between New Historicist practice and the Enlightenment science of human nature too far, I would suggest that anecdotes were valued for much the same reasons in the Enlightenment as they were in the heyday of the New Historicism. In both intellectual contexts, anecdotes were prized for their ability to point to hidden fissures and tensions in existing knowledge. Even the resistance to interpretation and integration that is commonly associated with the New Historicist anecdote is something that Enlightenment theorists of human nature also valued in the anecdotes they chose to tell. In *Practicing New Historicism* (2000), Catherine Gallagher and Stephen Greenblatt associate the New Historicist anecdote with a "vehement and cryptic particularity that would make one pause or even stumble on the threshold of history."[92] An anecdote unexpectedly unearthed in the archive may just succeed in pitching the historian into the full alterity of the past, where more direct routes to understanding history would fail. In Enlightenment writing on human nature, we often find anecdotes producing a similar kind of intellectual stumbling or stuttering on the threshold of human nature. Anecdotes did seem to illuminate human nature in the Enlightenment, but not as a neat table of patterns and principles but rather as a tangle of problems and paradoxes.

The ambition to account for everything touching the human in universal terms did, however, provide the rationale for the search for anecdotes in the Enlightenment science of human nature. In this book, then, the anecdote takes on some different associations from those it acquires in *Practicing New Historicism*. Where Gallagher and Greenblatt emphasize the anecdote's particularity, I emphasize its movement toward universality; where they emphasize its deviancy, I emphasize its rule-boundedness; and where they emphasize its pull toward concrete reality, I emphasize its pull toward abstraction.[93] Or rather, I show how the anecdote participates in a dialectic between these categories, whose movement is essential to the specific kind of intellectual work done by the anecdote as a genre.[94] Indeed, to explore how Enlightenment writers used anecdotes to think about the problem of human nature is to appreciate the persistence of distinctively Enlightenment modes of thinking about the human in our own time. In reading eighteenth-century writers' speculations on anecdotes, we often find our own critical practices reflected back at us, though as if through a distorting mirror.

OVERVIEW

I have organized each of the chapters in this book on a different principle. Successive chapters use a literary genre (the essay), a single writer (Hume), a historical event (the voyage of the *Endeavour*), and a literary project (*Lyrical Ballads*) as nets for catching anecdotes. My book is not intended as a general account of the eighteenth-century anecdote, but rather as a more focused study of the anecdote's role in what Hume called "the science of human nature" (*EHU* 5). This is one reason why, for example, I have not given a more prominent role to Samuel Johnson in this book. I am primarily concerned not with individual persons like Johnson but rather the universal category of the human. The decision to deemphasize Johnson also freed me from having to retread ground already well covered by Helen Deutsch in *Loving Dr. Johnson*, a book that has nevertheless shaped my thinking on the eighteenth-century anecdote in ways not easily specifiable in the notes, although I acknowledge the influence here.

The first chapter of this book is concerned with the anecdote's ability to make human nature newly available for exploration. I show how the anecdote emerges in the essayistic writings of John Locke, Joseph Addison, Richard Steele, and Eliza Haywood as a genre positioned between the scientific experiment and the thought experiment. Much like the premeditated events that were detailed in experimental reports, anecdotes were narratives of spontaneous events that seemed to point toward the existence of general principles behind the diversity of the human world. I emphasize throughout this chapter the capacity of anecdotes to stage experiments of thought. They had the effect of making human nature seem newly strange, encouraging writers to try to explain this strangeness. These explanations remained provisional, for anecdotes in the Lockean tradition of essayistic writing also invited further interpretation and reinterpretation. I show, for example, how one of Locke's anecdotes was directly answered by another anecdote of Hume's that served to unsettle the conclusions that Locke had reached on the basis of the original anecdote. I also examine how the antifeminist classical anecdote of the Ephesian matron was answered by Steele's anecdote of Inkle and Yarico, as well as how Haywood, in turn, tells an anecdote in order to trump one of the many anecdotes of female nature that appear in Addison's and Steele's *Spectator*.

My second chapter on Hume's literary career centers on the capacity of the anecdote to enable philosophers to take speculative flights from common life but also to pull them back down to earth again. I examine anecdotes of Hume's own odd behavior in public, anecdotes that seemed to imply a relationship between Hume's personal eccentricity and the eccentricity of his philosophical thought. Many of the anecdotes about Hume—anecdotes told by others and by Hume himself—frame Hume's philosophy as founded on Hume's self-alienation from common life. At the same time, however, the anecdotes present this self-alienation as a process that itself happens within common life. I argue that these anecdotes of Hume's oddness are continuous with Hume's own use of anecdotes throughout his literary career, in which anecdotes work as narrative islands that expose the constructed nature of the narratives human beings tell about themselves, as well as the narratives fashioned to explain the progress of England as a nation and the advance of religious belief from polytheism to monotheism. Finally, in my discussion of Hume's essay "On the Standard of Taste" (1757), I show the centrality of the anecdote Hume quotes from *Don Quixote* (1605–15) to Hume's attempt to explain the nature of aesthetic taste, a phenomenon that escapes easy definition but can nevertheless be exemplified through the *je-ne-sais-quoi* that the well-told anecdote is capable of producing.

While my first two chapters establish how anecdotes could function within the study of human nature, my third chapter looks at how the use of anecdotes as a tool for understanding the human could itself become a point of controversy in the Enlightenment. I focus on the divergences and disagreements about the use of anecdotes that surfaced in the wake of the first of James Cook's three voyages to the South Seas on the *Endeavour*. In their respective journals, Joseph Banks and Cook pursue different approaches to recording anecdotes, Banks seeking to fit anecdotal narratives into all-encompassing descriptions of the societies he encountered and Cook enacting a modest reticence to explain the larger meaning of the singular events he records in his journal. John Hawkesworth, the compiler of the official narrative of the voyage, would subsequently seek to mine the anecdotes he found in Banks's and Cook's journals for useful information for the study of human nature as a whole. His reliance on the anecdote as a form, however, opened him up to the scorn of many of his reviewers, who denied the relevance of the anecdotes on which he speculated for the science of man. Much as Hawkesworth was brought low by his association with the anecdote, Banks's association with the genre also worked to undermine his scientific authority as the president of the Royal Society. Finally, I contrast the Scottish conjectural historians' speculative use of anecdotes concerning the *Endeavour* voyage with Samuel Johnson's stubbornly commonsense reactions to the same material, which deny the need for any systematic framework at all in order to understand the anecdotes that the *Endeavour* brought in its wake.

In my final chapter on William Wordsworth and Samuel Taylor Coleridge's *Lyrical Ballads, with a Few Other Poems* (1798) I argue that Wordsworth reframes the anecdote as a distinctively poetic form of knowledge. As a genre embedded in the "real language of men," the anecdote helps Wordsworth bridge the gap between informal conversation and the language of poetry. In my reading of "Goody Blake and Harry Gill" in relation to the physiological writings of Thomas Beddoes and Erasmus Darwin, I show how the anecdote becomes a common ground on which men of science, poets, and the wider public can meet. The link between anecdotes and poetry thus underpins Wordsworth's claims that poetry can and should be written in ordinary language, that poetry is a "science of human feelings," and that the poet possesses a special claim to reveal the nature of human beings, a claim founded on the poet's special ability to transmute the anecdote into poetry. A brief coda juxtaposes Montesquieu's *Spirit of the Laws* (1748) with Laurence Sterne's *Tristram Shandy* (1759–1767), considering how both texts illustrate an animating illogicality that characterized the use of anecdotes to think systematically about the structuring principles of human nature.

This book was finished at a time of widespread anxiety over "fake news," falsehoods posing as actual news stories and disseminated rapidly through electronic social networks. These stories were, at the time of writing, often treated as if they had become malign agents in themselves, with powers to derange the whole public sphere. In the current climate, then, a book arguing for the enlightening potential of parafactual stories might appear a bit perverse.[95] But I would reply that the fact that Enlightenment writers did embrace anecdotes enjoins us to rethink what we mean by "enlightenment." For while anecdotes often led thinkers toward startling conclusions about the nature of human nature, they also brought the same thinkers perilously close to credulity, lunacy, and enthusiasm. This book takes notice of the darker side to Enlightenment anecdotes, which can depict cruel as well as whimsical incidents—and often themselves perform an intellectual cruelty toward the human beings they depict. Enlightenment anecdotes were, moreover, closely intertwined with transatlantic slavery, imperial expansion, and colonial prospecting, traveling along the routes these historical processes scored around the globe. Even as I have sought to acknowledge these entanglements, I have also tried to register the pleasures of reading and thinking with Enlightenment anecdotes—in our own time as well as in the long eighteenth century. For Enlightenment writers, this pleasure was no simple self-indulgence but a shared experience that served to bind them to their fellow human beings, even as their own efforts to expose the inner workings of human nature led them to depart from ordinary habits of thought. Anecdotes helped foster a certain self-consciousness about the embeddedness of intellectual work within the wider social world, as well as promoting an awareness on the oddness of studying the nature of human beings while at the same time being one. To trace the workings of anecdotes in the Enlightenment science of human nature may help us, in turn, become more conscious about the ways we think about the human now.

ONE

Anecdotal Experiments

***

In his *Dissertation on Anecdotes,* Isaac D'Israeli draws an analogy between the anecdotes of Addison and the experiments of seventeenth-century natural philosophers. "The science of human nature," D'Israeli writes, "like the science of physics, was never perfected till vague theory was rejected for certain experiment. An Addison and a Bruyere accompany their reflections by characters; an anecdote in their hand informs us better than a whole essay of Seneca. Opinions are fallible, but not examples."[1] Not all eighteenth-century writers agreed, however, that anecdotes supplied anything like "certain" knowledge of human nature. Voltaire, in his entry under "Ana, Anecdotes" in his *Questions sur l'Encyclopédie* (1770–72), for example, compares the blind acceptance of anecdotes to the blind acceptance of the assumptions of Aristotelian natural philosophy. He singles out the story of Polly Baker and the *Spectator*'s story of Inkle and Yarico as examples of the kind of false and misleading anecdote that is commonly passed off as genuine in the literary culture of his own time. "How many of our books are founded on nothing but the talk of the town," complains Voltaire, "just as physics was once founded on nothing but chimeras repeated from century to century up until our own time!"[2] (Notwithstanding this attack on anecdotes, Voltaire had himself foisted more than a few on the public.) In their respective remarks, D'Israeli and Voltaire make diametrically opposed arguments for the evidential value of anecdotes. But the associative leaps they both make from anecdotes to physics suggest that the affinities between the anecdote and the experiment were unavoidable for them. After all, in Voltaire's animadversions on anecdotes, the anecdote occupies the same conceptual field as the experiment, even if it is placed in implicit opposition to it.

This chapter uncovers the affinity between the anecdote and the experiment as it emerges in the early British Enlightenment. It argues that anecdotes work as the human equivalents of natural philosophical experiments in the moral philosophy of John Locke, Joseph Addison, Richard Steele, and Eliza Haywood.[3] To study moral philosophy was not just to inquire into ethics and morals but to study human nature in toto, from the minute cogitations of the human mind up to the large-scale workings of society. Moral philosophy, the study of all things pertaining to the human, was defined by opposition to natural philosophy, the study of the nonhuman world of matter, motion, plants, and planets. An important generic link between the disciplines of moral and natural philosophy was the essay, a genre that was not originally defined by its length, but rather by its provisional way of treating its materials. Essays extend in length from the short essays collected in Francis Bacon's *Essays* (1597) to Locke's weighty *Essay Concerning Human Understanding*. The genre of the essay takes its name from Michel de Montaigne's *Essais*, where the term denotes a series of "trials" or "attempts." In his chapter on Montaigne in *Mimesis* (1946), Erich Auerbach argues that "Montaigne's apparently fanciful method, which obeys no preconceived plan but adapts itself elastically to the changes of his own being, is basically a strictly experimental method, the only method that conforms to such a subject."[4] Here Auerbach intuitively links Montaigne's essays with the experimental methodologies that would transform the practice of natural philosophy in the seventeenth century. There was, then, an affinity between the essay and the experiment from the beginning. Indeed, in his study of the early modern essay, Scott Black shows how the essay genre became a vehicle for the experimental philosophy, in which experimental reports assumed the role played by commonplaces taken from the writer's reading of ancient authors in previous essays.[5] Locke's *Essay* shows a similar turn toward contemporaneity, eschewing classical *exempla* in favor of anecdotes extracted from his reading of modern books and his own private conversations and observations.

Locke emphasizes the open-ended and provisional nature of his *Essay* in the "Epistle to the Reader," where he discovers an essayistic quality in the workings of the human mind itself, whose "searches after Truth, are a sort of Hawking and Hunting, wherein the very pursuit makes a great part of the Pleasure. Every step the Mind takes in its Progress towards Knowledge, makes some Discovery, which is not only new, but the best too, for the time at least" (*L* 6). Locke explains that the *Essay* itself was written as a series of "incoherent parcels" (*L* 7), a discontinuous process of composition that parallels the mind's "Hawking and Hunting." "New Discoveries led me still on," explains Locke, "and so it grew insensibly to the bulk it now appears in" (*L* 8).[6] The extensive revisions and additions Locke made in successive editions of the *Essay* express this ethos of openness and provisionally. Likewise, Addison emphasized the essayistic nature of the *Spectator* papers when he had Mr. Spectator remark, "When I make Choice of a Subject that has not been treated of by others, I throw together my Reflections on it without any Order or Method, so that they may appear rather in the Looseness and Freedom of an Essay, than in the Regularity of a Set Discourse" (*S* 2:465).[7] Locke and Addison position their own essays as forms turned toward an open future, experimental spaces for the making of new knowledge. Even in the *Spectator*, stories and quotations from classical writers are transformed by being brought into close conjunction with anecdotes of contemporary experience. I begin this chapter with an overview of the relationship between the anecdote and the experiment from Locke to Haywood. I then explore the anecdote's role as a literary device for investigating human nature, focusing on Locke's *Essay* and on Addison and Steele's *Spectator*. I end by considering how Haywood appropriates the practice of analyzing human nature through anecdotes in the *Female Spectator* (1744–46).

ANECDOTES AND EXPERIMENTS

I begin with the image that opens Joseph Petit Andrews's anecdote compendium *Anecdotes, & c. Ancient and Modern* (1789). The engraving on the frontispiece depicts an anecdote collector in the process of extracting anecdotes from the tomes in a large bookcase behind him, which contains works by Pliny, Rabelais, and Montaigne. The collector is processing his book collection, turning large tomes into small anecdotes. The image creates a visual metaphor for this process of extracting anecdotes from larger texts. The anecdotes are made by means of a large alchemical flask, which holds the weighty volumes that have just been taken down from the shelves. The flask is heated by the furnace, which the collector fans while seated on his chair. The tomes in the flask include Gilles Ménage's *Menagiana*, from which, as we have seen, Locke took his anecdote of the Abbot of St. Martin. Also being warmed in the flask is Pierre Bayle's *Dictionnaire historique et critique* (1697), a work that, according to one of Addison's late eighteenth-century biographers, was always to be seen open on the essayist's desk while he was writing the *Spectator*.[8] As the anecdotes are sublimed from the anecdote collector's books, they are wafted upward through the flask, pass through a winding and gradually narrowing funnel, and emerge as separate pieces of paper, each of which contains an anecdote. The anecdotes finally land in an urn on which the word "ANECDOTES" is engraved. By turning big books into small anecdotes, the collector is doing the textual equivalent of transmuting lead into gold. But the image suggests a chemical experiment as well as an alchemical process, not that there had been a sharp distinction between alchemy and chemistry in the seventeenth century.[9] The process of turning books into anecdotes is experimental in the broadest sense of the word, for nobody can know in advance—not even the anecdote collector himself—what anecdotes will end up in the urn or what significance they may hold.

Through their textual experiments with anecdotes sourced from published texts, correspondence, and their own observations of everyday life, Locke, Addison, Steele, and Haywood helped form the anecdote culture of the British Enlightenment, a culture in which human experiences both past and present were imbued with the sense of newness implied in the anecdote's etymological sense as "things unpublished." This anecdotal culture's compulsion to seek out unfamiliar and singular experiences also motivated the scientific researches of the early Royal Society. Peter Dear has argued that Robert Boyle and other members of the Royal Society departed from Aristotelian tradition by staging specific experiments that would help reveal the gaps in received understandings of the workings of the natural world. Dear sees Francis Bacon as anticipating the Royal Society's faith in the epistemic authority of singular and anomalous circumstances. Bacon, Dear writes, saw "deviations from the ordinary course of nature as providing privileged insights into its workings" whereas "to the scholastic Aristotelian they were 'monsters.'"[10] The planned and anticipated experiment was a means of manufacturing just this kind of singular event. However, since not all experiments could be staged for the benefit of eyewitnesses, the making of knowledge of the natural world came to depend on self-contained narratives that could be credited as accounts of events that had actually taken place in the laboratory.[11] As Tita Chico has recently pointed out, members of the Royal Society depended on specifically literary resources—including a facility for storytelling and figurative language—in order to make their experiments and observations intelligible.[12] In directing their attention to specific happenings in the world, Boyle and other early experimenters gave up the certainty of Aristotelian principles for the possibility of remaking the understanding of nature on the basis of singular narratives of singular experiments.

Fig. 1. Frontispiece to Joseph Petit Andrews, *Anecdotes, & c. Ancient and Modern* (London, 1789).

Writers on human nature took notice of the developments in natural philosophy and sought to bring experimental methodologies into their own researches into human nature. In empiricist moral philosophy, the anecdote came to operate as the moral-philosophical equivalent of the experiment. But the unplanned nature of the events described in the narratives that would come to be known in the eighteenth century as "anecdotes" tended to distinguish them from the premeditated experiments practiced by natural philosophers. In fact, in the *Treatise of Human Nature,* Hume queries whether premeditated experiments are even possible in the study of human nature. Although the subtitle to *Treatise* presents the work as "an Attempt to Introduce the Experimental Method of Reasoning into Moral Subjects," Hume notes in the preface:

> Moral philosophy has, indeed, this peculiar disadvantage, which is not found in natural, that in collecting its experiments, it cannot make them purposely, with premeditation, and after such a manner as to satisfy itself concerning every particular difficulty which may arise. When I am at a loss to know the effects of one body upon another in any situation, I need only put them in that situation, and observe what results from it. But shou'd I endeavour to clear up after the same manner any doubt in moral philosophy, by placing myself in the same case with that which I consider, 'tis evident this reflection and premeditation wou'd so disturb the operation of my natural principles, as must render it impossible to form any just conclusion from the phænomenon. We must therefore glean up our experiments in this science from a cautious observation of human life, and take them as they appear in the common course of the world, by men's behavior in company, in affairs, and in their pleasures. Where experiments of this kind are judiciously collected and compar'd, we may hope to establish on them a science, which will not be inferior in certainty, and will be much superior in utility to any other of human comprehension $(T6)$[13]

The metaphor of gleaning was, as we saw in the introduction, associated with the anecdote in both its "old" sense as secret history and its "new" sense as a narrative of a detached event or circumstance. Hume suggests that philosophers must ultimately "glean up" their experiments of human nature through what we would now call anecdotal narratives. Hume also identifies the necessity of gleaning experiments from unpremeditated experiences, rather than staging planned experiments, as an important methodological distinction between natural and moral philosophy. Anecdotes relayed information on spontaneous happenings in human life, as opposed to the deliberate experiments created in the natural philosopher's laboratory. At the same time, however, essayistic writers of moral philosophy turned the acts of writing, reading, and reflecting on anecdotes themselves into experimental trials. We can say that the anecdotal experiments in the essays of Locke, Addison, Steele, and Haywood happen primarily in the mind and on the page, even if we credit at least some of their anecdotes as narratives of actual historical occurrences.

Besides the difficulty of experimenting on human behavior and thought without changing it, another asymmetry between natural and moral philosophy was the apparent discrepancy between the rates at which the two disciplines seemed to advance. William Wotton in his attempt to adjudicate the quarrel between the ancients and the moderns, *Reflections upon Ancient and Modern Learning* (1694), allowed that the natural philosophy of the moderns was superior to that of the ancients. But he argued that the moderns had made little advance on the ancients in moral philosophy because it was

> not Strength of Imagination, nor Subtilty of Reasoning, but Constancy in making Observations upon the several Ways of [the] Working of Humane Nature, that first stored the World with Moral Truths, and put Mankind upon forming such Rules of Practice as best suited with these Observations. There is no Wonder therefore, that in a long Series of Ages, which preceded *Socrates* and *Plato,* these Matters were carried to a great Perfection; for as the Necessity of any Thing is greater, so it will be more and more generally studied. . . . [The] Necessity of conversing with each other put Men upon making numerous Observations upon the Tempers of Mankind: And their own Nature being the Thing enquired after, all Men could make their Experiments at home.[14]

Although Hume would later query whether the study of moral philosophy could be based on "true" experiments, Wotton suggests that any self-reflection is, in effect, a self-experiment. He further argues that if the moderns have not improved on the ancients in moral philosophy, then that is because people have been using the experimental method to study human nature all along.

Locke, Addison, Steele, and Haywood share Wotton's sense of moral philosophy as something any person can do. Indeed, they view moral philosophy as something that everybody to some extent already does. But they also propose that it is possible to discover new dimensions of the human world by studying the anecdotal flotsam to be found in books, conversation, and personal observation. As accounts of spontaneous happenings that break through the surface of human life, anecdotes work to produce the same disruptions of ordinary experience that natural philosophers had come to value as the initial sparks leading to new knowledge of the physical world. In his *New Organon* (1620), Bacon attested to the value of what he called *"unique instances"* (*instantiae monodicae*) that "reveal in concrete form bodies which seem to be extraordinary and isolated in nature, having very little in common with other things of the same kind." These "unique instances" help "sharpen and quicken inquiry, refreshing a mind staled by habit and by the usual course of things." Bacon recommends that "unique instances" be gathered both from direct observation and the reports of credible witnesses and then used as the starting points for inquiries that "should proceed until the properties and qualities found in things which can be regarded as wonders of nature are reduced and comprehended under some specific form or law."[15] In Locke's *Essay*, anecdotes serve as just such instances, albeit instances that hover just on the threshold of the "specific form or law" that would explain them. Locke's anecdotes thus open opportunities for putting the laws of human nature to the test.

LOCKE'S ANECDOTES

In the introduction to Book I of the *Essay*, Locke warns against the temptation to "let loose our Thoughts into the vast Ocean of *Being*" and engage in the kind of metaphysical speculations that had produced so much scholastic dispute and debate. Instead, Locke recommends that inquirers into the human mind set strict limits on the scope of their investigations, for "were the Capacities of our Understandings well considered, the Extent of our Knowledge once discovered, and the Horizon found, which sets the Bounds between the enlightned and dark Parts of Things; between what is, and what is not comprehensible by us, Men would perhaps with less scruple acquiesce in the avow'd Ignorance of the one, and imploy their Thoughts and Discourse, with the more Advantage and Satisfaction of the other" (*L* 47). Anecdotes in Locke's *Essay* exist at the "Horizon" between "the enlightned and dark Parts of Things." They are small candle-like narratives that tend to appear at those places in Locke's *Essay* in which the boundaries of what can or cannot be known become obscure and uncertain. In my discussion of the *Essay* I emphasize the capacity of anecdotes to provide sites for experiments of thought—a capacity that reveals their closeness to the experiments conducted by Locke's colleagues in the Royal Society.[16]

In Locke's anecdotes, the genre of the philosophical thought experiment is brought into the real world, or at least what may pass for the real world in the anecdotal menagerie contained in Locke's *Essay*.

I begin not with an anecdote but a thought experiment posed to Locke by the Irish politician and natural philosopher William Molyneux, with whom Locke exchanged many letters during the 1690s.[17] This thought experiment, which has come to be known as "Molyneux's problem," inspired the search for anecdotes that might stand as real-life trials of Molyneux's imaginary scenario. Here is the imaginary case as Molyneux originally presented it in his letter to Locke of March 2, 1693:

> Suppose a man born blind, and now adult, and taught by his Touch to Distinguish between a Cube and a Sphere (Suppose) of Ivory, nighly of the same Bignes, so as to tel, when he felt One and tother, Which is the Cube, which the Sphære. Suppose then, the Cube and Sphære placed on a Table, and the Blind man to be made to see; Quære whether by his sight, before he touched them, he could now Distinguish and tel which is the Globe which the Cube.

This hypothetical case enables Molyneux to ask a question about the nature of human perception in general. In considering it, Molyneux is led to a conclusion that seems to run directly counter to most people's intuitions about the nature of seeing. Molyneux told Locke that although he had put his problem "to Diverse very Ingenious Men," he "could hardly ever Meet with One that at first dash would give me the Answer to it, which I think true; till by hearing My Reasons they were Convinced."[18] The correct but counterintuitive answer to the question, according to Molyneux, is that the blind man would not be able to tell the globe from the cube. For, although he did have the experience of touching the globe and the cube, he had no experience of seeing either of them. The thought experiment contains within itself a narrative of enlightenment in which a blind man suddenly comes to acquire the powers of sight. It also implies another narrative of enlightenment in which people, after reflecting on Molyneux's problem, come to appreciate that sight does not give us direct access to objects. Instead, sight gives us a stream of visual information that must first be learned to be deciphered before the signatures of objects can be discerned within it. Locke agreed with Molyneux's answer to his own question and with the reasoning that led him to arrive at his answer. He went on to take up Molyneux's suggestion that he put the problem into the second edition of the *Essay*, published in 1694. In Molyneux's letter and in the *Essay*, Molyneux's problem exists only as a thought experiment. The hypothetical nature of the problem is marked by Molyneux's repeated injunctions to "Suppose": to suppose a man blind since birth suddenly able to see and to suppose a sphere and a cube placed on a table. There is no need, in Molyneux's original thought experiment, to explain exactly how it is that the blind man gains the power of sight. The infinitive "to be" in "Suppose . . . the blind man to be made to see" locates the event in an atemporal realm of pure conjuncture. But Molyneux's theoretical case inspired the search for an analogue of his thought experiment in actual experience, which then could be told in the form of an anecdote.

The English surgeon William Cheselden published what appeared to be just this empirical analogue to Molyneux's problem in the *Philosophical Transactions* in 1728. In his article, Cheselden reported what happened after his operation on a blind boy who had, Cheselden claimed, either been born with the condition or had lost his sight before he could remember having done so. Although the boy could tell day apart from night, his cataracts prevented him from distinguishing objects, which he saw, Cheselden writes, as "thro' a Glass of broken Jelly," without being able to bring them into focus.[19] Cheselden decided to try to give the boy the ability to see by "couching" his eyes. That is, he used a needle to penetrate the boy's pupils and work the cataracts into the surrounding tissue. In theory, if not always in practice, the procedure would enable the patient to see.[20] What happened after the couching of the boy appeared to corroborate Molyneux's and Locke's answer to Molyneux's question:

> He knew not the Shape of any Thing, nor any one Thing from another, however different in Shape, or Magnitude; but upon being told what Things were, whose Form he before knew from feeling, he would carefully observe, that he might know them again; but having too many Objects to learn at once, he forgot many of them; and (as he said) at first he learn'd to know, and again forgot a thousand Things in a Day. One Particular only (tho' it may appear trifling) I will relate; Having often forgot which was the Cat, and which the Dog, he was asham'd to ask; but catching the Cat (which he knew by feeling) he was observ'd to look at her stedfastly, and then setting her down, said, So Puss! I shall know you another Time.[21]

Although Cheselden dismisses the story of the cat and the dog as "trifling," he does seem well aware of its relevance to Molyneux's problem. In Cheselden's anecdote, Molyneux's austerely geometrical sphere and cube are, as it were, transmuted into the warm and furry bodies of the cat and the dog. Indeed, as Kate E. Tunstall observes, the phrase "which was the cat, and which the dog" in Cheselden's anecdote is the exact syntactic parallel of Molyneux's query, as quoted in Locke's *Essay*, of whether the newly sighted man would be able to tell "which is the globe, which the cube."[22] This syntactic correspondence between Cheselden's anecdote and Molyneux's thought experiment suggests an important qualification to Jessica Riskin's argument that Cheselden represents a sharp break in the continuing conversation on Molyneux's problem: that by making Molyneux's "thought experiment real" Cheselden had "launched a new tradition that was primarily experimental rather than philosophical" in the study of the nature of human perception.[23] The formal resemblance of Cheselden's anecdote and Molyneux's thought experiment indicates the potential reversibility of the movement from thought experiment to empirically grounded inquiry. Cheselden's anecdote suggests that a happening told in an anecdote may be as fertile a source of philosophical speculation as any contrived thought experiment.

One indication of the continuity between the anecdote and the thought experiment is Julien Offray de La Mettrie's comments in his *Histoire naturelle de l'âme* (1745) on Cheselden's operation, for which he relied on Voltaire's account in *Éléments de la philosophie de Newton* (1738). Here, La Mettrie reinterprets Cheselden's original anecdote to fit what he thought was the correct answer to Molyneux's problem: namely that the newly sighted blind man would indeed be able to tell a cube apart from the sphere by sight alone. Although La Mettrie did agree with Locke and Molyneux on the nonexistence of innate ideas, he argued that the blind boy's knowledge of space, obtained through the sense of touch, would allow him to tell objects apart from one another upon gaining the power of vision. La Mettrie implied that Cheselden had already decided at the outset how the boy would respond to objects falling under his gaze. He hypothesized that either the boy's formerly afflicted eyes had not been given enough time to regain their normal function, or else that Cheselden had actually used some form of compulsion to "make the newly sighted boy say what he wanted him to say."[24] La Mettrie's criticism of Cheselden shows how similar the process of reasoning through anecdotes is to the process of reasoning by thought experiments. The anecdote may appear to be, by contrast to the thought experiment, closed rather than open-ended. But La Mettrie shows how easy it is to make an anecdote point toward another conclusion. Anecdotes turn out to be just as open-ended as thought experiments are.

Indeed, I would argue that the anecdote can perform much the same function of galvanizing reflection on human nature as the thought experiment. In her study of the philosophical uses of thought experiments, Tamar Szabó Gendler sees the genre as a means of producing new knowledge "by forcing us to make sense of an exceptional case."[25] The difference is that the thought experiment's scenario is presented in the anecdote as an actual occurrence, even if the anecdote's claim to historicity may be shaky at best. The formal geometry of the thought experiment may often be discerned beneath the anecdote's tactile immediacy and specificity.

Even in the first edition of the *Essay*, Locke had already told an anecdote that is very similar to Molyneux's problem in its concern with a blind person's experience—or lack thereof—of the visual world: "A studious blind Man, who had mightily beat his Head about visible Objects, and made use of the explication of his Books and Friends, to understand those names of Light, and Colours, which often came in his way; bragg'd one day, That he now understood what *Scarlet* signified. Upon which his Friend demanding, what *Scarlet* was? the blind Man answered, It was like the Sound of a Trumpet." Locke invites his readers to laugh at the "studious blind man" and to see his attempts to describe the colors he has never seen in terms of sounds as transparently absurd. Locke uses the anecdote to point out the general error of believing that words alone can communicate what it is like to have a simple idea, in the absence of any preceding experience of the idea itself. "Just such an Understanding of the name of any other simple *Idea* will he have," writes Locke, "who hopes to get it only from Definition, or other Words made use of to explain it" (*L* 425). Learned philosophers are just as foolish as the "studious blind man" when they claim that words are capable of giving us ideas that we have never experienced before.

Much like Molyneux's thought experiment of the blind man who suddenly comes to see, however, the anecdote of the blind man who thought that scarlet was like the sound of a trumpet was capable of producing different interpretations, not all of which accepted the self-evident absurdity of thinking that the human mind might have some kind of access to ideas it had not directly experienced before. In a letter to Joseph Spence of October 15, 1754, for example, Hume interprets Locke's anecdote more sympathetically than Locke had, in part by telling another anecdote that directly references Locke's anecdote but in many ways stands at cross purposes to it. Hume tells Spence in his letter that a thought had, twelve years before, occurred to him to ask his blind friend, the poet Thomas Blacklock, about his own understanding of colors:

> I remembered a story in Locke of a blind man, who said that he knew very well what scarlet was: it was like the sound of a trumpet. I therefore asked him, whether he had not formed associations of that kind, and whether he did not connect colour and sound together. He answered, that as he met so often, both in books and conversation, with the terms expressing colours, he had formed some false associations, which supported him when he read, wrote, or talked of colours: but that the associations were of the intellectual kind. The illumination of the sun, for instance, he supposed to resemble the presence of a friend; the cheerful colour of green, to be like an amiable sympathy, &c. It was not altogether easy for me to understand him: though I believe, in much of our own thinking, there will be found some species of association. 'Tis certain we always think in some language, viz. in that which is most familiar to us; and 'tis but too frequent to substitute words instead of ideas. (*LDH* 1:201)

Much as Molyneux's problem gives rise to Cheselden's anecdote of the formerly blind boy's discovery of the visual differences between the cat and the dog, Locke's anecdote of the blind man and the trumpet gives rise to Hume's anecdote describing how another blind person had associated colors instead with social affections. The fact that Hume counts Blacklock as a friend makes it that much more difficult for him to dismiss the blind poet's account of how he understands "the illumination of the sun" as akin to "the presence of a friend" as sheer nonsense. Hume writes instead, "It was not altogether easy for me to understand him"—a confession that hints that it is Hume that is the one who lacks understanding and not Blacklock. The blind poet's account of the workings of his mind leads Hume to reflect on the ways sensory perceptions and language are intertwined, even to hazard the thought that Locke might have been mistaken in thinking that words and ideas are entirely separable. Hume adduces Blacklock's account of the workings of his mind as an important piece of evidence for understanding the associating faculty of the mind in general. The reinterpretation of Locke's anecdote that Hume's letter enacts—one performed in part through the telling of another anecdote of an event that would never have happened but for Hume's prior reading of Locke's anecdote—shows how Locke's anecdotes exceed his intentions for them, potentially leading to descriptions of the limits and powers of the mind not countenanced by Locke.

If the figure of the blind man stands at the horizon "between the enlightned and dark Parts of Things" in the *Essay*, then figures from the geographical peripheries serve a similar role in testing the limits of human understanding. A case in point is the anecdote of the "*Indian* philosopher" (*L* 175), who believes that the entire world rests on the back of an elephant. What makes the case of the Indian philosopher an anecdote is the presence of an unnamed questioner who asks the philosopher what holds the elephant up and receives the answer that it rests upon a tortoise. After this point, however, the philosopher can go no further: "But being again pressed to know what gave support to the broad-back'd Tortoise, replied, something, he knew not what" (*L* 296). The anecdote begins as a story that makes fun of the "Indian philosopher's" literally unsupported explanation of how the world is kept from falling. But Locke makes occidental thinkers the anecdote's ultimate targets. He compares the Indian philosopher to those "*European* Philosophers" who "first ran into the Notion of *Accidents*, as a sort of real Beings, that needed something to inhere in" and "were forced to find out the word *Substance*, to support them" (*L* 175).[26] Locke goes on to suggest that the universal proclivity "to suppose some *Substratum*" that underlies the ideas given to us through our senses, "wherein they do subsist, and from which they do result, which we call *Substance*" (*L* 295), may be just as absurd and baseless as the Indian philosopher's explanation of how the world is held up. As a result of being associated with an eccentric anecdote, the very idea of substance is transformed into a strangely insubstantial "something," of which "we have no *Idea* of what it is, but only a confused obscure one of what it does" (*L* 175). Substance emerges in Locke's *Essay* as an unsubstantial *je-ne-sais-quoi* on which the human capacity to posit a world outside the mind depends. The true target of Locke's anecdote of the Indian philosopher turns out not to be the Indian philosopher at all. Rather it is the common proclivity to posit the existence of substances outside the mind that do not reduce to collocations of ideas. Locke's anecdotal excursions to the peripheries of the world serve much the same purpose as the anecdotal accounts of the perceptions of the blind, allowing the normal workings of the mind to be assessed from a newly estranged perspective.

The same pattern in which Locke uses an anecdotal exception to reexamine the presumptively normal case is also to be found in the chapter "Of Probability," in which Locke reflects on the tendency for people to accept testimonies of events that conform to their previous experiences and dismiss those that do not. Locke writes that if someone were to tell him that a man had walked on water that had frozen over in the winter, he would be pre-disposed to believe the account, since the narrative "has so great conformity with what is usually observed to happen, that I am disposed by the nature of the thing it self to assent to it, unless some manifest suspicion attend the Relation of that matter of fact." However, Locke notes that if the same story were told to someone "born between the Tropics, who never saw or heard of any such Thing before" (*L* 656), then this person would be less likely to credit its truth. Locke goes on to tell what would later be a much-retold anecdote of the king of Siam's disbelief in a Dutch ambassador's account of how water became solid in his home country in the winter: "it hap-pened to a *Dutch* Ambassador, who entertaining the King of *Siam* with the particularities of *Holland,* which he was inquisitive after, amongst other things told him, that the Water in his Country, would sometimes, in cold weather, be so hard, that Men walked upon it, and that it would bear an Elephant, if he were there. To which the king replied, *Hitherto I have be-lieved the strange Things you have told me, because I look upon you as a sober fair man, but now I am sure you lye*" (*L* 656–57). This anecdote is a natural part-ner for the "Indian philosopher" anecdote, both of them being anecdotes emanating from the East involving precariously supported elephants.[27] The anecdote raises, but does not itself answer, the question of whether or not the king of Siam was justified in disbelieving the ambassador. Although Locke does expect his English readers to recognize that the king of Siam did indeed err in calling the ambassador a liar, it is by no means obvious that the process of reasoning by which the king came to his conclusion was itself unsound. Hume, for one, argued in the chapter "On Miracles" in the *Enquiry Concerning Human Understanding,* that the king of Siam "reasoned justly" (*EHU* 86). The implication that the king of Siam employs the very same principles that Locke and his readers use to reason about the validity of testimony goes against Steven Shapin's sense that the king is pictured as a figure who exists outside the community formed by Locke and his readers.[28] For the king appears to use exactly the same reasoning process Locke and his readers do in evaluating the testimony of others. Indeed, if we assume that the king "reasoned justly," then his reasonable but erroneous judgment implies the fragility of much of what Locke's English readers would have taken to be their own certain knowledge about the world.

In the last anecdote of Locke's that I discuss, the anecdote concerning a talking parrot who holds an extended conversation with a prince, Locke pushes toward the very limits of credibility, where the genre of the anecdote seems to border on that of the animal fable. In doing so, however, he shows how even the most farfetched anecdote may have value for the project of re-thinking human nature.[29] Locke took this story from Sir William Temple's *Memoirs of what Past in Christendom from the War Begun 1672 to the Peace Concluded 1679* (1691), in which Temple takes the time to tell an anecdote that he had heard in the course of his conversation with the former governor of the Dutch colony in Brazil, John Maurice, Prince of Nassau-Siegen.[30] In the passage quoted by Locke in the *Essay*, Temple claims that he had taken the opportunity to query Prince Maurice about the truth of "a common, but much credited Story, that I had heard so often from many others, of an old *Parrot* he had in Brasil, during his Government there, that spoke, and asked and answered common Questions like a reasonable Creature," who was widely believed to be under the influence of either "Witchery or Possession" (*L* 333). Prince Maurice is said to have replied to Temple's query "with his usual plainness, and dryness in talk, there was something true, but a great deal false, of what had been reported" and to have then proceeded to give his own account of the talking parrot:

> he told me short and coldly, that he had heard of such an old *Parrot* when he had been at *Brasil,* and though he believed nothing of it, and 'twas a good way off, yet he had so much Curiosity as to send for it, that 'twas a very great and a very old one; and when it came first into the Room where the Prince was, with a great many *Dutch-men* about him, it said presently, *What a company of white Men are here?* They asked it what he thought that Man was, pointing at the Prince? It answered, *Some General or other;* when they brought it close to him, he asked it, *D'ou venes vous?* it answered, *De Marinnan.* The Prince, *A qui estes vous?* The Parrot, *A un Portugais.* Prince, *Que fais tu la?* Parrot, *Je garde les poulles.* The Prince laughed and said, *Vous gardez les poulles?* The Parrot answered, *Ouy, moy et je scay bien faire;* and made the Chuck four or five times that People use to make to Chickens when they call them. (*L* 333–34)

Locke uses this anecdote to illustrate the point that it is not rationality that divides human beings from other animals but rather the shape of their bod-ies. Locke argues that if anyone "should see a Creature of his own Shape and Make, though it had no more reason all its Life, than a *Cat* or a *Parrot,*" then they would "call him still a *Man,*" but if the same person were to "hear a *Cat* or a *Parrot* discourse, reason, and philosophize," then that person "would call or think it nothing but a *Cat* or a *Parrot;* and say, the one was a dull irrational *Man,* and the other a very intelligent rational *Parrot*" (*L* 333).

Prince Maurice's parrot story helps Locke distinguish humanness from self-consciousness. As Heather Keenleyside observes, the anecdote implies that "the person and the human are distinct sorts of identity: a rational and conversible parrot is not human, for all that it might be a person."[31] As a thought experiment anchored in what appears to be an actual traveler's tale, the parrot anecdote suggests that the distinguishing feature of the human is not the capacity to reason but rather a conformity to a shape that is recognizable as human. The larger implication of the parrot anecdote in the context of the *Essay* as a whole is that the very idea of the human itself, as something reliably distinguishable from other kinds of beings, is a kind of mental fiction. As we saw in the introduction to this book, Locke shows elsewhere in the *Essay* that shape itself is no reliable way of distinguishing human beings. The inconsistency remains unresolved in the last version of the *Essay* Locke completed before his death. Between them, the parrot and the Abbot of St. Martin raise doubts about the possibility of ever establishing the horizon dividing human from nonhuman nature. The anecdotes suggest that the human is itself a nominal category created by minds that may or may not be human.

I find that the anecdotes in Locke's *Essay* work less to define the human and its margins as to destabilize the very concept of the human. Before moving on to Addison and Steele's uses of anecdotes in the *Spectator,* then, I would like to reconsider Laura Brown's argument in *Fables of Modernity* (2001) that the parrot anecdote implies the existence of a fundamental distinction between Europeans and non-Europeans and works to associate the latter with animals. Brown remarks that with the parrot's first question: "What a company of white Men are here?" Prince Maurice and his party "are immediately singled out by the 'rational' parrot, in contrast to a non-white group with which the parrot by this observation implicitly links himself." Thus, in Brown's reading of it, the parrot anecdote in the *Essay* implies that the non-Europeans are less secure in their humanity than are Prince Maurice and the other Europeans: "'Man,'" writes Brown, "is conceived through the story of an animal that sees itself as a native."[32] Brown thus aligns Locke's parrot anecdote with David Hume's racist footnote in his essay "Of National Characters" (1748), in which Hume argues for the natural inferiority of blacks to whites, comparing the learned black poet Francis Williams to a parrot who "speaks a few words plainly" (*EMPL* 208).[33]

Europeans in the parrot anecdote, Brown suggests, are similarly seen to occupy the center of humanity, with non-Europeans pushed to the borderlands between the human and the animal.

But to follow the anecdote closely as it moves from Temple to Locke is to find that the story's implications are not so straightforward. In Temple's original telling of the anecdote, for example, the affinity of the "very great" and "very old" parrot and the prince is especially marked. Temple introduces the prince as "old Prince *Maurice* of *Nassau*" and relates the story that the prince "sought all occasions of dying fairly at the Battel of *Senesse* without succeeding, which had given him great regrets; and I did not wonder at it, considering his Age, of about Seventy-six, and his long habits both of Gout and Stone."[34] In both Locke's and Temple's tellings of the anecdote, the parrot's guardianship of the chickens is easily read as a parody of Prince Maurice's governorship of the colony in Brazil—whether the agent responsible for the joke is understood to be the parrot himself or Temple in putting words into the parrot's mouth. Locke's retelling of Temple's anecdote adds a further point of comparison between the parrot and the beings that the parrot identifies as "*white men*," for there is something unmistakably parrot-like about Locke's own reproduction of the anecdote from Temple, which itself concerns a speech delivered by a parrot that has, so it appears, been repeated over and over again. As Annabel Patterson observes, "in regaling his audience in 1700 with the anecdote of the rational parrot," John Locke "was only the fifth in a sequence of 'Hear-say': Parrot; the interpreters; Prince Maurice; Sir William Temple; John Locke."[35] The very act of reproducing the anecdote from Temple, who himself quotes the words of Prince Maurice, involves a parroting of a speech that had already passed, both figuratively and literally, through many tongues. The tendency of Locke's anecdotes in general is to trouble any complacent claim on the part of Locke or his readers to reside at the center of the human. Even if the anecdotes move to what are initially taken to be the peripheries of the human, the act of reflecting on them tends to lead to the conclusion that the distinction between center and a periphery is itself a fiction of the understanding. Indeed, the idea of the human itself in the *Essay Concerning Human Understanding* tends to disappear into the general operations of the understanding, operations by no means necessarily exclusive to human beings, however they are defined.

The figures appearing in the anecdotes that are either included in or closely related to Locke's *Essay*—the blind boy who is given the power of sight, the blind man who thinks the color scarlet is like the sound of a trumpet, the Indian philosopher who cannot explain what holds up the tortoise that supports the elephant supporting the world, the king of Siam who disbelieves the Dutch ambassador's story of water holding up an elephant, and the parrot who holds a conversation with Prince Maurice of Nassau—all tend to draw attention to the limits imposed by the understanding itself on our ability to fathom the outside world, the nature of the human, or even the workings of our own minds. Locke's anecdotes do not so much serve to confirm the *Essay*'s arguments about the nature of the understanding so much as draw attention to problems and paradoxes whose solutions must be perpetually hawked and hunted after. The anecdote in Locke is to be found at the line between "the enlightened and dark Parts of Things," illuminating new dimensions of human nature and disclosing unsuspected abysses within it.

MR. SPECTATOR'S ANECDOTES

In the *Spectator*, Addison and Steele not only helped to popularize many of the ideas of Locke's *Essay*, they also took up Locke's method of using anecdotes to explore the margins of human nature. Addison and Steele also shared with Locke a fascination with the new natural science. The young Addison delivered a Latin defense of natural philosophy at Oxford in 1693, in which he celebrated its capacity to open new insights into nature.[36] Soon after the *Spectator*'s first run had ended, Addison and Steele collaborated in arranging for William Whiston to read a series of astronomical lectures at Button's Coffee House.[37] And, like Locke's *Essay*, the *Spectator* even includes its own anecdote of a human-like avian that puts the boundaries between human and animal nature in question. This bird appears in *Spectator* 376 in a letter written by a correspondent calling himself "Michael Gander," who describes seeing a man "performing the Office of a *Day-Watchman*" (*S* 3:413) while accompanied by a goose who quacks every time the man calls out the hour. Subsequently inquiring into the watchman's "history," Gander learned from a friend that the watchman was once a regular night-watchman before he found that the goose had become attached to him, regularly echoing his voice with quacks. Discovering the goose's popularity, as well as its money-making potential, the man bought the bird and switched his working hours from night to day. Steele's correspondent proposes on the basis of his own anecdote that even apparently reasonable beings like the day-watchman may, like the goose, be more under the thrall of instinct than they realize. In a précis of the reflective essay that could have emerged from the anecdote of the day-watchman and his goose, had Mr. Spectator chosen to elaborate on it, "Gander" writes:

This is the Matter of Fact: Now I desire you, who are a profound Philosopher, to consider this Alliance of Instinct and Reason; your Speculation may turn very naturally upon the Force the superiour Part of Mankind may have upon the Spirits of such as, like this Watchman, may be very near the Standard of Geese. And you may add to this practical Observations, how in all Ages and Times the World has been carried away by odd unaccountable things, which one would think would pass upon no Creature which had Reason; and under the Symbol of this Goose, you may enter into the Manner and Method of leading Creatures, with their Eyes open, through thick and thin, for they know not what they know not why. (*S* 3:414)

The parrot in Locke's *Essay* talks like a man, whereas the goose in the *Spectator* walks like one. The parrot converses with a prince on equal terms, while the watchman descends to the level of the goose. Both the parrot anecdote and the goose anecdote are marshaled as tools for thinking about the relationship between human and animal behavior. Both are made to suggest that the borders of human nature may be more permeable than they may at first appear. At the very least, they imply that any individual human being might be studied in much the same way as a specimen of a plant or an animal could. In Gander's letter, human beings and animals alike are seen to act according to principles of which they remain, for the most part, wholly ignorant: "for they know not what they know not why."

Mr. Spectator, the periodical's self-appointed judge of human nature, himself is often seen to occupy the margins of the human. He is estranged from his fellow humans by the preternatural silence he maintains in public. This refusal to speak means that Mr. Spectator must develop a simple sign language in order to make his desires known to his landlady: "my Coffee comes into my Chamber every Morning without asking for it; if I want Fire I point to my Chimney, if Water to my Bason: Upon which my Land-lady nods, as much as to say she takes my Meaning, and immediately obeys my Signals" (*S* 1:52). He communicates with his landlady, that is, at much the same level of complexity as a cat or a dog. Mr. Spectator's refusal to engage in social interaction outside his own club enables him, he claims, to "discern the Errors in the Oeconomy, Business, and Diversion of others, better than those who are engaged in them; as Standers-by discover Blots, which are apt to escape those who are in the Game" (*S* 1:5). But this refusal to engage in social interaction also marks out Mr. Spectator as figure on the fringes of society on those rare occasions when he is noticed in public, as when Mr. Spectator overhears himself referred to as "*That strange Fellow*" (*S* 1:19).

An anecdote that was widely circulated about Addison in the latter half of the eighteenth century suggests that Addison shared Mr. Spectator's aversion to speaking in public. This is the anecdote as it appears in *Interesting Anecdotes, Memoirs, Allegories, Essays, and Poetical Fragments* (1794–97), a series of miscellaneous volumes attributed to another pseudonymous "Mr. Addison" entirely:

> It is related of Mr. Addison, who, though an elegant writer, was so diffident of himself ever to shine as a public speaker, that at the time of debating the Union act in the House of Commons, he rose up, and addressing himself to the Speaker, said, "Mr. Speaker, I conceive,"— but could go no farther; then rising again, he said, "Mr. Speaker, I conceive,"—still unable to proceed, he sat down again. A third time he rose, and was still unable to say anything more than.—"Mr. Speaker, I conceive,"—when a certain young member, who was possessed of more effrontery and volubility, arose, and said, "Mr. Speaker, I am sorry to find that the Honourable Gentleman over the way has conceived three times, and brought forth nothing."[38]

The two distinct senses of the verb "to conceive" conflated by the young wit are also conflated in the *Spectator* itself, when Mr. Spectator observes in *Spectator* 135, "The *English* delight in Silence more than any other *European* Nation" and "to favour our Natural Taciturnity, when we are obliged to utter our Thoughts, we do it in the shortest way we are able, and give as quick a Birth to our Conceptions as possible" (*S* 2:32). The anecdote emerges in the *Spectator* as the vital seed that generates new conceptions of the human. Mr. Spectator's essays frequently take their starting points from anecdotes that give rise to short sallies of thought—or "speculations" as he frequently calls them—that may or may not illuminate human nature. But the anecdote of Addison having fitful conceptions that produce nothing reads as a parodic metaphor for the whole *Spectator* project. The anecdote of Addison's threefold "conceivings" in the House of Commons reminds us that there is a distinction between the conception and the birth of an idea: the process of forming a mental conception about human nature on the basis of an anecdote may well fail to produce useful knowledge of human nature, giving birth only to a nonsensical "nothing."

The *Spectator* itself intimates that a risk of misconception inevitably attends the process of thinking with anecdotes. Addison has Mr. Spectator explain the origins of each number's "Sheet-full of Thoughts" (*S* 1:5) in "Sheet full of Hints" (*S* 1:196), in which Mr. Spectator records his notes on people and events that might provide material for essays. Mr. Spectator explains that he often takes a sheet with him on his travels "abroad in quest of Game," and "when I meet any proper Subject, I take the first Opportunity of setting down an Hint of it upon paper" (*S* 1:195–96). But the "Sheet full of Hints" also leads to Mr. Spectator himself becoming the subject of speculation when he accidentally loses the sheet containing the notes in a coffeehouse, where it is discovered and read out aloud to everyone present. The coffeehouse patrons hardly know how to interpret the apparently nonsensical inventory of "Hints" that contains such strange items as "*Childermasday*, Saltseller, House-Dog, Screech-Owl, Cricket,—Mr. *Thomas Inkle* of *London*, in the good Ship called the *Achilles. Yarico—Egrescitque medendo*" and so on (*S* 1:196–97). Explanations for the notes begin to multiply uncontrollably in the coffeehouse. The patrons hypothesize the list to be the ravings of a madman, a coded defamation of an individual and, closest to the truth, a series of notes taken from someone's reading of the *Spectator.* The conjectures only end when Mr. Spectator uses the notes to light his pipe, which at once destroys the notes and dispels any suspicions the coffeehouse patrons may have of his having authored them.

The anecdote of the mislaid notes offers Mr. Spectator the opportunity to reflect on his own practice of recording and disseminating anecdotes.[39] Like the notes, the anecdotes told in the *Spectator* are short, disjointed, and peculiar. They produce what Addison describes in the series of papers on the "Pleasures of the Imagination" as the "*new* or *uncommon*," which "contributes a little to vary Human Life, and to divert our Minds, for a while, with the Strangeness of its Appearance" and "bestows Charms on a Monster, and makes even the imperfections of Nature please us" (*S* 3:541). Many of the notes refer to what we would now call anecdotes: little stories of peculiar circumstances in human life previously told in the *Spectator.* These anecdotes give rise to hints for speculating on the human world by drawing attention to moments of otherness within it.

The note "*Childermas-day*, Saltseller, House-Dog, Screech-Owl, Cricket" is the seed for *Spectator* 7, which begins with Mr. Spectator's report of his dinner in the company of a family under the grip of superstition. The matriarch prevents one of the sons from beginning work on Childermas Day and is horrified when Mr. Spectator spills salt on the table. The incident reminds Mr. Spectator of other examples of irrational fear: families who are alarmed by the screeching of owls or the chirping of crickets and an "old Maid" who is frightened by the howling of a dog. Mr. Spectator has a theory that accounts for these odd superstitions that plague seemingly sane and rational people. He frames these melancholic "Apprehensions and Suspicions" and "Prodigies and Predictions" as so many little and various attempts to master the universal fear of death: "The Horrour with which we entertain the Thoughts of Death (or indeed of any future Evil) and the Uncertainty of its Approach, fill a melancholy Mind with innumerable Apprehensions and Suspicions, and consequently dispose it to the Observation of such groundless Prodigies and Predictions" (*S* 1:34).[40] These anecdotes of odd superstitions are treated in the number as clues that imply the existence of underlying principles of human nature. In this case, Mr. Spectator finds in all human superstitions a single origin in the universal fear of death.

But if this number appears to succeed in generating a principle of human nature, the sheet of hints as a whole emphasizes that the process of examining anecdotal circumstances for insights into human nature necessarily entails the possibility of failure. About half of Mr. Spectator's "notes" in the "Sheet of Hints" fail even to become essays at all, and we can only guess what the essays inspired by "Old Woman with a Beard married to a smock-faced Boy," "Fable of Tongs and Gridiron," and "*Cæsar*'s Behaviour and my own in Parallel Circumstances" would have been like (*S* 1:197). The list illustrates how close the *Spectator* as a whole comes to logical and formal incoherence. The tendency of the papers toward becoming an anarchic miscellany of irrelevant anecdotes haphazardly joined to unfounded claims about human nature was noted by the anonymous author who described the papers as "a disjoyn'd and confused huddle of unmethodiz'd Notions" in *A Spy upon the Spectator* (1711).[41] Mr. Spectator repeatedly fails to extract straightforward laws of human nature from the anecdotes that he and his correspondents recount. Even when he is able to make the leap from event to law, as he does in the number to which the note "*Childermas-day,* Saltseller, House-Dog, Screech-Owl, Cricket" refers, the very length of the list suggests an unmanageable excess of incidents that threaten to overwhelm any law that tries to contain them. Indeed, Mr. Spectator's continual search for small circumstances in human life in the belief that they may shine light on human nature is itself very similar to superstition. His method, after all, involves placing a disproportionate importance on things that would usually pass beneath notice.

Mr. Spectator's own effort to make everything in human life conform to abstract principles is obliquely satirized in the paper that results from another entry in Mr. Spectator's notes—"*Egrescitque mendendo.*" This "hint" reproduces the motto for *Spectator* 25, which Thomas Broughton translated as "By being cur'd grows sick" in *The Mottoes of the Spectators, Tatlers, and Guardians, Translated into English* (1735).[42] This number is largely devoted to a correspondent's letter detailing his attempts to regulate his health by compulsively measuring himself on a specially designed weighing chair. The idea of the weighing chair derives from the Italian physician Sanctorius's *Medicina Statica*, which first appeared in 1614 and was translated into English in 1676. This book introduced the invention and proposed its use as both a means of promoting healthiness and of determining the precise amount of perspiration given off by the body. Mr. Spectator's correspondent has ended up almost permanently ensconcing himself within his own version of the machine, spending most of his waking and sleeping hours measuring the fluctuations of his own weight. Addison's correspondent is physically self-imprisoned within the weighing chair and narratively imprisoned, as well, in his report of his own life on the chair, which has the effect of making his whole existence an anecdotal circumstance. Constantly performing both mentally and physically the "swaying and swinging of the mental disposition of weighing and judging," with which Jolles associates the simple form of the "case," the man brings to mind the unfortunate dove in the air pump in Joseph Wright's painting, except he is a willing participant in what is, in effect, an experiment that he is undertaking upon himself. The correspondent's efforts to measure and regulate the fluctuations of his own body—even to the extent of attempting to weigh the time he spends in sleep—only lead to him wasting away in his chair:

> I allow my self, one Night with another, a Quarter of a Pound of Sleep within a few Grains more or less; and if upon my rising I find that I have not consumed my whole quantity, I take out the rest in my Chair. Upon an exact Calculation of what I expended and received the last Year, which I always register in a Book, I find the Medium to be two hundred weight, so that I cannot discover that I am impaired one Ounce in my Health during a whole Twelve-month. And yet, Sir, notwithstanding this my great Care to ballast my self equally every Day, and to keep my Body in its proper Poise, so it is that I find my self in a sick and languishing Condition. My Complexion is grown very sallow, my Pulse low, and my Body Hydropical.

Although the man asks Mr. Spectator to provide him with "more certain Rules to walk by than those I have already observed," (*S* 1:107), Mr. Spectator refrains from giving him any. The Latin motto to the number implies, however, that the correspondent's sickened condition is the result of an un-suspected "rule" at work, one that predicts that too much self-regulation will end up destroying one's health. But the man in the weighing chair's very failure to find the "rules" for which he is to live, for all his weighing and calculating, embodies the way anecdotal cases in the *Spectator* in general are suspended before the general laws of human nature, whose existence they imply but never actually prove. Anecdotes are perennially "before the law" in the *Spectator*, suggesting the existence of regularities behind the human world but never quite clinching them.

The last entry of the notes I discuss, "Mr. *Thomas Inkle* of London, in the good Ship called the *Achilles*. Yarico—" refers to the story whose telling

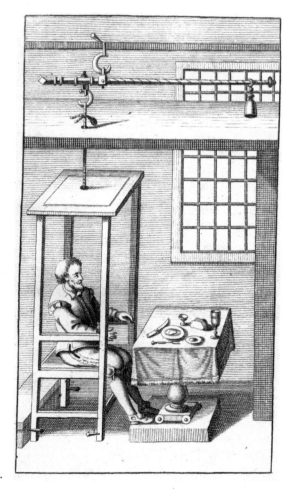

Fig. 2. Frontispiece from Sanctorius, *Medicina Statica: or Rules of Health in Eight Sections of Aphorisms* (London, 1704).

takes up most of Steele's *Spectator* 11. This number begins with the telling of an ancient anecdote by a "Common-Place Talker" to "Arietta," who is hosting him along with Mr. Spectator himself. This man discourses on "the old Topick, of Constancy in Love," tying together "Quotations out of Plays and Songs, which allude to the Perjuries of the Fair, and the general Levity of Women" in a monologue that does not end "till he had repeated and murdered the celebrated Story of the *Ephesian* Matron" (*S* 1:48). In the story of the matron, told most famously by Petronius in the first century CE, a woman elects to starve herself to death by the tomb of her husband. She changes her mind, however, when she encounters a soldier charged with guarding the dead bodies that hang on the crosses nearby. While the woman sleeps with the soldier, the parents of one of the crucified thieves take their son's body down from one of the crosses, leaving the soldier likely to be put to death for neglecting his duties. The widowed woman saves her new lover by offering her husband's body to the soldier to be hung up on the cross in place of the thief's stolen body.[43]

Arietta answers her guest's antifeminist story with a story of her own, which she tells on the authority of "*Ligon*'s Account of *Barbadoes*" (*S* 1:49). The book to which Arietta refers, Richard Ligon's *A True & Exact History of the Island of Barbados* (1657), tells the story of Yarico, an Amerindian woman from the mainland of South America. In Ligon's original anecdote, Yarico encounters an unnamed man recently arrived on an English ship on the coast of South America, who is left alone after his party is attacked by her own people. Yarico falls in love with the man and, sheltering him in a cave, feeds and protects him until it is safe for the two to return to shore. When the two lovers are taken on board a ship, Ligon writes, the youth "forgot the kindness of the poor maid, that had ventured her life for his safety, and sold her for a slave, who was as free born as he: And so poor *Yarico* for her love, lost her liberty." Yarico ends up as a slave on the island of Barbados, where she and her story attract Ligon's attention. He describes her going to a river to give birth to a baby, fathered by a servant on the island, and returning "with her Childe in her arms, a lusty Boy, frolick and lively."[44] She is also described pulling some of the ants that infest the island out of Ligon's feet.[45] In having Arietta retell the story, Steele excises Ligon's prefatory account of Yarico's life after her enslavement in order to create a self-contained anecdote that can serve to answer the story of the Ephesian matron. At the same time, Steele also greatly expands on Ligon's story of how Yarico came to be enslaved, naming the faithless man "Thomas Inkle" and adding the detail of Yarico's revelation to Inkle that she is pregnant by him, which only leads him to negotiate a higher price for her. Thanks to its inclusion in the *Spectator,* Yarico's story became a proverbial anecdote in the eighteenth century, endlessly told and retold in poems, fictional epistles, and plays.[46] Mr. Spectator himself thinks the story "should be always a Counterpart to the *Ephesian* Matron" (*S* 1:51), adducing the story as evidence that men may be just as prone to inconstancy as women are in matters of the heart.

The relationship of the Inkle and Yarico anecdote to the classical story of the Ephesian Matron exemplifies the *Spectator's* experimental ethos, which dictates that no one story, or even an interpretation of one, be allowed to have the final word. The problem with the commonplace talker's story of the Ephesian matron is that the story itself, and the antifeminist construction put on it, has become overfamiliar and fossilized into a standard *exemplum.* Like the flask that appears in the frontispiece for Joseph Petit Andrews's *Anecdotes, &c. Ancient and Modern,* the *Spectator* is a textual space in which ancient and modern stories collide and jostle, rather than falling into neat one-to-one relationships. The anecdote of Inkle and Yarico, for example, invokes other narratives besides the Ephesian matron, notably the ancient story of Dido and Aeneas and the modern story of Pocahontas and John Smith.[47] The anecdote fails to act as the simple "counterpart" of the story of the Ephesian matron, for the motivations for the betrayals in both stories are completely different, as are their consequences for the people betrayed. The emotional response that the two stories produce within the fictional situations in which they are told are, again, quite unlike. Petronius's anecdote of the Ephesian matron provokes the sailors who hear it to laugh while Arietta's story of Inkle and Yarico prompts Mr. Spectator to weep.

The word "counterpart" itself carries a specific legal sense as the copy of a document held by the other party to an indenture. The fact that both the anecdote of the Ephesian matron and the anecdote of Inkle and Yarico themselves revolve around broken promises, then, ought to make readers wary of treating either story as simply the "counterpart" of the other.[48] The *Spectator* papers in general tend to "introduce doubts, uneasy parallels between ancients and moderns that idealization cannot neutralize or assuage," as Nicole Horejsi writes in her essay on the *Spectator's* telling of the Inkle and Yarico story.[49] The trailing dash that ends the entry in Mr. Spectator's notes "Mr. *Thomas Inkle* of London, in the good Ship called the *Achilles.* Yarico—" suggests an awareness that part of Yarico's story has been excised and also a sense that the full implications of the story have not been accounted for. Although the subject of slavery is deemphasized in Steele's retelling of Ligon's anecdote, which cuts Yarico's story off at the point at which Inkle sells her into slavery along with her unborn child, in the latter half of the eighteenth century the story was reinterpreted as a narrative about the evils of the slave trade.[50]

The framing context of the *Spectator* thus tends to pull against Mr. Spectator's own sense that the Inkle and Yarico anecdote stands to the anecdote of the Ephesian matron in the simple relation of counterpart to original. Indeed, the number hints that to treat the two anecdotes as exactly equivalent would be to fall into a similar kind of abstract thinking that Thomas Inkle practices, when he begins "seriously to reflect upon his loss of Time, to weigh with himself how many Days Interest of his Mony he had lost during his Stay with *Yarico*," before making the decision to sell her so as not to appear to his friends to have made no profit from his voyage (*S* 1:51). The faithless man's last name, "Inkle," is, as Frank Felsenstein notes, the name for a type of linen tape used for shoelaces and other miscellaneous purposes, an appropriate name for a trader who begins to see his native lover as a commodity. The name also suggests the ink that Inkle would have frequently been using to draw up his accounts, including the one in which he presumably records the profit from the sale of his lover and unborn son.[51] Mr. Spectator similarly seeks to move from anecdotes to the abstract laws of human nature, much as Inkle moves from the things and persons in which he trades to the abstract entries of his account book. But the papers also stage Mr. Spectator's repeated failure to account entirely for the stories he tells. The number containing Steele's anecdote also seems conscious of the parallels between Inkle's exploitation of Yarico's body and Mr. Spectator's efforts to transform Yarico's story into useful knowledge by drawing attention to its exchangeability with the story of the Ephesian matron. Yarico herself might be said, to use Ian Baucom's words in *Specters of the Atlantic* (2005), to suffer both the violence of becoming a slave and "the violence of becoming a 'type': a type of person, or, terribly, not even that, a type of nonperson, a type of property, a type of commodity, a type of money."[52] The number at once gestures toward making Yarico into the type of the "betrayed woman" that can serve to counterpart the Ephesian matron's dead husband and draws attention, in Mr. Spectator's tears, to an affective surplus that exceeds the story's explicit role as a modern anecdote that can balance out Petronius's ancient one.[53]

Another anecdote of slavery in the New World that is included in Addison's *Spectator* 215—a story recounting an incident that supposedly took place "about twelve years ago" on Saint Christopher Island (now St. Kitts) in the Caribbean—makes explicit the connection between the violence of slavery and what Baucom calls "the violence of becoming a 'type.'" The anecdote, which Mr. Spectator tells on the authority of an English slave owner, who subsequently returned to London "about thirteen years ago," gives the story of two male slaves who are in love with the same woman. Although the woman agrees to marry either man, they are unable come to an agreement on who is to marry her and who is to renounce her. The two men subsequently stab the woman to death and then turn their weapons upon themselves, leaving the Englishman who owned them to tell their tragic tale.[54] The anecdote, on Mr. Spectator's interpretation of it, shows "what strange Disorders are bred in the Minds of those Men whose Passions are not regulated by Vertue, and disciplined by Reason" (*S* 2:340). The story is, for Mr. Spectator at least, an illustration of human nature in its original rough condition. Comparing the "Human Soul without Education" to "Marble in the Quary" (*S* 2:338), Mr. Spectator explains that human nature is everywhere made out of the same material, but that the common substrate of human nature must be polished in order to shape its expression.[55] "Though the Action which I have recited is in it self full of Guilt and Horror," Mr. Spectator explains, "it proceeded from a Temper of Mind which might have produced very noble Fruits, had it been informed and guided by a suitable education" (*S* 2:340). The anecdote thus seems, explicitly at least, to make the slaves' racial difference irrelevant to answering the question of why they acted the way they did. Mr. Spectator does not argue that the slaves murdered the woman because they belong to a race or nation predisposed to violence, but rather because the nature that they share with Mr. Spectator has been insufficiently polished by education. (At the same time, however, the marble metaphor covertly works to align civilized behavior with the whiteness of polished marble.) As in *Spectator* 11, Mr. Spectator seems to see the tragedy at the center of *Spectator* 215 as if it were almost entirely disconnected from the overarching tragedy of slavery itself, the institution within which the whole action occurs. Nevertheless, the number containing the anecdote suggests a structural similarity between the slave trader who originally tells the anecdote and Mr. Spectator: if the slave owner profits financially from the slaves' labor, then Mr. Spectator (and his readers) profit intellectually from their deaths, with the story of their sufferings serving to illuminate the science of human nature.

The anecdote of Inkle and Yarico and the anecdote of the tragic love triangle between slaves illustrate how the program of rethinking human nature after Locke increasingly depended on stories of people on the apparent peripheries of the human: people in the grip of strange superstitions, the obsessed man on the weighing chair, the calculating trader who exchanges his native lover for money, and the slaves who murder the woman they love. Mr. Spectator tells anecdotes of people who seem distant from the assumed human norm, people he then attempts to integrate back into a controlling vision of a universal nature. However, this process of manufacturing examples of human nature from anecdotes remains incomplete. Both anecdotes and the human beings whose stories they tell also inevitably slide away from the laws they are supposed to exemplify, refusing to settle into the commonplace, the *exemplum,* or the type. This friction between anecdotal circumstance and human law is what makes the process of thinking with anecdotes "experimental" in the encompassing sense of the term, as an open-ended act of thinking about the human through storytelling. The presence of the anecdote of Inkle and Yarico in the Spectator's notes, however, suggests that this practice was not innocent, for all its open-endedness. The co-presence of comic anecdotes of commercial London society with a tragic anecdote from the New World in Mr. Spectator's notes underlines the point that empiricist moral philosophy depended in no small part upon slavery for its materials. This relationship between the study and the trade of human beings was especially visible in the coffeehouses of London, sites of financial and intellectual speculation both.[56]

HAYWOOD'S ANECDOTES

In this last section, I examine how Eliza Haywood enters into the experimental tradition in the *Female Spectator,* a periodical that asserts women's prerogative to pronounce judgments on human nature.[57] Haywood's periodical at once imitates the *Spectator* and counters its tendency to frame women as moral philosophy's objects of study and not its practitioners. In the *Spectator* Mr. Spectator pronounces not only on human nature in general but also on the specific nature of the female sex. In *Spectator* 128, for example, he affirms that "Women in their Nature are much more gay and joyous than Men" though he declares himself uncertain "whether it be that their Blood is more refined, their Fibres more delicate, and their animal Spirits more light and volatile; or whether as some have imagined, there may not be a kind of Sex in the very Soul" (*S* 2:8). The anecdotes that are used to anatomize female nature in the *Spectator* frequently reinterpret transient fashions as the expressions of the female sex's natural proclivity to ostentatious display. In *Spectator* 129, for example, an unnamed correspondent describes the astonishment that rippled through a country church service he was attending when it was interrupted by the unexpected entrance of a woman wearing a hoop petticoat:

> As we were in the midst of the Service a Lady who is the chief Woman of the Place, and had passed the Winter at *London* with her Husband, entered the Congregation in a little Head-dress and a Hoop'd-Petticoat. The People, who were wonderfully startled at such a Sight, all of them rose up. Some stared at the prodigious Bottom, and some at the little Top of this strange Dress. In the mean time the Lady of the Manor filled the *Area* of the Church, and walked up to her Pew with an unspeakable Satisfaction, amidst the Whispers, Conjectures and Astonishments of the whole Congregation. (*S* 2:14)

On witnessing the spectacular entrance of the petticoat, the parishioners are moved to wonder at it, in both senses of the word. The petticoat breaks an implicit social law, and in doing so it gives rise to "Whispers, Conjectures, and Astonishments." The anecdote of the entrance of the hoop petticoat into the church prompts an opening query into the motivating causes that might lead women to wear such a garment in such a place and, by extension, the motivating causes that might lead women in general to make spectacles of themselves. By writing against the hoop petticoat, Mr. Spectator may, the correspondent hopes, cause women's petticoats once again to assume their natural shape, much as a flower responds to nightfall by closing in upon itself.[58] As Joanna Picciotto writes, in this letter to Mr. Spectator, women seem to "merge with botanical specimens, or vivisected experimental subjects, yielding to the pressure of his penetrating scrutiny."[59]

In the *Female Spectator*, however, Haywood reclaims just this power of "penetrating scrutiny" on behalf of women, moving women from specimens of human nature to speculators on it. This project to enlist women in the advancement of knowledge is made apparent in Book 15 of the periodical, in which *Philo-Naturae*, the *Female Spectator's* possibly fictional correspondent, encourages women to become natural philosophers. He recommends that when women go out into the countryside, they make sure to bring with them their microscopes, for if they were to do so then "They would doubtless perceive Animals which are not to be found in the most accurate Volumes of Natural Philosophy; and the *Royal Society* might be indebted to every fair *Columbus* for a new World of Beings to employ their Speculations" (*EH* 2.3:88). The Female Spectator, along with her companions, take *Philo-Naturae's* advice in Book 17 during a wet summer in the country, albeit with mixed results. Whenever a break in the rain allows, the women go out into the open air armed with their microscopes. Although they find that the small animals they hoped to find in drops of water have been washed away by the rain, their attention is captured by the numerous caterpillars they see. They note how these beings curl up into "a little Heap, or Ball, by the Help of Rings placed at certain Distances round their Bodies" at the touch of their fingers. They also take note of "those beautiful gold Specks" that some of the caterpillars display, which they are at a loss to explain, until "a very ingenious Gentleman, who sometimes assisted our Speculations," explains that "these Insects had small Fibres between their outward Coat and Skin, filled with a thinner and more delicate Juice than that which supplies them with Strength . . . and that this fine Liquid, transpiring by the Heat of the Sun, becomes of the same Colour with the Rays that called it forth" (*EH* 2.3.161). We might read the "Gentleman, who sometimes assisted our Speculations," as a stand-in for Mr. Spectator himself, who inspires the Female Spectator and her club but also makes way for them to assume the task of inquiring into the natural world, noticing anomalies in nature and attempting to discover the underlying principles that produce them.[60]

Yet Haywood also claims for women the prerogative to speculate on human nature, in ways that suggest an aggressive attempt to wrest the license to speculate on human anomalies away from Mr. Spectator. In the fifteenth number, a correspondent identified as "Leucothea" tells an anecdote that at once parodies the *Spectator*'s anecdotes of female nature and asserts women's prerogative to judge the nature of men.[61] Leucothea complains about the ridiculous length of the swords that fashion-conscious men have taken to carrying about, describing a discombobulating incident that recently happened to her involving one of them:

> I will tell you how I was served the other Day in the Mall:–There were five of us perfectly well dress'd; for my Part I had a new Suit of Cloaths on, I had never wore before, and every body says is the sweetest fancied Thing in the World:—To speak Truth we took up the whole Breadth of the Walk; unfortunately for me, I happened to be on the outside, when a Creature, who I afterward heard was a *Dettingem* Hero, came hurrying along, with a Sword as long as himself, hanging dangling at his Knee, and pushing roughly by me, his ugly Weapon hitched in the pink'd Trimming of my Petticoat, and tore it in the most rueful Manner imaginable. (*EH* 2.3.102)

Leucothea ends her letter with a request that the Female Spectator demon-
strate her impartiality by writing a similar exposure of the ridiculousness of
the male practice of going out in public "as if they were in a Field of Battle,
just going upon an Engagement" (*EH* 2.3:103), though she in fact supplies
more than enough satire of male vanity herself. Leucothea's anecdote acts
as the *Female Spectator*'s own "counterpart" to the *Spectator*'s anecdote of
the hoop petticoat's appearance in the parochial church.[62] Like the story
of Inkle and Yarico, of course, the anecdote does not merely "counterpart"
its equivalent in the *Spectator* but acquires implications of its own. One is to
associate Mr. Spectator's speculations on the nature of female nature with
the veteran of Dettingem's transparently phallic "weapon," which pokes at
women's dresses as its owner rudely pushes by them. What Picciotto calls
Mr. Spectator's "penetrating scrutiny" is thus unmasked in the anecdote as
an expression of a brutish male nature.

I use the *Parrot* (1746), the short-lived periodical that Haywood published after the *Female Spectator*'s run had ended, to draw to a close this
chapter on the experimental uses of the anecdote in the English essay from
Locke to Haywood. In the *Parrot*, Haywood adopted the eidolon of a parrot born on the island of Java who has, after a period of traveling around
continental Europe in the company of various owners, been moving from
owner to owner in England. The parrot reflects, in the first number, on
its own natural proclivity for "*Chit-Chat*":

> PHILOSOPHERS may argue as they please, but there is no such thing as
> totally changing Nature:—What is born with us will sometimes peep
> out, in spite of Precept or Education; unless, as some have endeav-
> oured to prove, the *Humours* and *Will of Action* is lodged in the *Blood,*
> which, by being drained out and exchanged for that of another Crea-
> ture, the System of the *Mind* would be reversed, and different *Pro-
> pensities* arise with the different *Animalculæ;* but should I, in order to
> get rid of this Tale-telling Inclination, submit to such an Experiment,
> which (by the bye) not the whole Royal Society, not all the Virtuosoes
> in the World should prevail on me to do, pray who can answer that I
> might not imbibe some other as *bad,* or perhaps *worse* Property than
> that which had been expunged? (*EH* 2.1.184)

The parrot engages here in a complicated reflection on tale-telling and its
relationship to the natural world. Most straightforwardly, the parrot asserts
that its compulsion to repeat whatever stories are told to it is an expression

of its unchangeable nature as a parrot. But the parrot also draws attention to the "Tale-telling Inclination" as something that it shares with human beings, including the philosophers of his own times who, as Hume suggested, must rely on tale-telling rather than experiments in order to understand their own nature.[63] Indeed, the parrot draws attention to the inappropriateness of conducting natural-philosophical experiments on conscious beings, pointedly refusing to countenance submitting himself to an experiment involving the complete replacement of its blood by another animal, so to ascertain whether the bent of his nature is to be located in the small "animalculæ" circulating around his body, or somewhere else. Despite the parrot's refusal to allow himself to be experimented upon, the essayistic writings of Locke, Addison, Steele, and Haywood posit the anecdotal tale itself as a kind of literary experiment, which allows human nature to "peep out" unexpectedly through the stray incidents of human life. As an "Inclination" characteristic of human beings as much as parrots, the telling of anecdotes is itself a fundamental phenomenon of human (and parrot) nature. As such, the anecdote is both a way of understanding human nature and itself a manifestation of that nature.

Across the essay tradition running from Locke to Haywood, anecdotes allowed deviant phenomena in human life to be mined for insights into the deeper regularities of human nature. Locke's anecdotes concern figures who are disabled or barred from the domains of experience that are shared by Locke and the majority of his readers: a blind man, an Indian philosopher, a king of Siam, and a Brazilian parrot. Mr. Spectator's notes contain jottings from the margins of human experience, including anecdotes of odd beliefs and superstitions, the case of the man who condemns himself to living his life on a weighing chair, and stories of betrayal and murder that play out against the backdrop of the Atlantic trade in slaves. Anecdotes served the science of human nature with narratives analogous to natural philosophers' accounts of experiments, which, as Hume argued, could not be conducted on human beings in the same way as they could on animals or inanimate matter. The narratives shared with the natural philosophical experiment and the philosophical thought experiment, however, an open-endedness that meant that their meaning could never fully be fixed or settled. Often these reinterpretations of existing anecdotes involved the tellings of new anecdotes that veered away from the old ones, as when Hume responds to Locke's story of the blind man who thought that scarlet was like the sound of a trumpet by telling the story of his blind friend's association of colors with the pleasures of society, when the *Spectator* responds to the familiar story of the Ephesian matron story by telling the story of Inkle and Yarico, or when the *Female Spectator* responds to the *Spectator's* anecdote of the hoop petticoat by telling the anecdote of the oversized sword. The work of anecdotes in the English essay from Locke to Haywood was to open up the human as an object of inquiry like any other phenomenon in nature, with the result that human nature became increasingly difficult to distinguish from the natural world that enfolded it. The only response to this newly estranged human landscape was to keep "Hawking and hunting" after an elusive human nature through the telling and retelling of anecdotes.

TWO

Hume and the Laws of Anecdote

ᵕᏙᵕ

David Hume's love of anecdotes is well known. Hume's biographer, Ernest Campbell Mossner, informs us that Hume "displayed a fondness for a large and well-prepared meal, for good drink (claret or port), and for the conviviality that good food and good drink in the proper proportions inspire—the witty anecdote, the spicy story, the friendly raillery, the practical joke."[1] Duncan Forbes finds that many of Hume's letters are "largely exclamation, banter, anecdote or just plain fun."[2] And John Richetti remarks on the role anecdotes play in Hume's philosophy, observing that "Even more than Locke or Berkeley and with a much greater spirit of fun" Hume "loves to ground his arguments in personal anecdote in which the process of thinking is dramatized and thereby redefined into a combination of perception and intellectual formulation after the fact of sense impressions."[3] This chapter offers plenty of evidence for Hume's delight in anecdotes. I aim to go, however, beyond the simple observation that anecdotes frequently appear in Hume's writings. My larger argument is that anecdotes and anecdotal thinking are woven into the very texture of Hume's thought.

Donald W. Livingston has argued that the contradiction between philosophy and what Hume calls "common life"—the everyday world with its unreflective habits of thinking and conversing that even philosophers fall into when they are not doing philosophy—is the central problem for Hume across his career. Livingston sees Hume as elaborating an account of human nature that starts out from the assumption that the philosopher stands above common life, scrutinizing its unexamined assumptions and finding them wanting. However, Livingston argues that this process of rigorously questioning the grounds of our knowledge of ourselves and our world leads to the ultimate conclusion that philosophers must depend on the commonsense beliefs that they thought to surmount.[4] This chapter suggests that the anecdote operates in Hume's writings as a way station between philosophy and common life, a means of traveling from the one to the other. Hume's anecdotes open routes leading away from common life, appearing to invite skepticism about the very possibility of maintaining a coherent sense of self, world, and past. At the same time, Hume's anecdotes also enable an escape from skepticism into a renewed sense of a shared reality, founded on the possibility of sharing stories with other people. Hume's anecdotes help him submit commonsense notions of mind and world to the skeptical labor of reason, which fragments these entities into a multitude of impressions and ideas. But anecdotes also play a restorative role in Hume's writings, affirming the possibility of approaching an understanding of human nature through storytelling. As a means of moving the dialectic between philosophy and common life forward, the anecdote in Hume's hands becomes a way of understanding perceptual experience as a vast midden made up of "broken appearances" (*T* 133; 136). Yet, as Annette C. Baier stresses in *A Progress of Sentiments* (1991), Hume also reveals how these "broken appearances" inhere within a world cemented together through social relationships.[5]

This chapter surveys how Hume grappled with anecdotes and anecdotal ways of thinking, over the course of his career as a man of letters. The first half of the chapter uses anecdotes told by Hume and anecdotes told about him to read the *Treatise of Human Nature*, the *Enquiry Concerning Human Understanding* (1748), and the *Enquiry Concerning the Principles of Morals* (1751) as advancing a distinctively anecdotal approach to the science of human nature. I then turn to Hume's later career, picking up the anecdotes scattered across Hume's major historical works: the *History of England* (1754–61) and the *Natural History of Religion* (1757). In these works, the anecdote helps situate historical and religious thought in common experience and question the teleological kinds of thinking that underlie history and religion. Finally, in the late essay "Of the Standard of Taste," the anecdote becomes a means of showing the faculty of aesthetic taste in action.

HUMEAN ANECDOTES

Hume was not just a teller of anecdotes; he was also the subject of anecdotes that circulated in his own lifetime and after his death. In this section I move between anecdotes told by Hume himself and anecdotes told by others about him, all of which are situated on the threshold between common life and philosophy. The anecdotes thus dramatize in human terms the way Hume's philosophical project is both alienated from and anchored in the assumptions of common life. In this context, the anecdotes about Hume appear not as trivial distractions from a serious reading of his writings. Instead they emerge as philosophical parables that illuminate the essentially anecdotal nature of Hume's thinking on human nature. The anecdotes that contemporary observers told about Hume not only resonate with the counterintuitive conclusions of his philosophy, they also condense the larger narrative that is presented in Hume's philosophical works in which Hume casts himself as a Sisyphus-like figure, attempting to push himself above common life, becoming bewildered and humiliated in the attempt, and subsequently accepting the authority of the beliefs that hold the social world together.

In his short manuscript memoirs entitled "Anecdotes of Hume" (written c. 1780), the Irish politician James Caulfeild, 1st Earl of Charlemont speculates on the causes of the contemporary obsession with anecdotes:

> Whether it be from that Portion of Envy which Nature seems to have implanted in our Disposition, and which, however misused and perverted by us, was probably intended by Providence as a Principle of virtuous Emulation, or from what other cause I know not, certain it is that We always behold with a Degree of Pleasure the Weaknesses of those whose Abilities and consequent Reputation have rendered them Objects of Respect and universal Applause. Perhaps also our innate Propensity to be amused by Absurdity and Inconsistency may strongly co'operate to this Point, and we contemplate a great and wise Man sinking into Childishness, and debasing his Character by rediculous Pursuits and incongruous Situations with a similar Delight to that which we feel when we see an Elephant dancing on the Ropes.[6]

Charlemont offers his anecdotes about Hume's "rediculous Pursuits" as accounts of occasions when the intelligence that Hume shows in his philosophical writing failed him. He also hints, however, that the anecdotes of Hume's absurd behavior can be read as tokens of the absurdity of his philosophical principles. Charlemont's "Anecdotes of Hume" ends with a diagnosis of how Hume's intellectual vanity led him down the path to irreligion and philosophical perversity: "He grew fond of Paradoxes, which his Abilities enabled him successfully to support, and his Understanding was so far warped and bent by this unfortunate Predilection that He had well nigh lost that best Faculty of the Mind, the almost intuitive Perception of Truth."[7] Hume's ridiculous behavior flows naturally, Charlemont hints, from the deeply ridiculous nature of his philosophy.

The first anecdote told in the "Anecdotes of Hume" is written according to what Charlemont calls "the Laws of Anecdote," which require the anecdote teller to poke fun at celebrated people by representing them in their frail and foolish moments.[8] The anecdote is taken from the period in which Charlemont first came to know Hume, in the middle of the 1740s, when Hume was acting as secretary to Lieutenant General James St Clair at Turin. The future Earl of Charlemont was also studying at the Military Academy there, where he was courting a beautiful young countess. In the anecdote, Hume asks Charlemont to introduce him to the countess so that he might have the benefit of female conversation and company, a request to which Charlemont readily consents. The countess soon informs Charlemont, however, that Hume has been making his own addresses to her and invites her incredulous lover to hide himself behind a curtain so as to observe Hume's behavior for himself. Observing the unfolding scene from his hiding place, Charlemont is more amused than angry to see "my old fat philosopher" going down on his knees to propose marriage to the young woman:

> And now indeed began the most rediculous of all possible Farces—
> The Violence of his unwieldy Passion, joined to his Want of French,
> rendered his Language almost inarticulate—He panted—He sighed—
> He groaned—Ah, Madame—Madame—J'estouffe *avec* l'amour! and
> then again He groaned—Chere—Chere Dame—Je suis desolè—
> abimè—aneanti!—Oh, pour *aneanti*, dit Elle, ce n'est en effat qu'une
> Operation très naturelle de votre Systeme—Mais levez vous de grace—
> Je ne veus plus vous soufrir dans cette Posture—allons—levez vous, je
> vous en prie—Je vous l'ordonne—Here He endeavoured to embrace
> her knees, and, turning his Face a little towards my hiding Place, ex-
> hibited to my View such a Picture of old, ugly, blubbering, fat, ungainly
> Passion as had well nigh forced me to discover myself by laughing.[9]

Charlemont has difficulty suppressing his hilarity at the contrast between Hume's foolish behavior and his reputation for philosophical sagacity. Hume's meeting with the countess was, Charlemont writes, an occasion on which Hume "forgot his philosophy." But it is the countess, in the anecdote, who is closer to the mark when she wittily comments after Hume has confessed to have been "annihilated" (*aneanti*) by love that his annihilation "is nothing but a very natural operation of your system" (*ce n'est en effat qu'une Operation très naturelle de votre Systeme*).

"Annihilate," as Charlemont might well have known, is a key word in the *Treatise of Human Nature,* in which Hume shows that his system of impressions and ideas, taken to its logical conclusion, implies the annihilation of the self as something distinct from the multitude of perceptions that comprise it. Hume writes:

> For my part, when I enter most intimately into what I call *myself,* I always stumble on some particular perception or other, of heat or cold, light or shade, love or hatred, pain or pleasure. I can never catch *myself* at any time without a perception, and never can observe any thing but the perception. When my perceptions are remov'd for any time, as by sound sleep; so long am I insensible of *myself,* and may truly be said not to exist. And were all my perceptions remov'd by death, and cou'd I neither think, nor feel, nor see, nor love, nor hate after the dissolution of my body, I shou'd be entirely annihilated, nor do I conceive what is farther requisite to make me a perfect non-entity.

Hume goes on to invite readers to consider the self not as a stable entity but rather as "a bundle or collection of different perceptions, which succeed each other with an inconceivable rapidity, and are in a perpetual flux and movement" (*T* 165). Perceptions persist no longer than the moment at which they appear before the mind. And these perceptions are not even "before a mind" since there is strictly speaking no mind behind the play of perceptions. As Hume writes in the 1740 *Abstract* to the *Treatise,* perceptions "*compose* the mind, not *belong* to it" (*T* 414). At a certain point in the mind's reflection on its own operations, the mind's own sense of itself as something apart from its perceptions disappears. All that apparently remains are orphaned perceptions whirling about in a great nothingness. Hume's philosophy appears to end in the dissolution of the self and the world outside it into a swarm of perceptions.

But Hume also suggests that the rupture between the lessons of philosophy and the beliefs of common life will begin to heal, once the philosopher admits philosophy's dependence on the intuitive ways of understanding the world that everyone, the philosopher included, makes do with most of the time. Philosophers, outside their moments of philosophical contemplation, perceive the world in much the same way as do the "vulgar," who have never been exposed to philosophical doubt and to whose naive ways of thinking even the most skeptical philosophers return when they are not doing philosophy. For Hume, this does not mean we should abandon skepticism entirely. "In all the incidents of life," Hume affirms, "we ought still to preserve our scepticism." But Hume thinks that skepticism should not lead us to reject all our experience (which is psychologically and practically impossible in any case) but to treat it with the same spirit that we hear anecdotes, with what he calls a "serious good-humoured disposition" (*T* 176), tempered with a measure of doubt.[10]

As Annette Baier notes in her reading of Hume's *Treatise,* social relationships place a natural limit on skepticism. We do not simply believe or disbelieve our ideas. Rather, we believe in and with other people, whom we try to persuade to share our own beliefs, while they try to persuade us to share in theirs in turn. Baier points out that we judge the truth of our senses in the same way that we judge the truthfulness of historical accounts of the past and of the anecdotal stories we encounter in informal conversation: "We trust the 'testimony' of our senses, more or less as we do the testimony of our fellows. We learn from experience, and from reflection on that experience, that most testifiers can, in some conditions and on some matters, speak falsely, and maybe that few rarely speak truly. But to judge that all speak falsely, when (as they all sometimes do) they attribute color to things, would be like resolving to disbelieve anybody who reported seeing the Loch Ness monster, because one's theory told one there could not be such a thing, even if one seemed to see it oneself."[11] For his part, Hume claims that this willingness not to insist on the absolute verifiability of the testimony of our senses and the testimony of others is an indulgence we are especially apt to extend to people telling funny stories. Hume notes in the *Enquiry Concerning the Principles of Morals,* that although the practice of passing off untrue stories as fact is usually condemned, "Some indulgence, however, to lying or fiction is given in *humorous* stories; because it is there really agreeable and entertaining; and truth is not of any importance" (*EPM* 68). In the *Enquiry Concerning the Principles of Morals* itself, Hume tells a number of such stories, one of which derives cruel humor from the spectacle of a hump-backed man used as a piece of furniture.[12] "It is a vulgar story at PARIS," Hume writes, "that, during the rage of the MISSISSIPPI, a hump-backed fellow went every day into the RUE DE QUINCEMPOIX, where the stock-jobbers met in great crowds, and was well paid for allowing them to make use of his hump as a desk, in order to sign their contracts upon it" (*EPM* 29). This anecdote, set during the frenzied speculation in John Law's Mississippi Scheme in the late 1710s, is intended to illustrate the exceptions that attend the general principle that beauty has its origin in utility. The story, set just before the Mississippi bubble burst, may itself be seen as a bubble, in the sense of being "unsubstantial, empty, or worthless."[13]

Yet even as a seeming "bubble" in itself, anecdote does perform an important role in the *Enquiry Concerning the Principles of Morals,* acting at once to circumscribe the application of general principles of human nature and to illustrate how philosophical reflection is indebted to the unverifiable stories of common life.

If Hume's *Treatise* as a whole tells a comic narrative of the philosopher's exile from common life and subsequent reconciliation with it, then contemporary reports of Hume's own appearance and behavior retell this story in the language of common life. Observers of the flesh-and-blood Hume often remarked on his appearance of mental absence in public. In Charlemont's "Anecdotes of Hume," for example, we find an extended description of Hume's oblivious expression that works to distance Hume from regular society: "The Powers of Physiognomy were baffled by his Countenance, neither cou'd the most skillful in that Science pretend to discover the smallest Trace of the Faculties of his Mind in the unmeaning Features of his Visage—His Face was broad and fat—His mouth wide, and without any other Expression than that of Imbecility—His eyes vacant and spiritless, and the Corpulence of his whole Person was far better fitted to communicate the Idea of a Turtle-eating Alderman than of a refined Philosopher."[14] Angela Coventry and Emilio Mazza have compiled a large number of similar eighteenth-century accounts that testify to Hume's blankness of expression.[15] Another contemporary description of Hume, for example, claims that Hume's "countenance was not very promising, being upon the whole rather heavy; tho' when he was engaged in conversation, or otherwise annimated, it lightened up considerably and it became very agreeable. He was of a Swarthy complexion, with grey eyes, very little collourd, and his features, upon the whole, rather flat than otherwise."[16] Hume's face is a stagnant pool that becomes animated only when it is stirred up by conversation with others, embodying, as it does so, the movement in Hume's own thought from philosophy to a renewed engagement with common life.

Hume's erstwhile friend, Jean-Jacques Rousseau, was also struck by Hume's facial expressions—one of which would become an important contributing factor in the well-publicized falling-out between the two men.[17] Addressing Hume in an accusatory letter, Rousseau remembers how, when the two were sitting in front of the fire, "I caught his [i.e., Hume's] eyes intently fixed on mine, as indeed happened very often; and that in a manner of which it is very difficult to give an idea; at that time he gave me a stedfast, piercing look, mixed with a sneer, which greatly disturbed me."[18] In his reply to Rousseau's letter, Hume protested that Rousseau had projected a sneer onto his perfectly expressionless face: "What! because sometimes, when absent in thought, I have a fixed Look or Stare, you suspect me to be a Traytor, and you have the Assurance to tell me of such black and ridiculous Suspicions! Are not most studious Men (and many of them more than I) subject to like Reveries or Fits of Absence, without being exposed to such Suspicions?" (July 22, 1766, *LDH* 2:68). Rousseau had, according to Hume, wrongly seen an attempt to express contempt when, on Hume's account, all he had really seen was a moment of absentmindedness. Hume's face, at least as its owner represented it, was in fact a total void, and Rousseau had perversely made an eventful something out of nothing.

A vacant stare is inherently ambiguous. It can suggest naïveté or hostility, deep thought or mental vacuity. In his *Life of David Hume* (1954), Mossner is careful to defend Hume's habitual absent look from those contemporaries who saw it as a sign of stupidity, affirming that he "exhibited that preoccupied stare of the thoughtful scholar that so commonly impresses the undiscerning as imbecile."[19] Yet to rush to interpret Hume's vacant look as a sign of intelligence is to miss the extent to which Hume's own philosophical writings depend on the literary performance of naïveté, even idiocy, as a means of disrupting commonsense assumptions that underpin everyday life. The vacancy of expression and mind to which many anecdotes about Hume attest is a physiognomic counterpart to the nothingness that lies at the very center of Hume's philosophical project. Ian Duncan points to the important part that nothingness plays in Hume's philosophy as a whole, in which "'Nothing' denotes the absence of divine agency and transcendental forms of meaning from the world (such as metaphysical causality)—and thus the abyss behind appearances, disclosed by the skeptical work of reason" and "also designates the phenomenological substance that covers up that abyss: the imaginary fabric of 'customary conjunctions' or habitual associations that make up our positive knowledge of the world."[20] If Hume's own face embodies the nothingness that Duncan discovers behind Hume's philosophy, many of the anecdotes told about Hume dramatize and personify it.

As Donald W. Livingston observes in *Philosophical Melancholy and Delirium* (1998), Hume delights in playing "the *fool*" for his readers, as in the moment in the *Enquiry Concerning Human Understanding* in which Hume says that when the skeptical philosopher "awakes from his dream, he will be the first to join in the laugh against himself."[21] In same paragraph, Hume argues that the small incidents of everyday life are all it takes to dispel the skeptic's dream: "a PYRRHONIAN may throw himself or others into a momentary amazement and confusion by his profound reasonings; the first and most trivial event in life will put to flight all his doubts and scruples" (*EHU* 119). As narratives of frequently trivial events, anecdotes might appear to belong naturally to unphilosophical and naive ways of thinking. Yet as Livingston observes, for Hume, "The act of philosophical reflection occurs when there is a break in what had been the seamless whole of custom brought on by an unexpected experience which is contrary to established belief."[22] As a genre drawing attention to "unexpected experiences" in common life, the anecdote can work as a threshold between common life and the work of reflecting philosophically on that life from an estranged perspective. Anecdotes describe occurrences that deviate from usual expectations about how people think and behave. They tend to introduce interruptions into talk and texts: breaks in the flow of conversation, the line of narrative, or the elaboration of an argument. In this way, they can supply potential starting points that allow philosophical thought to venture beyond the unreflective beliefs that underpin our usual transactions in the world. But they also act as anchors preventing philosophers moving too far away from the tacit knowledge of the wider community, drawing them back into everyday life, and humbling their pretensions.

In the *Treatise*, Hume illustrates how anecdotes can assist in prying apart the unexamined assumptions through which we make sense of ourselves and our shared world. He tells a personal anecdote in which he again pretends to be ridiculously obtuse in order to show up the disjunction between philosophical and commonsense accounts of perception. In this and in other moments in the *Treatise*, Hume breaks into a form of storytelling that resembles Samuel Richardson's "New manner of writing—to the moment" in the contemporaneous novel *Pamela* (1740).[23] Hume affects to describe what is going on around him as he writes in his closet and writes an odd kind of present-tense anecdote on the spot, where the strangeness of the story derives in part from the tininess of the gap that is implied between events and their subsequent narration. Hume pretends to be so naive that the sound of an unseen door opening is, for him, a wholly unprecedented and unaccountable event: "When therefore I am thus seated, and revolve over these thoughts, I hear on a sudden a noise as of a door turning upon its hinges; and a little after see a porter, who advances towards me. This gives occasion to many new reflexions and reasonings. First, I never have observ'd, that this noise cou'd proceed from any thing but the motion of a door; and therefore conclude, that this present phænomenon is a contradiction to all past experience, unless the door, which I remember on the other side of the chamber, be still in being" (*T* 130–31). Hume goes on to register amazement that the porter has defied gravity by levitating up to his room, which he must have done, Hume reasons, "unless the stairs I remember be not annihilated by my absence." He is unnerved at the letter from a friend sent across the English Channel that the porter hands him, a phenomenon he finds himself unable to explain "without spreading out in my mind the whole sea and continent betwixt us, and supposing the effects and continu'd existence of posts and ferries" (*T* 131). The simple act of a porter handing Hume a letter from a friend turns out to be an almost miraculous event, or at least it would be so to a person who doubted that objects and people continue to exist even when they are not being perceived.[24] Hume goes on to acknowledge that he is not really as obtuse as he pretends to be in this little story, whose purpose it is to illustrate the absurdity of regarding objects and other people as entities whose existence are dependent on our ability to perceive them. Yet a willingness to play the idiot is necessary to move beyond commonsensical means of construing the world. Like the story of the porter's letter, anecdotes in general are capable of producing a sense of immersion in the minutiae of everyday life. But, again like the letter, they are capable of drawing attention to the implicit rules and assumptions that underpin everyday life by showing what happens when they are suspended.

As we have seen in the case of Charlemont's anecdote of Hume and the countess, Hume's positioning of philosophy both inside and outside common life is paralleled in many anecdotes about Hume's own odd behavior in social situations. Another strikingly similar anecdote has Hume again behaving as a "strange uncouth monster" (*T* 172), struggling to speak fluently, and failing to behave appropriately in female company. The anecdote concerns Hume's behavior after being introduced to two women in a Parisian salon:

> he had been cast for the part of a sultan sitting between two slaves, and employing all his eloquence to win their love. Finding them inexorable, he had to try to find out the reason for their resistance. He was placed upon a sofa between the two prettiest women in Paris; he looked at them fixedly, smote the pit of his stomach and his knees several times, and could find nothing to say to them but, "Well, young ladies; well, there you are, then? well, there you are! there you are, then?" He kept on saying this for a quarter of an hour, without being able to think of anything else. At last one of the young ladies got up

and said impatiently: "Ah! I suspected as much; this man is good for nothing except to eat veal!" Since then he has been banished to the *rôle* of spectator, but is none the less fêted and flattered.[25]

We might read this anecdote as a kind of reductio ad absurdum of Hume's philosophy, which, in its most skeptical cast, renders the philosopher incapable of doing much more than registering the bare fact of perceptions appearing in the mind, resulting in an incapacity to say anything more about them than "there you are."

Stumbling over his words and saying the same thing over and over again, Hume falls in this anecdote into a kind of stammering or stuttering, verbal afflictions that Gilles Deleuze associates with the way many literary and philosophical texts place language under pressure, so that "the language system overstrains itself" to the extent "that it begins to stutter, to murmur, or to mumble," and "the entire language reaches the limit that sketches the outside and confronts silence."[26] In an interview with Claire Parnet, Deleuze linked stuttering with empiricist philosophy's penchant for fragmenting experience into its constituent parts.[27] Hume himself, like Deleuze, had an interest in speech impediments. He remarks in the *Enquiry Concerning the Principles of Morals* on the way stuttering both separates stutterers from society but also invites others to identify sympathetically with their disability: "When a person stutters, and pronounces with difficulty, we even sympathize with this trivial uneasiness, and suffer for him" (*EPM* 41). Like the stutterer whose stuttering both separates him from society and causes him to become an object of sympathetic attachment, Hume's philosophy at once distances him from common life and reels him all the more strongly into it. Anecdotes in general can work to pull philosophers out of their examinations of the workings of their own minds and into the realm of common life, just as Hume is pulled from the speculations of the closet and into a game of backgammon with his friends at the end of Book One of the *Treatise*. But anecdotes can also pull people out of a complacent immersion in common life and tip them into philosophical reflection.

ANECDOTAL RELATIONS

Anecdotes help Hume situate philosophy within the social world that sustains it. Annette Baier observes that even in Hume's analysis of the workings of the solitary mind, relationships between perceptions are personified as "biological and social ties, writ small in the soul."[28] If Hume presents the relations that tie individual perceptions together as analogous to the ties between people, then he also presents them as analogous to the relations between stories in extended narratives. In a section included in all editions up to the seventh edition of the *Enquiry Concerning Human Understanding*, Hume drew out the implications of Locke's concept of the "association of ideas" for the study of narrative. As Robin Valenza points out, Hume suggests here that narratives are tied together in much the same way that ideas are tied together in the human mind.[29] Just as the association of ideas allows the mind to construct sense of a continuous lifeworld, in literary works the association of ideas produces a sense of a coherent and continuous narrative. The association of ideas allows the mind to escape being utterly bewildered by the deluge of disjointed perceptions flowing into it. As Hume had observed in the *Treatise*, "Were ideas entirely loose and unconnected, chance alone wou'd join them" (*T* 12). In practice, the mind links individual ideas together in regular patterns that make the perceptions that form our experience comprehensible. The task of creating connections between perceptions is thus comparable to the task of making connections between anecdotes.

In Section 3 of the *Enquiry Concerning Human Understanding*, Hume attempts to establish a theory of narrative on the basis of the association of ideas. Hume assumes that an idea is analogous to the narration of a particular event. Longer narratives coordinate many individual narratives with one another in ways that resemble the association of ideas in the mind. Particular kinds of narrative are drawn to some kinds of relations more than others. For example, Hume identifies the organizing principle of Ovid's *Metamorphoses* as resemblance, not so much because the poem frequently uses the literary trope of metaphor, but rather because it is structurally founded on the resemblance of events. He observes of Ovid's poem: "Every fabulous transformation, produced by the miraculous power of the gods, falls within the compass of his work. There needs but this one circumstance in any event to bring it under his original plan or intention" (*EHU* 19–20). If poets in general are attracted to the relation of resemblance, then historians are drawn to the relation of contiguity. Hume observes that the historian writing a history of Europe for a particular century will tend to organize events more by contiguity than resemblance: "All events, which happen in that portion of space and period of time, are comprehended in his design, though in other respects different and unconnected" (*EHU* 19). The distinction between genres, for Hume, lies not in their content but rather in the characteristic ways they connect events together. Hume writes, for example, that since the difference between history and epic poetry "consists only in the degrees of connexion, which bind together those several events, of which their subject is composed, it will be difficult, if not impossible, by words, to determine the bounds, which separate them from each other" (*EHU* 22). This suggests that narrative genres are not so much defined by the degree to which they adhere to the past as it really happened as by their methods of arranging small narratives into larger ones. In associating the relation of resemblance with myth and the relation of contiguity with history, Hume anticipates Roman Jakobson's argument that literary genres and modes are characterized by the extent to which they gravitate toward metaphor or metonymy.[30]

After discussing the relations of resemblance and contiguity as principles of tying large narratives together, Hume turns to the relation of cause and effect. He identifies cause and effect as the most common principle of association in "narrative composition" in general and in history in particular. The narrative historian, Hume writes,

> chooses for his subject a certain portion of that great chain of events, which compose the history of mankind: Each link in this chain he endeavours to touch in his narration: Sometimes unavoidable ignorance renders all his attempts fruitless: Sometimes, he supplies by conjecture, what is wanting in knowledge: And always, he is sensible, that the more unbroken the chain is, which he presents to his reader, the more perfect is his production. He sees, that the knowledge of causes is not only the most satisfactory; this relation or connexion being the strongest of all others; but also the most instructive; since it is by this knowledge alone, we are enabled to controul events, and govern futurity. (*EHU* 19)

Hume's philosophical account of this "connextion," however, famously undermines the sense of necessity on which the relation between cause and effect depends.[31] Causal relationships, for Hume, are inferred only on the basis of seeing many like effects succeed on like causes, and it is "impossible for us to satisfy ourselves by our reason, why we shou'd extend that experience beyond those particular instances, which have fallen under our observation" (*T* 64). The inference of causality, for Hume, rests on what we would now call anecdotal evidence: it emerges only through the collation and comparison of many cases.

Hume did, however, often insist on the relation of causation's importance as the best means we have for understanding the workings of the world around us. He saw the need to establish causality correctly as important enough that he included a checklist of *"Rules by which to judge of causes and effects"* in the *Treatise* (*T* 116–18). The relation of cause and effect ties our ideas together and makes them useful to us. "Bodies often change their position and qualities," Hume observes, "and after a little absence or interruption may become hardly knowable. But here 'tis observable, that even in these changes they preserve a *coherence*, and have a regular dependence on each other; which is the foundation of a kind of reasoning from causation, and produces the opinion of their continu'd existence" (*T* 130). Hume gives as his example the fire left blazing in a hearth that has died down to embers by the time the owner has come home. By reasoning from cause to effect the returning owner is able to understand it as the same fire, despite the difference in the impressions on either side of the interval. The world simply would not make sense if we could not reason from cause and effect. As we saw earlier, Hume shows that without causal thinking we would not be able to receive a letter without utter bewilderment.

A sense of the coherence of things, founded on the relation of cause and effect, is as necessary in the theater as it is in life. In the *Enquiry Concerning Human Understanding,* Hume writes:

> The spectator's concern must not be diverted by any scenes disjoined and separated from the rest. This breaks the course of the passions, and prevents that communication of the several emotions, by which one scene adds force to another, and transfuses the pity and terror, which it excites, upon each succeeding scene, till the whole produces that rapidity of movement, which is peculiar to the theatre. How must it extinguish this warmth of affection, to be entertained, on a sudden, with a new action and new personages, nowise related to the former; to find so sensible a breach or vacuity in the course of the passions, by means of this breach in the connexion of ideas; and instead of carrying the sympathy of one scene into the following, to be obliged, every moment, to excite a new concern, and take part in a new scene of action? (*EHU* 21)

The breaking of the chain of cause and effect can be experienced as an unpleasant interruption for the reader of a narrative as much as it can for the spectator of a play. But the anecdote, when nestled within a longer narrative, presents an exception to the general rule that the reader's or spectator's attention must not be diverted by disconnected events. Anecdotes, by their very nature, tend to be unrelated to the causal structures that underlie large-scale historical narratives. What, then, is the use of them?

One answer is that anecdotes provide spaces for resisting the unreflective habits of mind that can result from causal thinking. A feature that defines the anecdote formally is our intuition that it narrates an event that is isolated from longer chains of cause and effect. The anecdote is a narrative isolate that interrupts the sense of forward progression that makes selves and narratives alike seem to cohere. But this interruption may be useful in certain cases precisely because it draws attention to the causal inferences that underlie the acts of storytelling and thinking. In doing so, anecdotes can allow for possibility of questioning or reevaluating the stories we tell ourselves about ourselves and the world. As Robin Valenza observes, in Hume's account of selfhood, "The unconscious habit of narrating a sequence of perceptions into a single identity is exposed only in cases when the narrative process breaks down."[32] Anecdotes can interrupt larger narratives temporarily, but in doing so they draw attention to the narrative process itself.

When historians embrace anecdotes, they come close to their apparent opposites: the poets. Hume saw poetry in general as more amenable to those events that do not fit logically into chains of cause and effect but that nonetheless seem to shed light on a historical person or a situation. "All poetry," Hume writes in the *Enquiry Concerning Human Understanding*, "being a species of painting, brings us nearer to the objects than any other species of narration, throws a stronger light on them, and delineates more distinctly those minute circumstances, which, though to the historian they seem superfluous, serve mightily to enliven the imagery and gratify the fancy." Hume notes, however, that it is not necessary for the poet "to inform us each time the hero buckles his shoes, and ties his garters" (*EHU* 20). The minute circumstances of poetry and of anecdotal history must somehow engage our attention as significant events in themselves. Hume reflects in one of the passages that appeared first in the appendix to the first edition of the *Treatise* on the way minute details can unexpectedly illuminate the past. He invokes a familiar quandary in ordinary conversation when one person tries to get the other to remember a past event: "He runs over several circumstances in vain; mentions the time, the place, the company, what was said, what was done on all sides; till at last he hits on some lucky circumstance, that revives the whole, and gives his friend a perfect memory of everything" (*T* 60). Leaving aside the question of whether it describes an actual event or not, the anecdote often acts as the "lucky circumstance" that makes the past suddenly appear present to the mind.

Even though he acknowledges the capacity of anecdotal narratives to bring past moments forcefully into the present, Hume often seems ambivalent on the question of whether anecdotes could actually yield reliable historical knowledge. At several points in the *Treatise*, Hume appears to regard history as built on a special order of narratives whose correspondence to independently occurring events cannot be reasonably questioned. Hume gives as his example Julius Caesar being assassinated in the Capitol on the Ides of March. His explanation of why Caesar's death is widely credited as a historical fact oddly succeeds in making the grounds for belief in the historicity of this incident shakier than it might otherwise have appeared. He begins asserting that everyone believes the event really took place "because this fact is establish'd on the unanimous testimony of historians, who agree to assign this precise time and place to that event." Why, we might ask, do historians believe this event really did happen? The answer for Hume lies in the sequence of cause and effect that runs from eyewitnesses through to the narrative histories of the present. "Here are certain characters present either to our memory or senses," writes Hume, "which characters we likewise remember to have been us'd as the signs of certain ideas; and these ideas were either in the minds of such as were immediately present at that action, and receiv'd the ideas directly from its existence; or they were deriv'd from the testimony of others, and that again from another testimony, by a visible gradation, till we arrive at those who were eye-witnesses and spectators of the event" (*T* 58). The human ability to imagine a continuous chain of tellings and retellings of the assassination winding its away from eyewitness accounts, through manuscripts, and, finally, to modern printed histories underpins the belief that this event did indeed take place.

After writing the *Treatise,* however, Hume would note the vulnerability of these mechanisms through which narratives of historical events come down to us from the past. Hume comments in the *Natural History of Religion* on the way the links between event and the subsequent narration of that event can become attenuated, especially when they are mediated by the testimony of the spoken word: "An historical fact, while it passes by oral tradition from eye-witnesses and contemporaries, is disguised in every successive narration, and may at last retain but very small, if any, resemblance of the original truth, on which it was founded" (*NHR* 36). The apparent certainty with which historical occurrences like Caesar's assassination in the Capitol are credited begins to seem less justified once the historical expanse that divides Hume and his contemporaries from the event is considered.

The existence of widespread belief in central historical occurrences like Caesar's assassination, then, might be better explained, to use Hume's own explanatory framework, by the way these kinds of historical events produce a large number of historical effects beyond themselves. If we are to doubt Julius Caesar's assassination in the Capitol ever took place, then we must also doubt a very large number of independent accounts of events that would not have happened but for Caesar's murder. If all historians were to direct this level of skepticism toward the historical archive, then it would be difficult to imagine how the writing of history could continue as a communal enterprise. The reason why we are often reluctant to place our faith in those narratives that have come to be known as anecdotes, on this view, would be that these narratives do not produce obvious consequences.

The question of what it means to believe or not to believe in an anecdote, however, is complicated by Hume's difficulty in specifying exactly what belief itself is. He finds no particular idea or impression to which belief corresponds. The quiddity of belief, he argues, is instead to be found in the way the ideas in which we believe appear before our minds. In the *Treatise,* Hume defines belief as "a lively idea related to or associated with a present impression" (*T* 67).[33] Hume, however, found it impossible to say exactly what this "liveliness" was. Belief, for Hume, is "that certain *je-ne-scai-quoi,* of which 'tis impossible to give any definition or description, but which every one sufficiently understands" (*T* 74). Hume's invocation of the *je-ne-sais-quoi* is only the most obvious example of what John Richetti calls the "strikingly aesthetic," terms with which Hume describes the nature of belief, adding that in Hume "The epistemological process takes place within a naturalistic psychology that resembles a rhetorical situation."[34] Expanding on Richetti's insight, Adam Potkay argues that much of the vocabulary that Hume uses to describe belief—including "force," "vivacity," and "liveliness"—was inspired by his extensive reading in classical rhetoric.[35] The well-told anecdote is full of what Aristotle called *energia:* the capacity of language to make an audience appear to see things vividly.[36] And this vividness can produce at least a temporary and transient belief in the idea before the mind.

The characteristic "coloring" of the anecdote that is told and of the language used to tell it can, according to Hume, lead us to invest a temporary belief in narratives that we might, in our soberer moments, be apt to dismiss as unreliable fictions. As Hume admits in the *Treatise,* "'Tis difficult for us to withhold our assent from what is painted out to us in all the colours of eloquence," even going on to allow that "the vivacity produc'd by the fancy is in many cases greater than that which arises from custom and experience"

(*T* 84). As lively stories full of *energia,* anecdotes can play an essential role in revivifying our sense of the past as a whole, if necessarily only for a short time. And as forms cut adrift from history as a series of events linked by relations of cause and effect, anecdotes can also allow the historian to attain a detached perspective on the writing of history. This capacity of the anecdote to enable reflection on how historical narratives are fashioned was what made the genre important for Hume the historian.

ANECDOTES IN THE *HISTORY OF ENGLAND*

Hume tells a multitude of anecdotes in his major historical work, the *History of England.* In doing so, he breaks with his own stated intention to write a history concerned solely with the well-attested historical happenings that determine and set constraints on future events, eschewing stories of minor and unverifiable events. At the beginning of the second volume of the *History of England,* Hume suggests that just as natural philosophy has made progress by becoming more systematic, so too must history if it is to advance as a discipline:

> Most sciences, in proportion as they increase and improve, invent methods by which they facilitate their reasonings; and, employing general theorems, are enabled to comprehend, in a few propositions a great number of inferences and conclusions. History also, being a collection of facts which are multiplying without end, is obliged to adopt such arts of abridgment, to retain the more material events, and to drop all the minute circumstances, which are only interesting during the time, or to the persons engaged in the transactions. (*HE* 2:3–4)

Anecdotes are exactly the kind of "minute circumstances" that may be found in the historical record, but that have no obvious historical consequences. And yet, as Hume writes in a letter of September 12, 1734, to Michael Ramsay, "'tis with Nations as with particular Man, where one Trifle frequently serves more to discover the Character, than a whole Train of considerable Actions" (*LDH* 2:21). Anecdotes in Hume's *History of England* often point to the insufficiency of historical methods that restrict themselves to discussing only the great political events that seem to determine the direction of history.[37] Anecdotes facilitate ways of thinking about the past that are not wholly beholden to cause and effect. They help maintain a certain skepticism toward modes of historical thinking that arise out of the desire to justify the present. They also can make historians and their readers more aware of the extent to which history itself is "a great anecdote . . . a series of anecdotes that have been welded together or have flowed into each other in a continuum," as Novalis observed in one of the notebooks he kept at the end of the eighteenth century.[38] Apparently free-standing anecdotes provide a means of appreciating the anecdotal construction of history itself: they draw attention to the seams and joins that allow a coherent historical narrative to be fashioned out of many disparate stories.

Anecdotes frequently mark a sense of conflict within the very process of writing history in the *History of England.* J. G. A. Pocock has discerned the presence of two types of history in Hume's *History of England:* one that is concerned with "changes in the actions and thoughts of large numbers of people" and the other with "the actions of a finite number of particular persons." In the former kind of history, relations of cause and effect can be drawn with reasonable certainty since the patterns may be discerned from the morass of individual deeds and inclinations. In the latter kind of history, drawing clear lines of causality from antecedent causes to the deeds of historical agents is more difficult. "It follows," Pocock writes, "that there are always two histories to be written: that of cultural change, and that of particular actions; and the relations between them are necessarily anomalous."[39] In what follows, I want to develop James Noggle's suggestion that the anecdotes of the *History of England* draw attention to the dissonance between Pocock's two types of history.[40] Anecdotes in the *History of England* serve to mark the disjunction between the large-scale movements of national histories and the particular actions of individuals.

We can see this disjunction between the histories of nations and of individuals staged in the fourth volume of the *History of England,* in which Hume quotes a series of anecdotes that he took from the *Memoires of Sir James Melvil of Hal-hill,* first published in an edited version by George Scott in 1683, which anglicized Melville's original Scots. In this work, Melville writes of his career as an ambassador for Mary Queen of Scots, which included liaising with Elizabeth I during Mary's preparations to marry Robert Darnley. Melville claims that Elizabeth constantly asked to be compared with Mary, inquiring which of the two was the taller and the fairer. Elizabeth's efforts to outdo Mary run to ridiculous extremes. Paraphrasing and compressing one of Melville's first-person accounts of a personal encounter with Queen Elizabeth, Hume writes:

> Having learned from him [i.e., Melville], that his mistress [i.e., Mary Queen of Scots] sometimes recreated herself by playing on the harpsichord, an instrument on which she herself excelled, she gave orders

to Lord Hunsdon, that he should lead the ambassador, as if were casually, into an apartment, where he might hear her perform; and when Melvil, as if ravished with the harmony, broke into the queen's apartment, she pretended to be displeased with his intrusion; but still took care to ask him whether he thought Mary or her the best performer on that instrument. From the whole of her behaviour, Melvil thought he might, on his return, assure his mistress, that she had no reason ever to expect any cordial friendship from Elizabeth, and that all her professions of amity were full of falsehood and dissimilation. (*HE* 4:68–69)

Hume frames Melville's anecdote as a story that illuminates Elizabeth's and Mary's mutual antipathy. Hume gives the story an ability to represent the conflict between Elizabeth and Mary partly through Hume's telescoping of Melville's much longer account into a short comic anecdote.[41] But the story also works self-reflectively to bring into question Hume's ability as a historian to lay bare the motives that lead to decisions that influence the course of history. Assessing Elizabeth's statecraft after telling the Melville anecdote, Hume observes:

The politics of Elizabeth, though judicious, were usually full of duplicity and artifice: but never more so than in her transactions with the queen of Scots, where there entered so many little passions and narrow jealousies, that she durst not avow to the world the reasons for her conduct, scarcely to her ministers, and scarcely even to herself. Besides a womanish rivalship and envy against the marriage of this princess, she had some motives of interest for feigning a displeasure on the present occasion. It served her as a pretense for refusing to acknowledge Mary's title to the succession of England; a point to which, for good reasons, she was determined never to consent. And it was useful to her for a purpose, still more unfriendly and dangerous, for encouraging the discontents and rebellion of the Scottish nobility and ecclesiastics. (*HE* 4:70)

Looking beyond the obvious chauvinism of presuming that Elizabeth's gender made her more prone to the influence of petty passions, what is striking about this passage is the way that it shows how Elizabeth's "womanish rivalship and envy" are, for Hume, hopelessly entangled with the political motivations for her antipathy to Mary. The large-scale historical forces that shape the decisions of monarchs are difficult to separate out from the petty passions to which they are subject. The Melville anecdote marks a limit beyond which the efforts of the historian to discern the laws underlying the movement of history become frustrated. In this way, the anecdote draws attention to the limitations of historical understanding itself.

In his review of the first volume of the *History of England,* Tobias Smollett commented on the disruptive effect that anecdotes like Melville's have on Hume's historical narrative. Smollett wrote that "Mr. *Hume* has not (in our opinion) been very happy in his manner of relating some private incidents," singling out in particular "the adventure of king *Charles* II. and the Presbyterian minister in *Scotland;* the gallantry of captain *Douglas* in the river *Medway,* when he was attacked by the *Dutch;* and some other anecdotes which he has endeavoured to throw in by way of sudden apostrophe, in imitation of *Voltaire.*"[42] To tell an anecdote is to create a sense of diversion from the main discourse, which is also one of rhetorical apostrophe's hallmarks. George Puttenham in the *Art of English Poesy* (1589) writes of apostrophe, "Many times when we have run a long race in the tale spoken to the hearers, we do suddenly fly out and either speak or exclaim at some other person or thing," and translates the Greek word ἀποστροφή as "the Turn-Way or the Turn-Tale," which "breedeth by such exchange a certain recreation to the hearer's minds."[43] Anecdotes are little "Turn-Tales" in Hume's *History,* little diversions that open spaces for considering history as something more than the succession of important figures and events.

When Smollett criticizes Hume's retelling of "the adventure of king Charles II. and the Presbyterian minister in Scotland," he is referring to an anecdote that appears in the section of the narrative devoted to Charles's short residence in Scotland soon after the execution of his father. Here, Charles lived as the Scots' proclaimed king, but only on the condition that he sign a declaration in which he promised to reverse his father's policy of opposing Presbyterian reform in Scotland and to eschew his mother's Catholic faith. Hume paints the picture of a king almost entirely under the thumb of the covenanters, his temporary allies in the struggle to regain his crown. The anecdote of Charles and the Presbyterian minister appears in the section dealing with Charles's and the covenanters' different ideas about the behavior proper to a king:

> The king's passion for the fair could not altogether be restrained. He had once been observed using some familiarities with a young woman; and a committee of ministers was appointed to reprove him for a behaviour so unbecoming a covenanted monarch. The spokesman of the

committee, one Douglass, began with a severe aspect, informed the king that great scandal had been given to the godly, enlarged on the heinous nature of sin, and concluded with exhorting his majesty, whenever he was disposed to amuse himself, to be more careful, for the future, in shutting the windows. This delicacy, so unusual to the place and to the character of the man, was remarked by the king; and he never forgot the obligation. (*HE* 6:33)

The narrative is conspicuously irrelevant to what Hume presents elsewhere as a historian's proper self-restriction to a single narrative line of events linked by relations of cause and effect. The anecdote works instead as a synecdoche that encapsulates the larger conflict between Charles and the covenanters. Hume's ironic remark that Charles "never forgot the obligation" also anticipates his later decision to renege on his promise to uphold the Solemn League and Covenant after the Restoration and his administration's persecution of the Presbyterians—although we are also aware that to see these acts as payback for a single humiliation at the hands of the covenanters would be absurd. To use Hume's own terms, the relations of resemblance and contiguity play a greater role in justifying the story's place in the *History of England* than the relation of cause and effect does. In the context of a history that explicitly privileges the relation of cause and effect, however, the story registers as an unnecessary diversion from the narrative line. This little unverifiable story seems to be included mostly for the sheer pleasure of telling it: the unexpected exhortation for the king to keep his windows shut during his trysts (rather than the expected one to reform his promiscuous behavior) opens a small narrative window that allows Hume to escape from his own self-limitation in the *History of England* to telling only the consequential events of England's history.

Hume's historical anecdotes sometimes suggest a resistance from within the *History of England* itself to the master narrative of the rise of liberty that is told across its six volumes. One such anecdote that Hume relates tells of Charles's escape from Cromwell's forces after losing the Battle of Worcester. The anecdote works to pull against the sense of historical movement that holds sway over much of the *History of England*. In it, the fugitive king seeks the help of a farmer by the name of Penderell, who disguises the king as a laborer and shelters him in his house, despite the danger of doing so. While he was staying under Penderell's protection, Hume notes that Charles is said to have climbed an oak tree, "where he sheltered himself among the leaves and branches for twenty-four hours. He saw several soldiers pass bye. All of them were intent in search of the king; and some expressed in his hearing their earnest wishes of seizing him. This tree was afterwards denominated the *Royal Oak;* and for many years was regarded by the neighbourhood with great veneration" (*HE* 6:36). This anecdote allows the reader of the *History of England* a limited escape from the march of history, just as Charles escapes the soldiers who search for him. The anecdotes of Charles's escape from Cromwell do possess a clear causative significance: they explain how Charles survived to be crowned in 1660. But they also function as resting places within the narration itself, drawing attention to traditional forms of life that persist through wars and revolutions. At the end of the section dealing with Charles's escape, during which he is sheltered by farmers and country gentry, Hume observes, "From innumerable instances it appears how deep rooted in the minds of the English gentry of that age was the principle of loyalty to their sovereign; that noble and generous principle, inferior only in excellence to the more enlarged and more enlightened affection towards a legal constitution." The anecdotes of Charles's escape work as warrants for the persistence of tradition beneath the ongoing movement described in the *History of England* toward the creation of a constitutional monarchy. As Hume writes, "during those times of military usurpation, these passions were the same" (*HE* 6:38). The anecdotes of Charles's flight from Cromwell's army expose the disjunction between two historical temporalities, serving to contrast a period of political upheaval with the steady allegiances of the common people over the *longue durée.*

Hume's anecdotes in the *History of England* also pull against the larger narratives in which they are marshaled by exposing the post facto nature of history itself. They show how self-serving historical narratives are often fashioned by historical personages themselves and thus reflect ironically on the process of writing the *History of England*. In volume 1 of the *History of England,* for example, Hume narrates an anecdote of William the Conqueror's quick thinking after a tumble following his landing on English shores in 1066: "The duke himself, as he leaped on shore, happened to stumble and fall; but had the presence of mind, it is said, to turn the omen to his advantage, by calling aloud, that he had taken possession of the country. And a soldier, running to a neighbouring cottage, plucked some thatch, which, as if giving him seizine of the kingdom, he presented to his general" (*HE* 1:154–55). In the anecdote, the usual sequence of cause and effect is inverted. William becomes, in effect, his own historian, interpreting his fall not as a bad omen but a token that his conquest of England will be successful—and indeed as a sign of the fact that he has already taken possession of the country. A soldier reproduces this inverted causal logic, in which effects appear to precede their causes, by presenting William with some thatch as if to do so were the same as to confirm his conquest of England. The anecdote itself, of course, only has the resonance it does because readers are aware that William was in fact successful in conquering England. The whole episode is preposterous in the rhetorical sense of the word in which the speaker presents things back to front: "Having that first which ought to be last; wrong; absurd; perverted," as Samuel Johnson defines the word "preposterous" in the first edition of the *Dictionary of the English Language*.[44]

Mark Blackwell has shown that the movement of Hume's thought is frequently "preposterous" in this rhetorical sense. One of the examples Blackwell cites is Hume's brief remark prefacing his account of how the mind discovers a necessary connection between cause and effect: "Perhaps 'twill appear in the end, that the necessary connexion depends on the inference, instead of the inference's depending on the necessary connexion" (*T* 62). As Blackwell observes, "Hume's forecast of his conclusion is preposterous in two senses: it places early in the *Treatise* a hypothesis that may appear only 'in the end,' and it suggests the possibility of a reversal in the causality of causation."[45] Another prominent example of "preposterousness" in the *Treatise*, which Blackwell does not happen to discuss in his essay, is Hume's remarks on the way princes and emperors appear to derive their legitimacy from those who succeed them:

> Nothing is more usual, tho' nothing may, at first sight, appear more unreasonable, than this way of thinking. Princes often *seem* to acquire a right from their successors, as well as from their ancestors; and a king, who during this life-time might justly be deem'd an usurper, will be regarded by posterity as a lawful prince, because he has had the good fortune to settle his family on the throne, and entirely change the antient form of government. *Julius Cæsar* is regarded as the first *Roman* emperor; while *Sulla* and *Marius*, whose titles were really the same as his, are treated as tyrants and usurpers. Time and custom give authority to all forms of government, and all successions of princes; and that power, which at first was founded only on injustice and violence, becomes in time legal and obligatory. Nor does the mind rest there; but returning back upon its footsteps, transfers to their predecessors and ancestors that right, which it naturally ascribes to the posterity, as being related together, and united in the imagination. (*T* 362)

Hume emphasizes both the commonsensical character and the fundamental absurdity of this "way of thinking," in which the legitimacy of princes is seen to derive from their success in settling their crowns on their own descendants. His analysis suggests that this same preposterous "way of thinking" is, in fact, bound up with the work of the historian, who is consigned to rearranging the past in light of the present. An attention to the ways anecdotes have been used and abused by interested parties in the past helps Hume maintain a skeptical awareness of how historical narratives are manufactured. In the sixth and final volume of the *History of England*, Hume especially associates the nascent Whig faction with the preposterous practice of fabricating anecdotes to suit the present. The Whigs had already, Hume remarks, prepared a narrative designed to delegitimize the Duke of York's first child even before the baby's birth in 1682, which in the end did not have to be used, as the child turned out to be a girl. Hume comments in a footnote on this episode, "Party zeal is capable of swallowing the most incredible story; but it is surely singular, that the same calumny, when once baffled, should yet be renewed with such success" (*HE* 6.495). When a son was born to James, of course, the Whigs were ready with the warming-pan story. This episode shows that historical narratives, large and small, may themselves affect the course of history, a reminder that the historian is embroiled in the history of the present as he or she attempts to write the history of the past. Even if history is necessarily written ex post facto, the anecdote's preposterousness can at least enable the historian to attain self-consciousness about the deep preposterousness that is part and parcel of the writing of history. Precisely because anecdotes stand at awkward angles to the large-scale narratives of history, they can interrupt those ingrained habits of thought through which historians make sense of the past.

ANECDOTES IN THE *NATURAL HISTORY OF RELIGION*

Much as Hume's *History of England* is a history of the English nation in which anecdotes subvert the text's master narrative of the progress of liberty, so too Hume's *Natural History of Religion* is a history of religion in which anecdotes subvert the text's master narrative of the progress of European societies from polytheism to monotheism. In his historical study of religion, first published in the collection of essays *Four Dissertations* (1757), which also included "Of the Standard of Taste," Hume assembles a large number of anecdotes concerning the behavior of religious believers in order to trace the origins of religious belief in the general workings of the human mind. Although Hume did preface the *Natural History of Religion* with a disclaimer that "The whole frame of nature bespeaks an intelligent author" and that he merely proposes to investigate "the origin of religion in human nature" (*NHR* 33), he did not convince his critics, who detected in the work a corrosive skepticism directed toward religion in general. The very title bothered William Warburton, with its suggestion that religions could be studied at the same detached remove as fossils, insects, and plants. "Would not the *Moral history of Meteors*," Warburton asked, "be full as sensible as the *Natural history of Religion?*"[46] One irreligious implication of Hume's treatment of religion in the manner of natural history was that it implied that the history of religion is not, in fact, a narrative of progress from polytheism to monotheism, but one in which polytheism and monotheism represent different expressions of the same religious proclivities of human nature. In the *Natural History of Religion*, Hume treats the history of religion as a synchronic field from which he gleans anecdotal stories without much regard for their location in time or space.

Anecdotes thus tend to pull away from the *Natural History of Religion*'s diachronic narrative of ancient polytheism yielding to modern monotheism. The early sections of the essay do seem to promise a teleological narrative of how a more rational monotheism emerged from its polytheistic origins. Hume observes, for example, that "polytheism or idolatry was, and necessarily must have been, the first and most ancient religion of mankind" (*NHR* 34). Polytheism appears at the outset as an immature form of religious belief: "Agitated by hopes and fears," Hume writes, "men scrutinize, with a trembling curiosity, the course of future causes, and examine the various and contrary events of human life. And in this disordered scene, with eyes still more disordered and astonished, they see the first obscure traces of divinity" (*NHR* 39). This teleological narrative is, however, challenged as the history unfolds. "It is remarkable," Hume observes around the text's midpoint, "that the principles of religion have a kind of flux and reflux in the human mind, and that men have a natural tendency to rise from idolatry to theism, and to sink again from theism into idolatry" (*NHR* 58). Hume hints that what is true of the human mind is presumably also true of human history as a whole and that the apparent triumph of theism over idolatry might be an impermanent and reversible one.

When Hume in the later stages of the essay begins to compare polytheism and monotheism, it is monotheism that often emerges as the less "enlightened" of the two. Hume claims, for example, that polytheism is naturally more tolerant than monotheism, quoting in support of this position an anecdote from Xenophon's *Memorabilia:* "When the oracle of DELPHI was asked,

What rites or worship were most acceptable to the gods? 'Those which are legally established in each city,' replied the oracle" (*NHR* 61). Hume argues that the belief in a remote and infinitely powerful deity tends "to sink the human mind into the lowest submission and abasement," whereas when the gods are conceived as nearer to the people who worship them, "we are more at our ease in our addresses to them, and may even, without profaneness, aspire sometimes to a rivalship and emulation of them. Hence activity, spirit, courage, magnanimity, love of liberty, and all the virtues, which aggrandize a people" (*NHR* 63). The shift from the third-person singular into the first-person plural does a good deal of rhetorical work here, slipping readers by stealth into the pagan mindset.

Some of the satire against established religion in the *Natural History of Religion* comes from the ironic juxtaposition of anecdotes. Hume strikingly brings together two anecdotes, the first sourced from Plutarch's *Moralia* and the second from Pierre Bayle's *Dictionnaire historique et critique:* "BRASIDAS seized a mouse, and being bit by it, let it go. 'There is nothing so contemptible,' said he, 'but what may be safe, if it has but courage to defend itself.' BELLARMINE patiently and humbly allowed the fleas and other odious vermin to prey upon him. 'We shall have heaven,' says he, 'to reward us for our sufferings: But these poor creatures have nothing but the enjoyment of the present life.' Such difference is there between the maxims of a GREEK hero and a CATHOLIC saint" (*NHR* 64). The maxims voiced by Brasidas and Bellarmine are, of course, very different, and the discussion that precedes the anecdotes invites us to give preference to the hero's code of honor over the saint's passive suffering. But the resemblances between the pagan and the Catholic are more striking than the differences. Both men allow themselves, after all, to be eaten by vermin. The fact that their names both begin with a *B* reinforces the affinities between them—a comic collocation of personages that also evokes the alphabetical structure of Bayle's *Dictionnaire,* from which Hume extracts the anecdote of Bellarmine. Hume's juxtaposition of Brasidas with Ballarmine subtly punctures the pretensions of monotheists to greater rationality. The anecdotes of the *Natural History of Religion* thus provide a kind of counternarrative to the *Natural History of Religion*'s own master narrative of polytheism replacing monotheism, implying that monotheism and polytheism are simply different expressions of the universal workings of the human mind.

A TASTE FOR ANECDOTES

In "Of the Standard of Taste," the last surviving essay Hume wrote, apart from his short deathbed memoir "Of My Own Life" (1776), Hume presents the anecdote as a genre whose domain is, in the last analysis, the aesthetic. Hume does not simply use an anecdote to explain the nature of aesthetic taste at a crucial juncture in "Of the Standard of Taste." Rather, the anecdote's lightning-like effect on the mind, prior to any train of reasoning that might be drawn from it, becomes a means of staging the act of aesthetic judgment itself in the space between author and reader. The crux of "Of the Standard of Taste" is the problem of finding a way of reconciling the disparate "sentiments" that works of art engender in different people. By arguing that aesthetic taste is more a sentiment than a judgment, not so much an appraisal of objective features in an artistic work as a subjective response to it, Hume acknowledges the objection that he seems to leave no way of distinguishing right from wrong judgments, for "a thousand different sentiments, excited by the same object, are all right: Because no sentiment represents what is really in the object" (*EMPL* 230). The task Hume sets for himself in "Of the Standard of Taste" is to find a way of arguing that aesthetic judgments are indeed founded on sentiment, and yet some are more correct than others.

To illustrate how there is such a thing as a more or less accurate taste for art and literature, Hume tells an anecdote adapted from one told by Sancho Panza in *Don Quixote:*

> It is with good reason, says SANCHO to the squire with the great nose, that I pretend to have a judgment in wine: This is a quality hereditary in my family. Two of my kinsmen were once called to give their opinion of a hogshead, which was supposed to be excellent, being old and of a good vintage. One of them tastes it; considers it; and after mature reflection pronounces the wine to be good, were it not for a small taste of leather, which he perceived in it. The other, after using the same precautions, gives also his verdict in favour of the wine; but with the reserve of a taste of iron, which he could easily distinguish. You cannot imagine how much they were both ridiculed for their judgment. But who laughed in the end? On emptying the hogshead, there was found at the bottom, an old key with a leathern thong tied to it. (*EMPL* 234–35)

This anecdote, appearing midway in "Of the Standard of Taste," follows the same general movement of the essay in which it is contained. Hume's essay begins, like the anecdote, with discord and disagreement: "The great variety of Taste, as well as of opinion, which prevails in the world, is too obvious not to have fallen under every one's observation" (*EMPL* 226). In the story that is told in the anecdote Hume adapts from *Don Quixote*, there is disagreement on the taste of the wine not only between Sancho's kinsmen but also between the two kinsmen and the rest of the village. The anecdote ends, however, with the validation of the judgment of both of Sancho's kinsmen, who, unlike the villagers, possess the special ability to detect the traces of iron and leather in the wine. The main argument of Hume's essay similarly ends with the affirmation that only a select few possess the highly refined sensibilities that qualify them to be true arbiters of taste.

In deploying this anecdote in his essay on taste, Hume betrays the influence of Joseph Addison, who is praised as "elegant writer" in the *Treatise* (*T* 186), especially Addison's papers on the "Pleasures of the Imagination." In *Spectator* 409, Addison had considered the nature of "Mental Taste" by comparing it to "that Sensitive Taste which gives us a Relish of every different Flavour that affects the Palate" (*S* 3:527). Mr. Spectator mentions an acquaintance who possesses such a fine palate that "after having tasted ten different Kinds of Tea, he would distinguish, without seeing the Colour of it, the particular Sort which was offered him; and not only so, but any two Sorts of them that were mixt together in an equal Proportion; nay, he has carried the Experiment so far, as upon tasting the Composition of three different sorts, to name the Parcels from whence the three several Ingredients were taken" (*S* 3:527–28). This is one of the moments in which the *Spectator* explicitly assumes the form of an experimental report. Mr. Spectator offers his anecdote as an argument by analogy for the proposition that just as one may have finely attuned powers of sensitive taste, so too one may have advanced powers of aesthetic taste.

Noting the closeness between Addison's and Hume's anecdotes, Denise Gigante comments: "The problem for all Enlightenment taste theorists was that while there may be empirical evidence for gustatory taste, there is no comparable key 'with a leathern thong tied to it' that can be produced to refute or confirm judgments of mental taste."[47] The anecdote itself, however, might just be the "key" that confirms the acuity of the teller's mental taste. As an anonymous reviewer of *Four Dissertations* in the *Critical Review* wrote, Hume "has shewn not only that he knows what a delicate taste is, but that he is himself possessed of it."[48] The reviewer went on to quote Hume's use of an anecdote told by the fictional character Sancho Panza as an analogy for tasteful judgment as a case in point. This demonstration of tastefulness through praxis made amends for what this reviewer took to be Hume's failure to fix the standard of taste.

In his earlier essay "Of Simplicity and Refinement in Writing," Hume had held up Cervantes's characterization of Sancho Panza as an example of a grotesque character that can nevertheless please "persons of taste." For, Hume writes, "if we copy low life, the strokes must be strong and remarkable, and must convey a lively image to the mind. The absurd naivety of *Sancho Pancho* is represented in such inimitable colours by CERVANTES, that it entertains as much as the picture of the most magnanimous hero or softest lover" (*EMPL* 192). The anecdote as a genre, like Sancho Panza, can be grotesque and naive, but it nevertheless may exemplify the mental faculty of taste. Sancho Panza's anecdote, far from being an absurd digression, is central to "On the Standard of Taste" because it provides a narrative method of capturing a phenomenon that resists formal definition or description. Just as the judgments of Sancho Panza's kinsmen on the wine are transformed from wholly idiosyncratic and private opinions to publicly recognized displays of acute taste, so too is Sancho Panza's anecdote transformed from an idiosyncratic story into an exemplary narrative of aesthetic judgment. In this fictional anecdote in "Of the Standard of Taste," Sancho Panza and his relatives emerge as eccentric but authentic Men of Taste: a company in which Hume implicitly includes himself.

Humean anecdotes—both anecdotes about Hume and anecdotes told by him—are narratives balanced between the worlds of philosophy and common life. Anecdotes can take us away from common life by drawing attention to single and aberrant circumstances within it. They thus open holes in common life that enable its unexamined assumptions to be questioned. At the same time, however, as narratives that move in a social and conversable space, anecdotes also work to connect people in the shared investigation of the problems that arise from this anecdotal puncturing of experience. This withdrawal is recontextualized in the anecdotes told by Hume—and the anecdotes told about his own peculiar behavior—as a movement that itself takes place within common life, a temporary excursion that ends with a renewed understanding of habitual thoughts and practices that usually go without question. The Humean anecdote is, to borrow a grammatical metaphor from Samuel Taylor Coleridge, a *"conjunction disjunctive"* (*BL* 1:19) that leads both out and into the sociable world of common life. Anecdotes in Hume's writings join naive storytelling with philosophical penetration, allowing them to work not only as tools for gaining possible insights into human nature but also as satires of philosophy itself. They act both as tunnels through which to burrow into philosophy and as escape hatches opening out of it when philosophy threatens to become a prison of the mind. And this is why David Hume loved his anecdotes.

THREE

Anecdotes in the Wake of the *Endeavour*

In a manuscript collection of anecdotes that he entitled "Boswelliana," James Boswell recorded a *bon mot* delivered at a social gathering that included Daniel Solander and Joseph Banks, both newly returned from James Cook's first voyage to the South Seas on the HMS *Endeavour* (1768–71). On this occasion, Boswell, David Hume, and the Scottish composer Thomas Alexander Erskine, sixth Earl of Kellie, were discussing an unidentified globetrotting "Mr Wright," who, Lord Kellie remarked, "has been in several parts of the world; and I expect to see him in Otahite before he dies." This comment prompts a remark from Hume, who affects to take Kellie literally: "So then my Lord (said David Hume Esq.) you expect to be there yourself." Not to be bested, Kellie prepares a rejoinder: "In order to retort upon Hume for this catching at this word he set himself in a steady posture and said: My Dear David if you were to go there, you would be obliged to retract all your Essay on Miracles. O no my Lord said Hume, Everything there is in nature. Aye said the Earl. But there are different natures."[1] Kellie repays Hume for quibbling on his own use of the word "see" by playing in turn on Hume's use of the word "nature," which Hume seems to intend to mean the natural world as a whole (of which human nature is but one part) whereas Kellie takes it in its colloquial sense as describing the bent of an individual or the character of a society. Hume's and Kellie's exchange may be flippant, but their repartee nevertheless raises fundamental questions about human nature. Was human nature in actuality comprised of a multitude of different natures? If human behavior in Tahiti deviates so completely from European manners and morals as to appear miraculous from a European perspective, then its singularity would undermine not only Hume's arguments against miracles in the *Enquiry Concerning Human Understanding* but also his presumption of the universality of human nature itself.

Although Boswell did not record any response from Hume to Kellie's rejoinder, Hume had already considered whether there is one human nature or many by way of a fictional dialogue he had appended to the *Enquiry Concerning the Principles of Morals*. In this dialogue, an unnamed narrator debates a fictional scholar and traveler named Palamedes, a man, we are told, "who has run over, by study and travel, almost every region of the intellectual and material world" (*EPM* 110). Palamedes contends that societies differ radically from one another across time and space and that there is no overarching standard of morality against which to judge the particular standards that hold in individual societies. The narrator argues against this position, however, that just as the Rhone and the Rhine flow in opposite directions, even though they flow from the same mountain and are governed by the same law of gravity, what may appear to be divergent manners and customs are in fact expressions of the same laws of human nature that hold across all human societies (*EPM* 116). Although we do not know what Hume said after Kellie observed that there are "different natures," he could well have replied that however unusual instances of human behavior in Europe and its antipodes may appear, they will always be found to flow from the same basic human nature, just as the most dissimilar phenomena in nature may be shown to derive from the same set of laws.

In many respects, the contemporary reception of the anecdotes that arrived in the wake of the *Endeavour* voyage to the South Pacific is consistent with the assumption of a universal human nature whose workings could be explored through anecdotes. In his *Life of James Cook* (1788), for example, Andrew Kippis credited Cook with advancing the science of human nature, writing: "It is not to the enlargement of natural knowledge only, that the effects arising from Captain Cook's voyages are to be confined. Another important object of study has been opened by them; and that is, the study of human nature, in situations various, interesting, and uncommon."[2] Edmund Burke, in a letter of June 9, 1777, to the Scottish historian William Robertson, noted that the narratives of unfamiliar peoples written by explorers to remote areas of the world had given contemporaries "very great advantages towards the knowledge of human nature" and "the Great Map of Mankind is unrolld at once; and there is no state or Gradation of barbarism, and no mode of refinement which we have not at the same instant under our View."[3] In the journals they wrote on the *Endeavour*, Cook and Banks recorded anecdotes of singular examples of human behavior, both on the part of the visitors themselves and the people they encountered during their travels. Later, in *An Account of the Voyages Undertaken by the*

Order of his present Majesty for making Discoveries in the Southern Hemisphere (1773), John Hawkesworth combined narrative material from Cook's and Banks's onboard accounts with his own reflections on human nature. Anecdotes from Cook's first voyage were subsequently incorporated into the conjectural histories of the Scottish moral philosophers James Burnett, Lord Monboddo; Henry Home, Lord Kames; and John Millar. These writers envisaged human societies moving through a series of stages from "savagery" to "civilization." Monboddo, Kames, and Millar mined anecdotes from the *Endeavour* voyage for insights into what the precursors to modern commercial societies might have been like at the earlier stages of their history.

In the case of the anecdotes told and retold about the *Endeavour* voyage, however, we often find the relationship between anecdotal singularity and the idea of a universal human nature put under strain. The periodicals and satirical poetry of the 1770s and 1780s openly mocked Banks's and Hawkesworth's claims to superior knowledge of human nature. Satirical writers in the magazines linked the voyage and its anecdotal cargo not with the production of knowledge but with the immediate and transient pleasures of sex and food. Both these writers and Banks's critics in the Royal Society adduced Banks's collecting of curious flora, fauna, objects, and anecdotes as a sign of his unfitness to serve as president of the Royal Society. In his travels in Scotland, Samuel Johnson was recorded by Boswell as reflecting on South Sea anecdotes in ways that diverged from both Hawkesworth and the Scottish conjectural historians. In his account of his tour of Scotland with Johnson, James Boswell presents Johnson as a skeptic of the idea that anecdotes of the South Seas reveal human nature in its earliest stages of development. Johnson is seen to consider the anecdotes of the voyage as more revealing of the continuities of everyday practices between Europeans and Polynesians than the existence of fundamental differences between them that could be explained by recourse to conjectural theory. Unlike Hawkesworth and the Scottish conjectural historians, Johnson requires no abstract theory of human nature to make sense of the anecdotal flotsam of the *Endeavour* voyage. This chapter is organized around conflicts and divergences between relaters and readers of anecdotes: James Cook against Joseph Banks, Hawkesworth against his reviewers, Banks versus the satirical poet Peter Pindar, and Samuel Johnson against the Scottish conjectural historians. It begins, however, with a rare and unusual catalogue that holds both samples of anecdotes and samples of barkcloth that are claimed to have been collected on the course of Cook's voyages to the South Seas.

SCIENCE AND SINGULARITY

A recent census of Alexander Shaw's *A Catalogue of the Different Specimens of Cloth Collected in the Three Voyages of Captain Cook* (1787) records only sixty-six known copies worldwide.[4] Each copy contains what Shaw asserted were actual specimens of Polynesian barkcloth, cut from larger fabrics used for clothing, bedding, and mats, many of which are decorated with bright colors and geometric patterns. The catalogue entries provide information on the purpose and origin of each piece of barkcloth, with several entries containing anecdotes that tell the stories of how the pieces of cloth came to be acquired by the European visitors. The anecdote for barkcloth specimen 34, for example, describes how the visitors came to possess a piece of Tahitian barkcloth during one of Cook's two later voyages to the South Pacific:

> A number of the natives being on board of the Resolution, one of the chiefs took a particular liking to an old blunt iron, which lay upon one of the officer's chests, and taking hold of a boy about nine years of age, offered him in exchange, pointing to the iron. The gentleman, although he knew he could not keep the youth, yet willing to see if he would willingly stay; or if any of the rest would claim him, took the child and gave the savage the iron; upon which a woman, who appeared rather young for the mother, sprung from the other side of the ship, and with the highest emotions of grief seemed to bewail the loss of the infant: but the lieutenant, with a true British spirit, took him by the hand and presented him to her, upon which, after putting her hands twice upon her head, she unbound the roll of cloth which was round her body, and from which this specimen was cut, and having spread it before him, seized the boy, and jumping into the sea both swam ashore, nor could he ever learn whether she was the mother, sister, or relation, and this he lamented the more, as such affection was very seldom seen among those people.[5]

This anecdote centers on a series of exchanges: the "gentleman" onboard the *Resolution* exchanges the "old blunt iron" for the boy without meaning to keep him, the lieutenant "with a true British spirit" presents the boy to the Tahitian woman apparently without expecting anything in return, and the Tahitian woman gives the barkcloth to the lieutenant in exchange for the boy. A small sample of the barkcloth to which the story refers can be seen and touched by the reader of the catalogue, a textile specimen of Tahitian society to accompany the textual one supplied in the anecdote. Like the sample of barkcloth to which it is attached, the anecdote of the woman's distress at the trade of the iron for the boy is seen as valuable in its rarity, for "such affection was very seldom seen among those people." Both the piece of barkcloth and the anecdote itself are framed as rare and precious specimens of Tahitian society. Much like the anecdote to which it is attached, of course, the provenance that is claimed for the piece of barkcloth is impossible to prove—a point underlined by the fact that a second printing of the *Catalogue* seems to have used entirely different pieces of barkcloth for its samples.[6]

Just as the small square sample of the barkcloth attests to the absence of the garment from which it has been taken, the anecdote to which it is attached also draws attention to the absence of any full understanding of Tahitian society as a whole that would enable the English reader to make sense of the story. The anecdote ends in ignorance rather than knowledge, for the lieutenant cannot know whether the woman who cried out was "the mother, sister, or relation" of the boy. Indeed, the narrative is peppered with gaps and ambiguities. What, exactly, does the chief intend in proffering the boy in place of the iron? Are the woman's gestures unambiguous signs of grief for the loss of the boy or, as the interpolated "seemed" suggests, possibly something else? Is the barkcloth meant to be given in exchange for the boy or does its unraveling hold some other significance?[7] The intentions of the British themselves seem obscure. Does the "gentleman" really pretend to accept the boy in exchange for the iron only in order to perform an impromptu test to see what the Tahitians would do—or is this really an ex post facto rationalization for an impulsive action? Even the number of the participants in the narrative are difficult to count. Are the gentleman and the lieutenant the same person or two separate people? And, assuming gentleman and lieutenant are one and the same, is this the person who told the anecdote to Shaw? Even in their apparent tactile immediacy, the anecdotes and the pieces of barkcloth in the *Catalogue* exhibit their own failure to work as synecdoches that, taken together, would allow the keeper of the catalogue to grasp the nature of Tahitian society, much less the societies of the South Sea islands as a whole.

Jonathan Lamb has drawn attention to the ways in which small anecdotes and objects that voyagers to the South Seas recorded and collected on their travels resisted integration into larger classificatory orders or into tidy narratives of imperial progress. "At their first advent," writes Lamb, "these little circumstances, whether narrative or material, are not tokens of

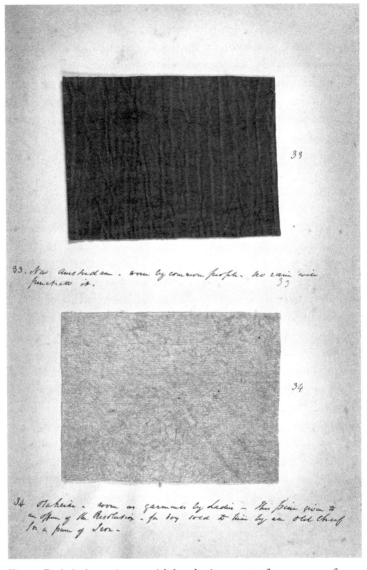

Fig. 3. Barkcloth specimens with handwritten notes from a copy of Alexander Shaw's *Catalogue of the Different Specimens of Cloth Collected in the Three Voyages of Captain Cook to the Southern Hemisphere* (London, 1787). The note for Specimen 33 reads "New Amsterdam—worn by the common people—no rain will penetrate it." The note for Specimen 34 reads "Otaheite, worn as garments by Ladies—this piece given to an officer of the Resolution—for boy sold to him by an old Chief for a piece of Iron—" (Object number ABDUA: 36921; courtesy of the University of Aberdeen)

anything: they act neither as information nor booty, neither as a gift nor as a commodity." These "minute particulars," for Lamb, mark "the boundary enclosing not a particularized universality, which is how the Enlightenment is usually supposed to have shaped the truth-claims of travelers, but an extravagant and utopian singularity."[8] Here, Lamb presents the anecdotal "minute particular" as operating in much the same way as utopian literature from Thomas More's *Utopia* (1516) to William Shakespeare's *The Tempest* (c. 1611). These texts place their alternate societies in islands cut off from the rest of the world and, in Roland Greene's words, "afford a perspective that can have only an oblique relation to the accumulating and totalizing worldview of the imperial and economic centres."[9] In the eighteenth century, utopias were not just to be found in the islands of the South Seas previously unknown to Europeans; little utopias were also contained within the anecdotal "minute particulars" that voyages such as Cook's brought back with them: islands of knowledge that appeared to float free of larger intellectual systems, even as they impelled the desire to incorporate them into these larger orders.

In this chapter I put the emphasis less on the *Endeavour* anecdotes' absolute resistance to intellectual integration and more on the way different ideas about the anecdotes' relationship to the science of human nature came to clash in the aftermath of the voyage. The question the *Endeavour* anecdotes raised about the explanatory power of isolated and unusual events reflects wider questions raised in the period about the evidentiary status of what Francis Bacon called the "unique instance," which for Lorraine Daston was the very model of the scientific fact for much of the seventeenth century. Daston suggests, however, that natural philosophers increasingly sought out demonstrable regularities in nature in preference to "unique instances," arguing that "the prototypical scientific fact mutated between circa 1660 and 1730, from a singular and striking event that could be replicated only with great difficulty, if at all, to a large and uniform class of events that could be produced at will."[10] Daston associates the later ideal of the scientific fact with Linnaean classification, which deliberately overlooks the infinite particularities and peculiarities of individual plants in order to taxonomize them on the basis of a restricted number of common features. Linnaeus does emphasize in his *Philosophia Botanica* (1751) that the definition of a plant should abstract away from particular features specific to individual specimens, instructing the botanist to "exclude from the specific name all accidental features that do not exist in the actual plant or are not palpable: for example, *place, time, duration,* and *use.*"[11] The scientific usefulness of the "singular instance" certainly was challenged by figures like Linneaus. But Linnaeus himself made extensive use of singular, unrepeatable events in his theological speculations, speculations that suggest the continuing attractions of singular anecdotes, even to one of the century's most notoriously systematizing minds.

While Linnaeus was publishing his taxonomies of animals, plants, and minerals, he was also working on his *Nemesis Divina,* a compilation of evidence of God's providence that included many tersely told anecdotes of sinful deeds punished by unfortunate accidents. "An Uppland farmhand," one of the collection's many anecdotes of divine punishments being meted out for various transgressions, reads as follows: "The farmhand makes two girls pregnant at about the same time. The first faces public disgrace as a whore; the second does away with her child in secret. The farmhand marries the second girl. On a certain occasion, while she is brewing, she has a fit of giddiness, falls into the brewing vat, and is boiled to death. The first girl marries and gets on well."[12] Taken individually, Linnaeus's anecdotes read as a series of exceptional misfortunes, told with clinical callousness. Collectively, however, they are intended to point to the existence of a general and ineluctable moral law ensuring that all misdeeds are eventually punished in this world and not only in the next.[13] As short stories stripped to the narrative bone, the anecdotes of *Nemesis Divina* resemble Linnaeus's botanical descriptions, with their drive to present observable features of plants as parsimoniously as possible. Daston calls Linnaeus's practice of stripping away superfluous detail "description by omission" and argues that this kind of description characterizes the scientific fact once it has shifted from Baconian singularity to Linnaean regularity. Yet Linnaeus's anecdotes in *Nemesis Divina* also show his abiding interest in Baconian "singular instances" that might inspire the discovery of new laws of earthy and divine nature.

The immediate motivation for the *Endeavour* voyage, moreover, was the epitome of what Daston calls a "singular and striking event that could be replicated only with great difficulty, if at all." Cook and the astronomical contingent on the *Endeavour* hoped to observe the 1769 Transit of Venus from Tahiti, which lay in the ideal area in the Southern Hemisphere for observing the event. Transits of Venus, in which Venus passes across the disc of the sun, are exceedingly rare astronomical phenomena. They occur every 243 years, in paired transits placed eight years apart. The transits were of central importance for astronomers because they theoretically could be used to estimate the distance from the Earth to the sun, which once known could then be used to calculate the distances to all the other visible planets and so reveal the true dimensions of the solar system. Because observers stationed at different points on the Earth's surface would see transits from different angles, it was predicted that they would record different timings for the period the planet takes to track across the disc of the sun. Using the parallax method, these timings could in turn be used to calculate the Earth's distance from the sun. The 1769 Transit of Venus would be the last chance to witness a transit of Venus until 1874. Much was riding on the accuracy of the observations made from Tahiti.

On June 6, 1769, the weather conditions happened to be ideal. "Not a Clowd was to be seen the whole day," wrote Cook in his journal, "and the Air was perfectly clear, so that we had every advantage we could desire in Observing the whole of the Passage of the Planet Venus over the Suns Disk." Despite this, the official observers on Tahiti—Cook, Solander, and Charles Green—all recorded different timings for the moments of contact between Venus and the sun.[14] In his journal, Cook reported that "we very distinctly saw an Atmosphere or dusky shade round the body of the Planet which very much disturbed the times of the Contacts particularly the two internal ones" (*C* 97–98). Consequently, the unwanted divergences between the three observers at Tahiti impeded the attempt to measure the meaningful divergences that were expected to be found between observers at different locations on the Earth's surface. The astronomers' conflicting observations of the moments of contact between Venus and the sun were not so far removed from the anecdotes of moments of contact between the Europeans and the peoples of the South Pacific. These anecdotes also differed from teller to teller. They created similar difficulties to those that confronted Hawkesworth, who was tasked with making a coherent story out of the journals that came down to him, much as the astronomer and mathematician Thomas Hornsby was tasked with reconciling the differences between Cook's, Green's, and Solander's observations of the Transit of Venus from Tahiti. The discrepancies between the three observers' timings of the Transits of Venus remind us that even when we are dealing with anecdotes whose correspondence to actual preexisting events seems stronger than is usually the case, an anecdote of even an eyewitnessed event is still subject to distortion and error. The next section takes its cue from these divergent accounts of the Transit of Venus. I read Cook's and Banks's journals in parallax, shuttling back and forth between them in order to highlight the differences between the ways both writers recorded anecdotes of the events they observed during the course of the voyage in their respective journals. These differences correspond, in turn, to Cook's and Banks's very different understandings of the anecdote itself as a vehicle for representing the experience of contact and of fathoming the workings of another culture.

BANKS'S AND COOK'S ANECDOTAL JOURNALS

In his firsthand journals kept over the course of the *Endeavour* voyage, Banks tries to account for the surprising actions of the people he saw by identifying them as customs peculiar to island societies. His journal attempts to move from anecdotal narratives of the islanders' actions to the understanding of common practices, shifting from puzzling and singular events to the comprehensible and general customs he deems to be characteristic of South Sea societies. The method of Cook's journal is different. Rather than recording anecdotes in order to explain them later, as Banks does, Cook tends to report the surface appearance of events but often refuses to speculate further, attempting to record, as far as possible, the "facts" of the voyage as they appeared to him without interpreting them. In their descriptions of unfamiliar peoples in the South Seas, Banks moves from the singularity of anecdote to the typicality of custom; whereas Cook tends to arrest just this movement from the singular to the typical.

Anecdotes of singular instances of human behavior are frequently linked to acts of violence in both Banks's and Cook's journals. Banks's account of his encounter with a singular way of treating the body of a dead man is linked, in turn, to a violent event perpetrated by the visitors themselves. In his journal entry for April 18, 1769, Banks mentions that the ship's surgeon, William Monkhouse, had discovered a man lying on a bier inside a small hut with his weapons, a hatchet, human hair, a coconut, and a cup of water beside him: "[a] custom so new as this appears to be surprised us all very much," writes Banks, "but whether all who die are thus disposd of or it is a peculiar honour shewn to those who dye in war is to be cleard up by future observation" (*B* 1:259). This surprising sight is later found to be the direct consequence of the events of April 15, 1769, in which members of the *Endeavour* crew, on the orders of the midshipman Jonathan Monkhouse, William Monkhouse's brother, fired hundreds of shots at a crowd of Tahitians after a man seized a musket and ran off with it. The man who took the musket was shot dead, and this was the man discovered by William Monkhouse lying dead in the hut. Neither Banks nor Cook fully account for the sequence of events that led to the man's death, though Banks hesitantly contemplates the possibility that "the midshipman (may be) impudently orderd the marines to fire" and writes that the visitors went back to the ship "guilty no doubt in some measure of the death of a man who the most severe laws of equity would not have condemnd to so severe a punishment" (*B* 1:240). Banks made his own visit to the hut in which the dead man's body was laid on April 22, when he lifted the cloth covering the corpse and "saw part of the body already dropping to pieces with putrefaction about him and indeed within all parts of his flesh were abundance of maggots of a species of Beetle very common here" (*B* 1:261). If Banks's taxonomic precision in noting the precise species of beetle consuming the body seems to distance him from the horror, the dead man is not allowed to recede into the past once good relations are seemingly restored with the Tahitians. He returns in the context of a burial practice that surprises and unsettles the visitors.

Banks witnesses the continuing effects of the man's death in the form of an event that leaves him initially mystified. Banks's entry for April 28 tells of how Terapo, a Tahitian woman, entered the European visitors' encampment Fort Venus and burst into tears. Ignoring Banks's attempts to "enquire the cause," and his efforts to comfort her, the woman "took from under her garment a sharks tooth and struck it into her head with great force 6 or 7 times. a profusion of Blood followd these strokes and alarmd me not a little; for two or 3 minutes she bled freely more than a pint in quantity, during that time she talkd loud in a most melancholy tone" (*B* 1:165). Banks provides a detailed account of the incident:

> I was not a little movd at so singular a spectacle and holding her in my arms did not cease to enquire what might be the cause of so strange an action, she took no notice of me till the bleeding ceas'd nor did any Indian in the tent take any of her, all talkd and laugh'd as if nothing melancholy was going forward; but what surpriz'd me most of all was that as soon as the bleeding ceas'd she lookd up smiling and immediately began to collect peices of cloth which during her bleeding she had thrown down to catch the blood. These she carried away out of the tents and threw into the sea, carefully dispersing them abroad as if desirous that no one should be reminded of her action by the sight of them; she then went into the river and after washing her whole body returnd to the tents as lively and chearfull as any one in them. (*B* 1:265–66)

What seems to perplex Banks most in his account of the incident is not the act itself but the apparent indifference that accompanies it: both the indifference of the woman to his attempts to comfort her and press her to explain her behavior and the indifference of the other Tahitians and the woman herself to her action once it is completed, which undercuts Banks's efforts to play the sentimental traveler.[15]

Only later, when Banks writes the ethnographic sketch after the *Endeavour* had moved on from Tahiti, does he present the two "surprising" circumstances—a burial of a man above ground and a woman's self-wounding with a shark tooth—as two separate moments in the same process of attending to the dead. In his descriptive survey of Tahitian manners, Banks explains that the dead bodies of high-ranking Tahitians are laid on biers surrounded by huts, whose Tahitian name Banks renders as "*Tu papow*" (*fare tupapa'u*). After this, Banks writes, the nearest female relative to the deceased leads a party of women up to the hut and "swimming almost in tears strikes a sharks tooth several times into the crown of her head, on which a large effusion of blood flows, which is carefully caught in their linnen and thrown under the Bier." The rest of the women do the same, and the women go on to wound their heads again every two or three days for "as long as the women chuse or can keep it up, the nearest relation thinking it her duty to Continue it longer than any one else" (*B* 1:377). The process of mourning ends with the washing, scraping, and burial of the bones, "unless some of the women who find themselves more than commonly afflicted by the Loss repeat the ceremony of *Poopooing* or bleeding themselves in the head, which they do at any time or in any place where they happen to be when the whim takes them" (*B* 1:378). The ethnographic sketch makes intelligible an event that would otherwise remain utterly bewildering.

Yet questions about the nature of the ceremony remain even in Banks's ethnographic sketch. Vanessa Smith observes that the odd description of women performing the ritual whenever "the whim takes them" suggests Bank's difficulty in its emotional significance: "For Banks, this persistent, melancholic version of mourning remains ambivalent: is it a genuine sign of uncommon affliction or simply 'whim?'"[16] The ambiguity suggests that even Banks is not entirely secure in his ability to describe Tahitian society for the benefit of his European readers. A sense of uncertainty arises again when Banks begins another section on Tahitian cosmology and prefaces it by observing, "Religion has been in ages, is still in all Countreys Cloak'd in mysteries unexplicable to human understanding." He notes that the difficulty of comprehending the nature of religious belief is compounded in the South Sea islands because "the Language in which it is conveyd, at least many words of it, are different from those usd in common conversation" (*B* 1:379). In general, however, the shift in Banks's journal from anecdote to survey is a movement from confusion to understanding and surprise to knowledge. By the time he gets to writing his survey, Banks seems more assured in his ability to understand Tahitian society. He says the Tahitians believe the blood on the cloths they throw into the "*Tu papow*" to be "an acceptable present to the deceasd, whose soule they beleive to exist and hover about the place where the body lays observing the actions of the survivors" (*B* 1:377). His confidence is underwritten by the stylistic markers that, as Mary Louise Pratt has shown, often characterize eighteenth-century ethnographies: the subsumption of individual people under a "collective *they*," coupled with the "timeless present tense."[17]

Cook presents himself in his own journal as much less certain in his ability to fathom the societies of the South Pacific. Cook's discussion of Tahitian burial practices is much more tentative than Banks's. Like Banks, Cook had made his own visit to observe the dead man in the Tahitian hut. In his descriptive overview of Tahitian customs, Banks would explain these huts as offerings for the gods, who would otherwise feast on the dead man's flesh. Cook is less sure of the custom's meaning, writing "if it is a Religious ceremoney we may not be able to understand it, for the Misteries of most Religions are dark and not easily understud even by those who profess them," and declining to speculate further as to its significance (*C* 84). Cook's journal documents instances of unaccountable behavior in the people he encounters, which he leaves largely unexplained, whereas Banks's journal often shifts from instances of unaccountable behavior to explications of their meaning.

Descriptions of people and practices in Cook's journal are regularly punctuated by qualifications that signal Cook's sense that his understanding is incomplete. The entry in Cook's journal from May 1, 1769, for example, mentions that "This day one of the Natives who appear'd to be a Chief dined with us as he had some days before," in which the "appear'd" shows that Cook is reluctant even to identify the man's social position. He recounts that the man refused to eat until one of the servants fed him, there being no Tahitian women around to perform this task. Cook surmises, "We have often found the Women very officious in feeding of us, from which it would seem that it is a Custom upon some occasions for them to feed the Chiefs, however this is the only instance of that kind we have seen" (*C* 86). What would now be recognized as a widespread taboo in Polynesian societies, which forbade certain people eating with their own hands, is hedged with qualifications that forestall any determinate judgment on the ritual's meaning.[18] In particular, Cook is careful not to extrapolate customs from singular instances: although the visitors have been fed by women often, Cook has only seen a chief—or someone who appears to be a chief—fed in this way only once.

Cook is more interested, then, in describing the dislocating events arising from cross-cultural contact than in explaining them. He leaves what would become the most notorious of the *Endeavour* anecdotes unexplained in his journal entry for Sunday, May 14, 1769:

> This day we perform'd divine Service in one of the Tents in the Fort where several of the Natives attended and behaved with great decency the whole time: this day closed with an odd Scene at the Gate of the Fort where a young fellow above 6 feet high lay with a little Girl about 10 or 12 years of age publickly before several of our people and a number of the Natives. What makes me mention this, is because, it appear'd to be done more from Custom than Lewdness, for there were several women present particularly Obarea and several others of the better sort and these were so far from shewing the least disaprobation that they instructed the girl how she should act her part, who young as she was, did not seem to want it. (*C* 93–94)

Cook's hesitance to account for this incident shows not only in the qualifiers "appear'd" and "seem" but in the very syntax of the last clause which is, as Neil Rennie points out, ambiguous: it could mean that the girl did not need to be instructed on how to act her part or that she did not want to have sex.[19] Hawkesworth would later attempt to draw out the event's "philosophical" implications. For his part, Cook characteristically performs a refusal to generalize from the event or to fully understand the mental states of the participants in the "odd Scene."[20]

Like Banks, Cook also produced a descriptive survey of Tahitian society and customs. By contrast to Banks, however, Cook's survey focuses on the external manifestations of Tahitian culture. Although he lingers on activities like tattooing, dancing, and cloth making, Cook declines to try to explain what they might have meant from the perspective of the people who performed them. Banks's ambition, by contrast, is to attain precisely this perspective. He even went as far as to participate in a Tahitian funeral ceremony, allowing himself to be stripped down to a single piece of barkcloth around his loins and daubed with soot and water. He then joined a party of similarly daubed Tahitian men in running through the European fort and the surrounding area, chasing Tahitians and scattering them wherever they found them "like sheep before a wolf" (*B* 1:289). Perhaps Banks thought that his active participation would give him a special insight into this ceremony, a practice whose meaning and purpose is still difficult to parse, since this particular custom lapsed in the immediate decades following the *Endeavour*'s visit.[21] In his survey of Tahitian customs, Banks relates that after the corpse has been interred in a *fare tupapa'u,* "2 or 3 boys," naked except for a "piece of Cloth round their wrists," are daubed with charcoal and run about the deceased "as if in pursuit of people on whoom he may vent the rage inspird by his sorrow, which he does most unmercifully if he catches any body, cutting them with his stick the edge of which is set with sharks teeth" (*B* 1:378). Cook in his own survey of Tahitian society and customs also mentions soot-besmeared Tahitians "runing here and there, and where ever they came the people would fly from them as tho they had been so many hobgoblins not one daring to come in their way," but he adds, "I know not the reason for their performing this ceremony" (*C* 1:136). Cook again prefers to profess ignorance than to advance claims to knowledge that may turn out to be unfounded.

The difference between Cook's and Banks's journals is exemplified, finally, in their different reactions to the evidence of cannibalism they encountered in the area Cook named "Queen Charlotte's Sound" in the South Island of New Zealand. Banks wrote in his journal that he chanced to see "2 bones, pretty clean pickd, which as apeard upon examination were undoubtedly human bones." He goes on to adduce these bones as positive "proof" of a custom that the visitors had already suspected was practiced among the natives: "Tho we had from the first of our arrival upon the coast constantly heard the Indians acknowledge the custom of eating their enemies we had never before had a proof of it, but this amounted almost to demonstration: the bones were clearly human, upon them were evident marks of their having been dressd on the fire, the meat was not intirely pickd off from them and on the grisly ends which were gnawd were evident marks of teeth, and these were accidentaly found in a provision basket." With the help of Tupaia, the Ra'iatean high priest and navigator who traveled on the *Endeavour* from Tahiti, Banks questioned the "Indians" about the bones, receiving apparent confirmation that they came from a man. Banks then turns to describing the reactions of the visitors to this seeming proof that the Māori were cannibals: "The horrour that apeard in the countenances of the seamen on hearing this discourse which was immediately translated for the good of the company is better conceivd than describd. For ourselves and myself in particular we were before too well convincd of the existence of such a custom to be surprizd, tho we were pleasd at having so strong a proof of a custom which human nature holds in too great abhorrence to give easy credit to" (*B* 1:455). Banks describes cannibalism as a practice held in abhorrence not simply by Europeans but by human nature itself. But the very confidence he expresses in the reality of the practice also inevitably raises the question of whether abhorrence of cannibalism is really innate in human nature. The incident, in which the visitors behold evidence of cannibalism but not the actual eating of human beings, produces various kinds of vacillation in Banks's journal. The "New Zealanders" appear to oscillate in and out of human nature, while the reactions of the European visitors oscillate between horror and pleasure in having their darkest suspicions confirmed. Anticipating the eventual publication of his own journal in some form or other, Banks himself acknowledges that his report of the practice of cannibalism will cause readers to doubt the veracity of his own narrative.

In his general ethnographic survey of the "New Zealanders," which he wrote down the day before the *Endeavour* departed their shores, Banks attempts to reconcile cannibalism with the idea of a universal human nature. Describing the diet of the natives, Banks writes:

> As for the flesh of men, although they certainly do eat it I cannot in my own opinion Debase human nature so much as to imagine that they relish as a dainty or even look upon it as a part of common food. Tho Thirst of Revenge may Drive men to great lengths when the Passions are allowd to take their full swing Yet nature through all the superior part of the creation shews how much she recoils at the thought of any species preying upon itself: Dogs and cats shew visible signs of disgust at the very sight of a dead carcass of their species, even Wolves or Bears were never sayd to eat one another except in cases of absolute nescessity, when the stings of hunger have overcome the precepts of nature, in which case the same has been done by the inhabitants of the most civilizd nations. (*B* 2:19–20)

Here the attempt to define cannibalism as an act contrary to human nature depends on the claim that cannibalism is unknown in the animal kingdom. Cannibals are unnatural, it seems, not because they act like animals but, on the contrary, because they depart from a nature common to both human beings and animals. Reasoning by analogy from the animal to the human world, Banks assumes that the eating of one's own kind only occurs when natural disgust is overcome by some stronger instinct: excessive hunger or excessive anger. In this way, Banks is able to accommodate cannibalism to human nature, although only by implying that Europeans might themselves become cannibals given the right circumstances. Indeed, the popular representations of Banks that circulated after the *Endeavour* voyage would burlesque the botanist's outsized appetite for women, food, curious objects, and decapitated heads, the sheer excessiveness of which tended to associate him, in the popular mind, with the cannibal's deviant taste.

In his own general account of the peoples he had seen in New Zealand, Cook was as convinced as Banks was in the reality of cannibalism, writing, "It is hard to account for what we have every w[h]ere been told of their eating their enimies kill'd in battle which they most certainly do, circumstance enough we have seen to convince of the truth of this" (*C* 282). But in his version of the anecdote of the encounter with the supposed cannibals in Queen Charlotte's Sound, Cook focuses not on the natives' words but on one Māori man's miming of the act of cannibalism. His account of the incident includes the detail, omitted by Banks, that the man made as if to eat his own arm, apparently to signify that the bone in his possession was indeed that of a man, after the visitors affected to believe that the bone was a dog's rather than that of a human being. He also recorded that the Māori "to shew us that they eat the flesh they bit a[nd] naw'd the bone and draw'd it thro' their mouth and this in such a manner as plainly shew'd that the flesh to them was a dainty bit" (*C* 236–37). Cook's own account suggests a charade of cannibalism more than it does a re-creation of an actual eating of enemies. As Gananath Obeyesekere observes, it appears that "the Maori are at great pains to prove that not only are they cannibals, but also they are truly horrible ones."[22] The anecdotes recorded by Cook and Banks suggest a strong performative dimension to the display, even assuming that the Māori had in fact eaten their enemies. Indeed, as Obeyesekere points out, even the apparently clinching evidence of the human bones is itself open to doubt. He speculates that the Māori may have endowed the bones with the marks of cannibalism after the fact, both to impress the British with their ferocity and also to furnish them with commodities for which the visitors were clearly interested in bartering.

Cook's trust in the visual over the verbal in his account of the interrogation of the natives is consistent with a comment attributed to him by James Boswell, who was present at a Royal Society dinner both men attended on April 18, 1776. On this occasion, Boswell writes, Cook "candidly confessed to me that he and his companions who visited the South Sea Islands could not be certain of any information they got, or supposed they got, except as to objects falling under the observation of the senses; their knowledge of the language was so imperfect they required the aid of their senses, and anything which they learnt about religion, government, or traditions might be quite erroneous."[23] This remark assumes that the evidence of the senses—especially sight—are more trustworthy witnesses to other societies than the words spoken in languages that the visitors barely understood. In fact, of course, the evidence of the senses could be just as ambiguous as words were in the South Seas, a point that Cook misses when he makes an uncharacteristic judgment that the men who made as if to gnaw on human bones "plainly shew'd that the flesh to them was a dainty bit," a conclusion that Banks, as we have seen, explicitly rejects. Cook's self-restriction in his journal of describing what he sees, as opposed to interpreting it, implies that what he does choose to set down is the unequivocal truth. Yet even the senses were not infallible witnesses to events in the South Seas, as Cook himself discovered when he compared his timings of the transit of Venus with those of Green. Cook would also discover that his own recorded observations were vulnerable to the depredations of his editor, John Hawkesworth, who would assume Cook's own voice, even though he would emulate little of Cook's display of interpretive austerity.

HAWKESWORTH'S ANECDOTAGE

Many of the anecdotes traded about the *Endeavour* voyage in eighteenth-century Britain were first communicated to the public through Hawkesworth's *Account of the Voyages*.[24] Hawkesworth compressed into the first volume of this work the narratives of the voyages of John Byron in the *Dolphin* and the joint voyage chartered by Philip Carteret and Samuel Wallis in the *Dolphin* and the *Swallow*. He signaled the special significance of the *Endeavour* voyage by devoting two volumes to it. In these volumes, Hawkesworth combined narrative material from Cook's and Banks's journals with his own moral speculations. He brought these disparate materials together in a first-person narrative that is ascribed to Cook himself, though Hawkesworth did admit to his readers that this voice was an editorial fiction from the outset. The resulting book was a major literary event. Hawkesworth's *Account of the Voyages* went through three editions in its first year in print alone and was the most borrowed item from the Bristol Library between 1773 and 1784, surpassing Hume's *History of England*, Laurence Sterne's *Tristram Shandy*, and Henry Fielding's *Works* in popularity among readers.[25] Hawkesworth drew on his own experience as a periodical essayist (in Johnson's *Adventurer*) to extrapolate moral lessons from the particular narratives he found in Cook's and Banks's journals. Hawkesworth's approach to the *Endeavour* anecdotes differs from that of the original journal keepers. He pushes beyond custom to a higher level of generality. Cook tends to stop once he has described the surface appearance of events and Banks tends to stop once he has explained particular events as instances of prevalent customs. But Hawkesworth tends to go further than either Cook or Banks had in looking beyond particular happenings and customary practices to their sources in a universal human nature. In his *Account of the Voyages,* Hawkesworth sought to move from narratives of singular events to the human condition in general.

Throughout the *Account of the Voyages,* Hawkesworth tries to tease out the implications of the events Cook and Banks witnessed for the study of human nature. He takes, for example, Banks's description of Tahitians using the stern of an old canoe to ride dangerous waves to a stony shore as a promising topic for moral-philosophical speculation. In his rendering of the event, Hawkesworth follows Banks's description closely, reproducing Banks's comment that the waves would have ended the lives of most Europeans. But Hawkesworth slips in his own infantilizing analogy, comparing the surfing Tahitians to "our holiday youth," who "climb the hill in Greenwich park for the pleasure of rolling down it." Hawkesworth follows his description of the Tahitians' riding the waves with his own speculations on the sources of unusual abilities in a universal human nature: "Upon this occasion it may be observed, that human nature is endued with powers which are only accidentally exerted to the utmost; and that all men are capable of what no man attains, except he is stimulated to the effort by some uncommon circumstances or situation. These Indians effected what to us appeared to be supernatural, merely by the application of such powers as they possessed in common with us, and all other men who have no particular infirmity or defect" (*H* 2:136). Hawkesworth compares the Tahitians not only to rope dancers and balance makers, who have cultivated their unusually fine sense of balance by honing abilities that are latently possessed by all human beings, but also to the blind, who develop unusually sharpened senses of hearing and touch as the direct result of lacking the sense of sight. Running through Hawkesworth's reworking of Banks's observations of the Tahitian surfers is the persistent implication that they are somehow immature or incapacitated. He suggests, but does not quite say, that the Tahitians' grace is the direct consequence of their moral and intellectual underdevelopment. Hawkesworth's narrative assumes the presence of a universal but malleable human nature, in which the cultivation of some latent abilities results in the atrophy of others.

Hawkesworth also attempts to tease out implications for the study of human nature from another anomalous event, one that, as we have seen, was witnessed and recorded by Cook, of a young man and a young girl copulating in front of the fort at Point Venus. After retelling the story, Hawkesworth writes, "This incident is not mentioned as an object of idle curiosity, but as it deserves consideration in determining a question which has been long debated in philosophy; Whether the shame attending certain actions, which are allowed on all sides to be in themselves innocent, is implanted in Nature, or superinduced by custom?" Hawkesworth hesitates at the crossroads between natural and cultural explanations of sexual shame, writing, "If it has its origin in custom, it will, perhaps, be found difficult to trace that custom, however general, to its source; if in instinct, it will be equally difficult to discover from what cause it is subdued or at least overruled among these people, in whose manners not the least trace of it is to be found" (*H* 2:128). He splits the difference between the two explanations for the embarrassment of sexuality, inviting the reader to decide between the options instead. The incident becomes a kind of *experimentum crucis* between two competing explanations for the phenomenon of sexual shame, although, as Rennie observes, Hawkesworth appears to lean toward the idea that shame about sex has its origin in custom rather than instinct.[26]

Hawkesworth's efforts to plumb Cook's and Banks's journals for insights into the nature of human beings were not universally judged to be successful. In a negative review of the *Account*, the *Edinburgh Magazine and Review* observed that even though the voyages described in Hawkesworth's book had "effected discoveries, and given occasion to nautical remarks of great utility" they nevertheless "communicate little that can gratify an intelligent inquirer into the history of mankind." In the reviewer's estimation, Hawkesworth had made "few observations of any importance" and, conversely, had "mentioned valuable facts in a manner as if they were of little consequence."[27] In criticizing the disproportionate attention Hawkesworth gives to the insignificant events of the voyages, the reviewer discounts the central principle guiding the use of anecdotes as tools for studying human nature: that those narratives that would typically be overlooked by historians are in fact most significant for learning about the nature of human beings. In the view of the reviewer, Hawkesworth's concern with inconsequential events is simply a sign of his inability to distinguish between important and unimportant matters. The fact that much of the information about the *Endeavour* voyage was communicated to the public through scattered and minute anecdotes helped create the impression that voyagers who had set out in the expectation of making great discoveries had returned with little to show for their pains. The anecdotes of the *Endeavour* also worked to diminish the reputations of the very people who helped put them into circulation. Hawkesworth's literary reputation was not the only casualty of the *Endeavour* anecdotes. The *Endeavour* anecdotes had a similarly deleterious effect on Banks's scientific reputation, as discussed in the next section.

BANKS'S ANECDOTAL BURLESQUING

In popular magazines and satirical poems, the anecdotes of the *Endeavour* voyages were framed as indulgences that entertain but could never provide the basis of a serious study of human nature. Individual anecdotes were lifted from Hawkesworth's weighty volumes and inserted into scurrilous poems and gossipy magazines. The anecdotes most often told and retold in the popular press were those that sated either the reading public's demand for peeks into the paradise of sexual delights, which Tahiti was widely imagined to be in the popular imagination, or else their desire to laugh at the expense of the *Endeavour* voyagers and the people they encountered. Although Hawkesworth died soon after publishing his *Account of the Voyages*, Banks lived to see his intellectual reputation besmirched much longer, in part by the publication of many of the same anecdotes he had himself set down in his journal. In their irreverent uses of the anecdotes surrounding the voyage, popular magazines and satirical poems tended to break the alliance between anecdotes and philosophy, which writers from Locke to Hume had tried to forge. They made fun of the very idea that anecdotes could provide a reliable source of knowledge. Banks was widely mocked both as a frequent subject of anecdotes and as someone fond of telling them.

One anecdote that was often extracted from Hawkesworth's narrative told the story of Banks surprising the highborn Tahitian woman, who came to be known as "Queen Oberea" (Purea), while she was lying in the arms of a young Tahitian man. Banks himself had first recorded this story in his journal: "On my return ashore I proceeded to pay a visit to her majesty *Obórea* [as] I shall for the future call her. She I was told was still asleep in her Canoe-awning, where I went intending to call up her majesty but was surprizd to find her in bed with a hansome lusty young man of about 25 whose name was *Obàdée*. I however soon understood that he was her gallant, a circumstance which she made not the least secret of" (*B* 1:267). Hawkesworth included this little story in his *Account of the Voyages* but told it in Cook's voice, transposing Banks's original narrative from the first person to the third, smoothing out Banks's style, and adding and amplifying some details:

On the 29th, not early in the forenoon Mr. Banks went to pay his court to Oberea, and was told she was still asleep under the awning of her canoe: thither therefore he went, intending to call her up, a liberty which he thought he might take, without any danger of giving offence: but, upon looking into her chamber, to his great astonishment, he found her in bed with a handsome young fellow about five and twenty, whose name was OBADÉE: he retreated with some haste and confusion, but was soon made to understand, that such amours gave no occasion to scandal, and that Obadée was universally known to have been selected by her as the object of her private favours. (*H* 2:107)

Hawkesworth, taking his cue from Banks's reference to Oberea as "her majesty," turns the scene into a parody of courtly romance: so, for example, Banks pays "court" to Oberea rather than just going to "visit" her, while the canoe becomes Oberea's "chamber." These changes work to frame a putatively "real" event as an episode in a mock romance, moving fact in the direction of fiction.

The anecdote of Banks surprising Purea in the canoe was subsequently reproduced as part of a running series of scandal chronicles in the *Town and Country Magazine*, entitled "Histories of the Tête à Tête annexed," in which the private affairs of public and semipublic figures were regularly exposed. In reproducing the anecdote from Hawkesworth's narrative, the only major change the *Town and Country* makes is to "disguise" Banks's name as "Mr. B," thus inevitably recalling the fictional character in Samuel Richardson's *Pamela*, the same book that Hawkesworth had named as a narrative model for his history of the recent British voyages to the Pacific, as well as Mr. Booby in Henry Fielding's parody *Shamela* (1741). The article focuses on Banks's infidelity toward Harriet Blossett ("Miss B—."), whom he had jilted soon after arriving back from his tour of the South Seas. The author of the broadside on Banks draws the obvious conclusion from Hawkesworth's depiction of Banks's behavior during the *Endeavour* voyage: "The queens, and women of the first class, we find constantly soliciting his company, or rather forcing their's upon him: at other times we find him visiting them in their bed-chambers, nay in their bed."[28] The magazine made the anecdote all the more delicious by pretending that the anecdotes of Banks in Hawkesworth's *Account of the Voyages* constitute a "secret history" that Banks would have had suppressed if he could.

Another widely circulated anecdote of the *Endeavour* voyage told how Banks lost his clothes during a night sleeping inside a canoe with Purea.

Adapting the account of the loss of the clothes from Banks's own journal, Hawkesworth recounted that the theft had left Banks with little more than his breeches: "his coat, and his waistcoat, with his pistols, powder-horn, and many other things that were in the pockets, were gone" (*H* 2:133). One of the many retellings of the story of the response to Banks's experiences on the *Endeavour* related the story of the lost garments in the voice of the "Injured Harriet." Seizing on the suspicions laid on Purea in Hawkesworth's account, "Harriet" accuses "Oberea" herself of stealing the clothes:

> Did'st thou not, crafty, subtle, sun-burnt Strum,
> Steal the silk breeches from his tawny bum?. . . .
> Call'st thou thyself a Queen? and thus could'st use
> And rob thy Swain of breeches and his shoes?
> Expose his flesh unto the bleak night-air,
> Then lend thy petticoat to shew thy care?[29]

Banks is made doubly ridiculous by wearing the clothes of another gender and another culture. Greg Dening has argued that this and other endlessly repeated stories of Banks's amours with "Queen Oberea" allowed the British reading public to take imaginative possession of "Tahitian otherness by laughing at it."[30] Although Dening does acknowledge that the public were laughing at Banks as well as "Queen Oberea," he misses the way that the anecdotes of Banks's erotic misadventures in the South Seas also constitute a burlesque of Banks's ethnographic project of understanding Pacific societies, especially insofar as this project depended on the interpretation and generalization of anecdotes.

One satirical poem, published long after the *Endeavour* voyage, explicitly mocked the idea that anecdotes might yield knowledge at all. Written by John Wolcot, who went under the pseudonym of Peter Pindar, the 1788 satire on Banks, *Peter's Prophecy*, identifies the latter's fondness for telling anecdotes as a sign of his unsuitability to serve as the president of the Royal Society. In the dialogue that is enacted in the poem between Pindar and Banks, Pindar says to Banks, "I grant you full of anecdote, my friend—/ *Bon Mots*, and wond'rous stories without end," but observes that "if a tale can claim, or jest so rare,/Ten thousand gossips might demand the chair."[31] The very public image of Banks was in large part formed through anecdotes: anecdotes of Banks falling into lakes, anecdotes of Banks being arrested on suspicion of being a highwayman while botanizing in a ditch, and anecdotes of Banks having sexual misadventures in the South Seas. Pindar's jibe that "Ten thousand gossips might demand the chair" if Banks's anecdote-telling were sufficient qualification for it associates Banks with a form of talk—gossiping—that was especially identified with women, thus implying that one of the qualities disqualifying Banks from the presidency of the Royal Society was that he was insufficiently masculine. Indeed, Banks cultivated a number of sociable relationships with fashionable women, including Lady Mary Coke and Margaret Cavendish Bentinck, who belonged to a female-centered network in which botanical information and gossip about the *Endeavour* voyage circulated.[32] A manuscript entitled "Banksiana," probably written by one of Banks's friends in the Royal Society, the chemist Charles Hatchett, suggests that Banks was indeed "full of anecdote": a fount of entertaining but frivolous stories.

These anecdotes in the "Banksiana" turn often to the theme of food and eating, and in doing so they present the anecdote form itself as a kind of delicacy meant for immediate consumption. Anecdotes in the "Banksiana" offer the easy satisfactions of an amusing story but little in the way of knowledge. Early on in the manuscript, Hatchett records that Banks had once claimed, "I have eaten all sorts of things and I believe I have eaten my way into the animal kingdom farther than any other man." When Hatchett asked Banks what he had *not* eaten, he replied:

> I never have eaten Monkey, although when at Batavia Captn Cooke Dr Solander and myself had determined to make the experiment but on the morning of our intended feast I happened to cross the yard of the House in which we resided and observed half a dozen of these poor little Devils with their arms tied upon cross sticks laying on their backs preparatory to their being killed. Now as I love all sorts of animals I walked up to them and in consequence of their primitive chattering and piteous looks I could not resist cutting the strings by which they were bound and they immediately scampered off so that we lost our monkey dinner.

The anecdote is saved from sentimentality when Hatchett goes on to say that Banks replied to his observation that the action did credit to his humanity by replying, "I don't know that . . . for I have been told that monkey makes a good dish, especially in the form of soup."[33] An image of Banks literally eating his way into the animal kingdom had already been publicized by the Thomas Rowlandson print that accompanied *Peter's Prophecy* entitled "The Fish Dinner," which shows Banks and his circle of fellow zoological enthusiasts in the Royal Society devouring a meal consisting of exotic animals, including a snake and an alligator. The print and the poem frame Banks's love of anecdotes as a reflection of his insatiable appetite for singularities of all kinds, anecdotal temptations that draw him away from both disciplined inquiry and tasteful consumption.

Although Hume had associated anecdotes with the performance of tasteful judgment, anecdotes were often linked with bad taste in the late eighteenth century. In a review of another satirical poem by Pindar attacking James Boswell's and Hester Lynch Piozzi's anecdotal memoirs of Samuel Johnson, the *English Review* remarked, "Every consideration must give place to the insatiable voracity of the anecdote-hunter; who, without any object but the satisfaction of his appetite, swallows and disembogues his trash with equal want of taste and discrimination."[34] The link between anecdotes and eating reappears in a more metaphorical guise in another of Hatchett's anecdotes, this one about the occasion on which Banks "boasted (to use his own expression) that he had tasted Womans flesh in almost every part of the Known habitable World." Banks's claims to sexual prowess are,

Fig. 4. Thomas Rowlandson, "The Fish Dinner," in Peter Pindar [John Wolcot], *Peter's Prophecy* (London, 1788). (Courtesy of Special Collections, University of East Anglia)

however, immediately undercut. Hatchett goes on to report that Banks followed up the boast with the admission that "he was severly Mortified when
having passed the Night with the Queen Oberrea, she dismissed him with
evident Contempt, informing him that he was not to be compared with her
own Men and requesting that for the future he would devote his attentions
to the Girls of her suite, who being comparatively ignorant might perhaps
be better satisfied with him than she was."[35] This anecdote is the sexual
counterpart to the anecdote that follows on Banks's claim to have eaten
nearly every species in the animal kingdom, though it ends with a note of
self-deprecation about his own prowess as a lover. In all, Hatchett's "Banksiana" frames Banks's zoological and anthropological interests as thin covers
for his pursuit of sensual pleasures.

The link between physical cravings and anecdotal pleasures resurfaces
in an anonymous anecdote that was printed in the *Attic Miscellany* in 1789,
where it appeared among other "Anecdotes and Bon Mots." The anecdote
is set at 32 Soho Square, which served both as Banks's home and a working
place for the study of natural history. Here, Banks collected and preserved
botanical specimens from around the world, kept an extensive library of
natural history, and employed engravers to work on the project (never completed) to produce a permanent record of prints of the flora and fauna gathered during the course of the *Endeavour* voyage. This program of research
was closely intertwined with Banks's deep involvement in the administration of Britain's empire. Banks took a leading role, for example, in a scheme
to transplant the breadfruit tree from the South Pacific to the West Indies to
provide a cheap source of food for the slaves who labored there.[36] The anecdote in the *Attic Miscellany* does not center, however, on Banks himself, but
rather on one of his engravers, who defies Banks's authority and seeks out
forbidden knowledge in the garden at Soho Square:

> One of these artists observing a jar in the garden, amidst other curi-
> osities, opened the covering; and perceiving a liquor, which afforded
> an aromatic flavour, he determined to taste it. Its delicious fragrance
> fully met his expectation; he therefore drank plentifully, naturally sup-
> posing it to be the produce of some happier clime than his own. At
> length, being satisfied with the surface, he felt as great an inclination
> to know what the bottom contained; he felt *something*; and, draw-
> ing it up, beheld––horrible to his imagination!––the preserved head
> of an Otaheitan, slain in battle! The punishment which Sir Joseph

inflicted—that of instant dismission—was the smallest part of the evils which resulted from this unwarrantable act of curiosity.[37]

This story is a fable of how the nominally dispassionate process of compiling knowledge of the South Seas was underlain by the baser motivations of curiosity. The story renders in literal terms Nicholas Thomas's argument that the "spirit of inquiry" that drove explorers to collect objects from the Pacific "could only be imperiled by some wider, positively hazardous, associations of the notion of curiosity."[38] It also serves as a narrative encapsulation of the way many readers were satisfied with the surfaces of the *Endeavour* anecdotes, enjoying their superficial pleasures (and occasional horrors) without looking any deeper for any insights they might hold for the science of human nature. The anecdote also pulls against what several recent critics describe as Soho Square's status as a "center of calculation," a phrase Bruno Latour uses to describe institutions in which objects, specimens, and knowledge from around the globe were consolidated, systematized, and transformed into objects of knowledge.[39] The anecdote from the *Attic Miscellany* suggests that these cycles of accumulation did not always run as smoothly as people such as Banks would have liked. Indeed, the anecdote begins by explaining that Banks had brought the engravers to work at his own house out of a desire "to preserve his plans as much as possible, from being pirated."[40] The anecdote presents the dispassionate work of gathering information as constantly endangered by intrusions of undisciplined curiosity and greed, passions of which Banks himself stood accused in Rowlandson's print.

The persistent framing of the anecdotes in circulation about Banks with the act of eating in turn helped frame the anecdote as a genre incompatible with serious disciplinary inquiries into the natural and human worlds. In his satirical poem *Peter's Prophecy*, mentioned above, Pindar opposes the anecdote-loving Banks to the "men of science" in the Royal Society who attempted to force him from the presidency of the Royal Society in early 1784. The faction was drawn from the society's "mathematicians," though most worked in the field of "mixed mathematics," or physics. The immediate spark for their rebellion was Banks's ousting of Charles Hutton, author of treatises on geometry and on the physics of bridges, from the post of foreign secretary in 1783. During a meeting held on January 8, 1784, Samuel Horsley, the editor of Newton's works, threatened that he and his fellow dissidents would secede from the Royal Society. He apparently announced to the assembled fellows, "I am united with a respectable and numerous band, embracing, I believe, a majority of the scientific part of this Society; of those who do its scientific business."[41] Horsley used the term "scientific" to mark off those fellows trained in mathematical and experimental kinds of inquiry, a select group that Horsley contrasted with Banks and "his train of feeble *Amateurs*."[42]

Although they ultimately failed to topple Banks from the presidency, the mutineers had succeeded in causing a fracas in the Royal Society, which spilled over into the wider arena of public debate. Pindar's *Peter's Prophecy* was a belated addition to the controversy surrounding Banks's fitness to lead the Royal Society.[43] In it, Pindar exhorts Banks to:

Think of the men, whom Science so reveres!
HORSLEY, and WILSON, MASKELYNE, MASERES,
LANDEN, and HORNSBY, ATWOOD, GLENIE, HUTTON,—

At which point Banks interrupts:

Blockheads! for whom I do not care a button!
Fools, who to *mathematics* would confine us,
And *bother* all our ears with *plus* and *minus*.[44]

The attacks launched against Banks by the mutinous mathematicians, whom Pindar names, made use of the same tropes used in popular satires against him. On December 27, 1783, for example, Banks's friend Charles Blagden wrote to him that the mathematicians were moving against him: "They give out that it is a struggle of the men of Science against the Macaroni's of the Society, dignifying your friends by the latter title."[45] The "macaroni" label identified Banks and his fellow dilettantes in the Royal Society as effeminate fops, lacking not only the intellectual discipline but also the requisite masculinity characterizing the true "Man of Science."

The attack on Banks's dilettantism overlooked Banks's concern, over the course of his career, for imposing discipline and order on his and his contemporaries' discoveries. John Gascoigne has described the whole of Banks's career as a general movement from the haphazard cultivation of human and natural curiosities to preoccupation with fitting discoveries into larger systems, moving Banks from "virtuoso to botanist" and from "antiquarian to anthropologist."[46] Despite the general shift from an interest in singularity to system that is traceable across Banks's career, Banks's correspondence shows his continuing faith that singular and striking events could contribute to the making of new knowledge. He sent, for example, a letter to his fellow member of the Royal Society Sir Everard Home, on September 30, 1798, in which he described his observations of a bird who bent back the stem of a plant overhanging a pond so that it could reach the ear of corn at its end and called the event "The strongest and most beautiful instance of the reasoning of a Bird I have seen."[47] This anecdote of a singular instance of avian reason shows how Banks continued to leave a place for anecdotes in the understanding of nature. The movement of the *Endeavour* anecdotes into Scottish moral philosophy likewise attests to the continuing role anecdotes played in the science of human nature.

CONJECTURAL ANECDOTES

Anecdotal reasoning on singular and unreproducible events is frequently to be found in the Scottish conjectural histories of John Millar; Henry Home, Lord Kames; and James Burnett, Lord Monboddo. These conjectural historians read the *Endeavour* anecdotes through the lens of stadial theories of human development, which envisaged human societies moving through a series of stages from savagery to civilization. In the four-stage model promulgated by Adam Smith, Adam Ferguson, and James Millar, for example, societies were envisaged as passing from hunting to pasturage, to agriculture, and finally to commerce. Conjectural history offered both a method of classifying societies and an explanation of large-scale societal change. By consulting accurate accounts of voyages to the South Seas, philosophers could peel back the stages of human progress and trace the general structure of societies occupying each stage of development. As the Scottish moral philosopher James Dunbar observed in his *Essays on the History of Mankind in Rude and Cultivated Ages* (1780), "the history . . . of some of the South Sea isles, which the late voyages of discovery have tended to disclose, enables us to glance at society in some of its earlier forms, and to mark, in some striking examples, the inviolable fidelity of social love."[48] Anecdotes acted as time machines that allowed conjectural historians to view human societies in their early stages of development.

Millar, Kames, and Monboddo believed that journeys to the far side of the world could furnish important evidence for their overarching theories of societal progress. Accounts of voyages, including the *Endeavour*, were mined for material for their inquiries into human development.[49] These writers used this material to make their histories seem less conjectural than they otherwise would have. Because they assumed that all societies begin in savagery and surmount the same series of steps on the way to civilization, they felt justified in using voyage narratives to the South Seas as evidence for the early history of the human species. They took the anecdotal narratives emanating from these expeditions as indications of both the general character of the societies encountered during the course of the voyage and the social conditions marking the more primitive stages of human society. The anecdote, ideally, would reconcile the two ideals of factuality Daston describes, the one resting on "striking and singular facts" and the other on a "large and uniform class of events." Anecdotes allowed conjectural historians to leap from stray events to the apprehension of the distinctive moral and social orders that are characteristic of each stage of development.

In the expanded edition of the *Origin of the Distinction of Ranks* published in 1779, for example, Millar quoted an anecdote from Hawkesworth's *Account* of a ceremony that had been performed in front of Banks by a Tahitian woman and the trading party that she appeared to lead. In Hawkesworth's rendering of the event, a woman ("Oorattooa") stepped on three pieces of barkcloth spread on top of one another and "taking up her garments all round her to the waist, turned about, and with great composure and deliberation, and with an air of perfect innocence and simplicity, three times" and then repeated the same procedure on another pile of cloth, and then another, before finally presenting Banks with the bundle of cloth used during the ceremony (*H* 2:135). Millar cites the story from Hawkesworth because it seems to support his theories about the social relations between men and women in "barbarous" societies, which he takes to be "chiefly regulated by the primary intention of nature"—that is, by the instinct to produce children.[50] The social and sexual codes that regulate commerce between the sexes in civilized nations are, in Millar's view, entirely lacking in barbarous societies: "From the extreme insensibility, observable in the character of all savage nations, it is no wonder they should entertain very gross ideas concerning those female virtues which, in a polished nation, are supposed to constitute the honour and dignity of the sex."[51] Millar takes the anecdote of the ceremony with the barkcloth, together with the instance of public copulation witnessed by Cook, as evidence for the absence of sexual propriety at the first stage of human development. Banks, Hawkesworth, and Millar all appear to have misinterpreted the meaning of this ceremony, at least if the historian Anne Salmond is correct when she argues that no sexual meaning attached to the ceremony at all.[52] Whatever the true significance of the ceremony, what is clear is that in their eagerness to find evidence for their theories of social development, the conjectural historians treat the anecdotes that emerged about the *Endeavour* voyage with little of the interpretive reticence Cook and (to a lesser extent) Banks show in their journals.

Although Scottish conjectural historians generally told a story of manners and civilization replacing original shamelessness and barbarity, this progressive narrative was often shadowed by a counternarrative of primitive virtue degenerating into hypocrisy and cowardice. Lord Kames, in his *Sketches of the History of Man*, illustrates this tendency to stress the loss of virtue that accompanied the advance of civilization when he writes that "When Mr. Banks and Dr. Solander were on the coast of New Holland, the natives, seeing some of our men fishing near the shore, singled out a number of their own equal to those in the boat, who marching down to the water-edge, challenged the strangers to fight them; an instance of true heroic courage." On the basis of a single anecdote, whose source he does not cite, Kames surmises that "the people in that part of New Holland must be a very different race from those Dampier saw."[53] Kames moves quickly from isolated narratives and descriptions to the character of a whole society: setting a single anecdote of native bravery against William Dampier's description of the indigenous New Hollanders he encountered in 1688 as the "miserablest People in the world" who "differ but little from Brutes."[54] Kames is motivated to find evidence of the differing characteristics of the peoples of New Holland (present-day Australia), because he wishes to contest the common assumption in stadial theory of a uniformity of culture and custom characterizing each stage of civilization. Kames posits a diversity of manners and customs within each stage of human development but assumes, at the same time, a uniformity within particular races, a uniformity he argues cannot be explained by climate or geographical factors but must derive instead from characteristics specific to a particular people. The use of the anecdote here departs from its usual role in conjectural history as practiced by Millar and others, of illustrating the characteristics of a particular stage in human society. In Kames's hands the anecdote pivots from the role of illustrating the effect of the environment on human nature to illustrating the characteristics of a "nation" or "race." His interpretation of the anecdote thus points away from conjectural history toward nineteenth-century conceptions of race, which would turn the term into an essentialist category marking out distinct divisions within humankind.[55]

Not all readers found Kames's practice of combining anecdote, conjectural history, and racial theorizing convincing. The reviewer in the *Critical Review*, for example, described *Sketches of the History of Man* as "Filled with curious erudition, entertaining anecdotes, and uncommon historical facts" and commented that Kames "has reared upon that foundation a specious fabric of whimsical systems and speculations, which at least yields amusement, if it produces not instruction."[56] This conflict could also be described as a disjunction between "deep" and "surface" readings of the anecdote: a "surface" reading orientated toward transient pleasure and a "deep" reading orientated toward the discovery of the underlying principles of human nature. Whereas the Scottish conjectural historians looked to *Endeavour* anecdotes for confirmations of their theories of the progress of human nature, their critics saw the same anecdotes as stories that might amuse but held none of the philosophical significance that the Scottish conjectural historians saw in them. This conflict between "deep" and "surface" readings of the *Endeavour* anecdotes was played out in the dispute between Lord Monboddo, an eccentric practitioner of Scottish conjectural history, and Dr. Johnson during his tour of Scotland with Boswell.

MONBODDO VS. JOHNSON

In a footnote in the 1860 edition of Boswell's *Journal of a Tour to the Hebrides with Samuel Johnson* (1785), Boswell's editor, Robert Carruthers, tells an anecdote about what the great critic and lexicographer did in Inverness during his tour of Scotland in 1773:

> Mr. Grant used to relate that on this occasion Johnson was in high spirits. In the course of conversation he mentioned that Mr. Banks (afterwards Sir Joseph) had, in his travels in New South Wales, discovered an extraordinary animal called the kangaroo. The appearance, conformation, and habits of this quadruped were of the most singular kind; and in order to render his description more vivid and graphic, Johnson rose from his chair and volunteered an imitation of the animal. The company stared; and Mr. Grant said nothing could be more ludicrous than the appearance of a tall, heavy, grave-looking man, like Dr. Johnson, standing up to mimic the shape and motions of a kangaroo. He stood erect, put out his hands like feelers, and, gathering up the tails of his huge brown coat so as to resemble the pouch of the animal, made two or three vigorous bounds across the room![57]

As this anecdote shows, anecdotes about the *Endeavour* voyage helped pollinate further anecdotes that could then be exchanged in conversation and in print. The anecdotes surrounding the *Endeavour* voyage were also much on the mind of Lord Monboddo, who would personally meet Banks and Solander a year after their trip around the world on the *Endeavour* in 1772 and, later on, Johnson during his 1773 tour of Scotland.[58] On both occasions, Boswell was present to record the meetings for posterity.

Monboddo notoriously argued in the second edition of *On the Origin and Progress of Language* (1774–92) for the humanity of "Orang Outang," a term that could refer to the great apes in general in the eighteenth century, including chimpanzees.[59] After surveying various accounts of the "Orang Outang," Monboddo concluded, "The substance of all these different relations is, that the Orang Outang is an animal of the human form, inside as well as outside."[60] He also suggested that the evidence for the existence of "men with tails, such as the antients gave to their satyrs, is a fact so well attested that I think it cannot be doubted."[61] In September 1772, Monboddo personally met Banks and Solander, who were journeying through Scotland on their way to Iceland, and during one of Monboddo's meetings with Solander, Boswell was on hand to record that Monboddo "listened with avidity to the Doctor's descriptions of the New Hollanders, almost brutes—but added with eagerness, 'Have they tails, Dr Solander?'" to which Solander replied, "'No, my Lord, they have not tails.'"[62] Later, Boswell would publish to the world Johnson's assessment of Monboddo's theories, delivered during their tour of Scotland: "Mr. Johnson said it is a pity to see Lord Monboddo publish such notions as he has done, a man of sense and of so much elegant learning. That there would be little in a fool doing it. We would only laugh. But that when a wise man does it, we are sorry. 'Other people,' said he, 'have strange notions; but they conceal them. If they have tails, they hide them; but Monboddo is as jealous of his tail as a squirrel'" (*J* 80). But the dispute between Monboddo and Johnson was not simply about tails—it was also about tales. The difference between Johnson's and Monboddo's responses to the anecdotal tales swirling around the *Endeavour*'s voyage emerges out of their differing assumptions about the nature of cultural difference. Johnson approaches the events witnessed by the crew of the *Endeavour* as illustrations of the commensurability of cultures, drawing lines of comparison between the South Seas and European cultural practices. Monboddo, on the contrary, sees the same anecdotal material as evidence for the profound changes that human beings and societies undergo as they progress from savagery to civilization. The contrast in the ways Johnson and Monboddo use anecdotes about the *Endeavour* reflect fundamental differences in their understandings of human nature.

Like his contemporaries in the Scottish Enlightenment, Monboddo attempted to integrate anomalous narratives from the South Seas into a general account of human development. In the fourth volume of his *Ancient Metaphysics*, published in 1795, Monboddo reported an anecdote of an instance in which Banks and Solander sailed out to an island with Tupaia, hoping to collect specimens of plants, but instead found themselves fighting for their lives. The anecdote in question reflects the fact that while Monboddo's conception of human nature was progressive, it also incorporated the myth of the noble savage. The natives do not simply attack Banks and Solander en masse but chivalrously give them the time and opportunity to join up with the boatload of fellow countrymen coming to save the two hapless botanists. Only then do the natives finally launch their attack:

> Dr Solander, now dead, who attended Captain Cook on that expedition, told me a story of them, of which Sir Joseph Banks is still a living witness. He said, while they were yet in terms of hostility with the New Zealanders, Sir Joseph and he went to a little island off the coast of New Zealand to botanize, which the New Zealanders observing, set off in their canoe, in order to intercept them; to prevent which, our people set out with their long boat. But the canoe got to the island before the boat, and laid hold of Sir Joseph and Dr Solander, who gave themselves up for lost: And Sir Joseph, he told me, had his hand at his pistol, resolved to sell his life as dear as he could. But those savages, as we call them, were so generous and noble minded, that they did not offer the least violence to them, but waiting till their countrymen came up to them, put them into their hands, and then bid them defend themselves, as the Otaheite man [i.e., Tupaia], who was with them, interpreted their words. Upon this they made a very fierce attack upon our people, who were obliged to kill some of them before they could beat them off.[63]

Since nothing like this incident appears in Banks's or Cook's journals, I suspect Monboddo's anecdote may be the result of Solander and Banks telling Monboddo tall tales of their South Sea adventures during their meeting with him in 1772—that is, if the story is not simply Monboddo's own invention. Whatever its origin, the anecdote of the chivalric "New Zealanders" allows Monboddo to present them as embodying the original nobility of humankind in the infancy of society.

Boswell and Johnson interpret the anecdotes of the *Endeavour* voyage as indications of the uniformity of human customs and behaviors, thus doing away with the need for a stadial theory of human development or even the need for philosophical speculations on the deep sources of human nature. The year before Boswell embarked on his tour of Scotland in the company of Johnson, for example, an anecdote recorded by Boswell evinces his own reluctance to believe in anecdotes that suggest a great difference between British and Pacific societies. In 1771, for example, Boswell recorded in his journal an anecdote of the *Endeavour* voyage he had heard in St. Paul's Coffee House, where he found himself in the company of Joseph Priestley, the physician and future discoverer of oxygen. Priestley appeared, Boswell writes, "happy in a story that a Methodist sailor who was along with Mr. Banks and Dr. Solander had brought several of the wild men to be pretty well disposed to Christianity; but whenever he showed them a print of Christ on the cross in his prayer-book and attempted to explain to them the doctrine of the Trinity, they all left him." Boswell goes on to speculate that the story may not be true and that, even if it is, "it only proves that the Methodist sailor was a bad explainer of a mystery, or that the savages had not patience or humility sufficient."[64] Priestley seems to enjoy the story because it confirms his own Unitarian beliefs. Boswell dismisses Priestley's interpretation of the story, however, in order to shore up his conviction in a three-part Godhead. Boswell assumes the essential sameness that links Britons and Tahitians, to whom the truth of the doctrine on the Trinity ought to be equally perspicuous.

A similar assumption of a continuity between European and antipodean societies also underlies Johnson's reaction to Boswell's description during their tour of Scotland of how Tahitians slaughter dogs for eating. In the *Journal of a Tour to the Hebrides,* Boswell reports a conversation that was prompted by his informing Johnson that the art of butchery was unknown in Tahiti: "for instead of bleeding their dogs to death, they strangle them" (*J* 208). Boswell's source for this piece of information was probably Hawkesworth's *Account of the Voyages,* in which Hawkesworth closely followed the version of the incident contained in Banks's *Endeavour* journal: "We had lately learnt, that these animals were esteemed by the Indians as more delicate food than their pork; and upon this occasion we were determined to try the experiment: the dog, which was very fat, we consigned over to Tupia, who undertook to perform the double office of butcher and cook. He killed him by stopping his hands close over his mouth and nose, an operation which continued above a quarter of an hour" (*H* 2:152). Johnson's response to Boswell's description of the Tahitian method of killing dogs is not to contrast Tahitian with English butchery nor, for that matter, Tahitian with English food. Rather he sees the Tahitian practice as basically continuous with comparable practices in his own culture. According to Banks, Johnson responded to the information about the Tahitian practice of strangling dogs by saying, "This would be owing to their not having knives, though they have sharp stones with which they can cut a carcass in pieces tolerably." Johnson goes on to remark on the different methods of killing animals: "An ox is knocked down and a calf stunned, but a sheep has its throat cut without anything done to stupefy it." Despite the differences in the methods of execution, those killing the animals are, in each case, indifferent as to whether their victims suffer or not. The bulls and calves are not hit in the head before being butchered out of concern for their distress: "The butchers have no view to the ease of the animals, but only to make them quiet, which they did not mind with sheep" (*J* 209). Here Johnson literally domesticates Banks's anecdote of the suffocated dog in Tahiti, associating it with what are to him familiar methods of butchering and eating animals. The anecdote reveals less the continuity of a deep human nature as the commonality of the repeated, and usually unreflective, acts of killing that provide both Tahitians and Britons with meat.

Whereas Monboddo thinks that anecdotes concerning Tahitian society are reports from human society at its first stage of development, Johnson thinks that they reveal that the general forms of life are the same from the South Seas to the Hebrides. But Monboddo's and Hawkesworth's divergent treatment of the same kind of anecdotal material surrounding the *Endeavour* voyage also reflects the difference between Monboddo's systematic and Johnson's antisystematic approach to the study of the human world. Mary Poovey has contrasted Johnson's observations on the Highlanders in his *Journey to the Western Islands of Scotland* (1775) with the Scottish conjectural historians' use of the same "rude" societies as illustrations of their own systems of societal progress. The noncoincidence between Johnson's observations of the Highlanders and what the conjectural historians predicted he should see led Johnson to meditate, in Poovey's words, "on the difficulty of producing systematic knowledge and the incentives that might lead an interlocutor to distort even firsthand accounts."[65] Johnson's resistance to system is also reflected in Boswell's account of his conversation during the tour of Scotland, in which he indicates a preference for an anecdotal plenty over the system builder's ambition to reduce human life to a small number of principles. Boswell reports Johnson as remarking in a conversation with the Scottish historian William Robertson, "I love anecdotes. I fancy mankind may come in time to write all aphoristically, except in narrative; grow weary of preparation, and connexion and illustration and all those arts by which a big book is made. If a man is to wait till he weaves anecdotes into a system, we may be long in getting them, and get but few in comparison of what we might get" (*J* 22). Anecdotes may be incorporated into a "system," a word that is defined in Johnson's *Dictionary* as "a scheme which reduces many things to regular dependence or co-operation."[66] But they can also be easily gathered and shared in less systematic ways, assembled into anecdote miscellanies, for example, or loosely strung together to form an episodic narrative, as they are in Boswell's *Journal of a Tour to the Hebrides with Samuel Johnson* as well as in his *Life of Samuel Johnson.* Johnson's and Boswell's meditations on the *Endeavour* anecdotes reflect a conception of history as underlain by the continuous weave of common life rather than the sharp discontinuities between societies that the conjectural historian assumes.

When Johnson did meet Monboddo on the 1773 tour, the intellectual brawl between the two men that Boswell had feared or perhaps hoped would break out did not, in the event, come to pass. The account of their conversation, as it is represented in Boswell's journal, nevertheless captures the difference between the two men over the use of anecdotes in history. Boswell's account of the encounter has Monboddo declaiming, "The history of manners is the most valuable. I never set a high value on any other history," to which Johnson replies, "Nor I; and therefore I esteem biography, as giving us what comes closest to ourselves, what we can turn to use." Here Boswell cuts into the conversation, saying, "But in the course of general history, we find manners. In wars, we see the dispositions of people, their degrees of humanity, and other particulars." Johnson replies, "Yes; but then you must take all the facts to get this, and it is but a little you get." To which Monboddo responds, "And it is that little which makes history valuable." At this point, Boswell gives a mental "Bravo!" and decides that Monboddo and Johnson, on this point at least, "agree like two brothers" (*J* 55).

In fact, this appearance of agreement between the two men may be illusory. In his conversation with Monboddo, Johnson reiterates his allegiance to the deracinated anecdote over the explanatory systems promulgated by the conjectural historians. Indeed, his comment that "it is but a little you get" if one waits to gather all the facts is a direct echo of his earlier observation, recorded by Boswell, that "If a man is to wait till he weaves anecdotes into a system, we may be long in getting them, and get but few, in comparison of what we might get." Although Monboddo also has uses for anecdotes of human behavior, he wants to find the overarching system into which these anecdotal particulars can be fitted. Johnson, at least as Boswell portrays him, has no need for such a system. Rather, he sees events in human life as testifying to the generally known continuities of human nature that require no overarching explanation. For Monboddo, anecdotal information about manners is important because it establishes how archaic people acted and still act in places that have not yet entered into modernity. On the contrary, for Johnson, anecdotes are useful because they reveal how human beings adapt themselves to specific circumstances, whether they are exploring the islands of the Hebrides or the South Pacific, slaughtering sheep or dogs for food, or hopping around like a kangaroo in a tavern in Inverness.

This chapter has tracked an interest in the singular anecdote in the journals kept by Banks and Cook, in Hawkesworth's speculative reworking of their journals, and in the Scottish conjectural historians' appropriation of the anecdotes circulating about the *Endeavour* voyage. I have also argued that the fortunes of the *Endeavour* anecdotes represent one significant occasion in which the anecdote's epistemic authority was put in question. A skepticism of the anecdote's epistemic authority underlies Pindar's association of Banks's penchant for anecdotes with the absence of the discipline and rigor expected of a "Man of Science." Scientists and satirists thus found common ground in attempting to exclude an interest in anecdotal singularity from serious inquiries into the natural world and the nature of human beings, even while anecdotes continued to play an important role in the science of man. In the next chapter, I argue that, in *Lyrical Ballads,* William Wordsworth reestablished the anecdote's authority on quite different grounds than those on which it had rested before: turning the anecdote into a distinctively poetic genre and making a facility with and appreciation of the anecdote central to the poet's special claim to chart the great map of mankind.

FOUR

Anecdotal Poetics in *Lyrical Ballads*

I n one of the notebooks that he kept between 1797 and 1799, Novalis remarks that the "true anecdote is of itself already poetic." Distinguishing
"true" anecdotes from merely "descriptive" anecdotes, Novalis writes that
"Descriptive anecdotes refer to an interesting subject, their interest only
relates to something outside," whereas "the purely poetic anecdote refers
to itself, it is interesting for its own sake." For Novalis the true anecdote's
self-referentiality made it already poetic, even if it happened to be written
in prose and not verse. This chapter argues that William Wordsworth in
the *Lyrical Ballads*, written in collaboration with Samuel Taylor Coleridge,
arrived independently at a similar conclusion as Novalis did. Wordsworth
drew attention to the anecdotal qualities of the volume in the first 1798 edition by entitling one of his contributions "Anecdote for Fathers." This poem
is only one of many poems by Wordsworth in the 1798 *Lyrical Ballads* that
read as versified tales spun from minor incidents. Others include "Simon
Lee, the Old Huntsman with an Incident in Which He was Concerned,"
"The Last of the Flock," "Old Man Travelling," and "We are Seven." Poems
in the collection as disparate as Coleridge's "The Rime of the Ancyent Marinere" and Wordsworth's "The Complaint of a Forsaken Indian Woman"
drew inspiration from prose anecdotes culled from travel literature. Even
the "Lucy" poems in the second volume of the 1800 *Lyrical Ballads*—poems
in which the narrative impulse seems to have been abandoned almost
altogether—retain vestigial links with anecdotal form. Anecdotes do not,
however, simply function as source material or as formal models for individual poems in *Lyrical Ballads*. The anecdote as a genre also shapes the theory
of poetry articulated in the critical writings that accompanied successive
editions of *Lyrical Ballads* and in the poems themselves.[1] In *Lyrical Ballads*,

Wordsworth and Coleridge positioned the anecdote as a prose genre poised on the threshold of poetry.

The dialogue staged in *Lyrical Ballads* between anecdotes and poetry informs the Preface that Wordsworth first placed at the beginning of the 1800 edition, which attempts to theorize both the poems that follow and the nature of poetry in general. Precisely because the usual associations of the anecdote were with prose, the generic borderland between anecdotes and poetry became an especially productive space for Wordsworth to think about the relationship between poetry and other forms of language.[2] The symbiosis between poems and anecdotes in *Lyrical Ballads* informs several disparate claims that Wordsworth makes about poetry in the Preface: that poetry is grounded in the incidents of real life, that it is or ought to be written in the language of everyday life, and that it can advance our knowledge of human feelings. The anecdote's capacity to mediate between prose and poetry helps Wordsworth advance the claim that the poems of *Lyrical Ballads* are shaped by the language of conversation and the contours of everyday life.

By envisaging his anecdotal poetry as a tool for discovering "the primary laws of our nature" (*PW* 1:122) in the incidents and language of daily life, Wordsworth associates *Lyrical Ballads* with Enlightenment "science of man," whose practitioners often used anecdotes to investigate the sources of human behavior in human nature.[3] In the process of making poetry anecdotal, however, Wordsworth also makes the anecdote poetic, allowing the poet to lay claim to a special insight into human nature that is in many respects superior to the philosopher working in prose. The meetings in *Lyrical Ballads* between anecdotes and poems illuminate not only the poetic theory Wordsworth develops in the Preface but also Coleridge's and Wordsworth's later divergence from each other on the question of poetic language's relationship to prose. I take up Coleridge's criticisms of Wordsworth in the latter part of this chapter, where I argue that Coleridge defined his own poetics in *Biographia Literaria* (1816) in part by emphasizing the very rift between prose anecdotes and poems that Wordsworth had tried to bridge in his own contributions to *Lyrical Ballads*. The differences that emerged between Wordsworth and Coleridge on the relationship between prose and poetry—and between poems and anecdotes in particular—remind us that the connection that is implicitly posited between anecdotes and poems in *Lyrical Ballads* was neither obvious nor inevitable. But neither was it completely idiosyncratic. The anecdote's capacity to act as a way station between poetic and nonpoetic language enabled Wordsworth to develop and theorize a poetry that would draw on, and yet remain autonomous from, the informal conversations of everyday life and the abstruse disquisitions of the figure Wordsworth dubs the "Man of Science."

This chapter explores the anecdote's role in *Lyrical Ballads* as a link connecting poems to the larger world of everyday life and language that surrounds them. The anecdote also allowed Wordsworth to link his own poetic practice to the researches of prominent figures in contemporary medical science such as Thomas Beddoes and Erasmus Darwin. The interplay between anecdotes and poems in *Lyrical Ballads* helped Wordsworth maintain a dialogue with the very type of language against which he defined his poetry: the specialized disquisitions of the Man of Science. I begin, however, with the question of how the anecdote might illuminate Wordsworth's attempts to ground *Lyrical Ballads* in "the real language of men" and the incidents of real life. The one poem in the collection that is explicitly identified as an anecdote, "Anecdote for Fathers," serves as my first example.

ANECDOTES FOR POETS

"Anecdote for Fathers" happens to be at the physical center of the first edition of *Lyrical Ballads,* beginning on page 105 of a volume numbering 210 pages. The poem is also a central case for the poetic theory that Wordsworth developed in the evolving set of critical writings that accompanied *Lyrical Ballads* from its first appearance as a single volume of poetry in 1798. Read in the context of Wordsworth's poetic theory, Wordsworth's "Anecdote for Fathers" is not simply a poem that happens to take the form of an anecdote. Rather, it emerges as a poem that uses the generic proximity of prose anecdote to verse poem to ask how poetry relates to everyday life and language. By announcing itself as an anecdote, "Anecdote for Fathers" draws attention to its groundedness in daily happenstance and idle talk. At the same time, the poem allows itself, through its anecdotal detachment from the regular flow of discussion, the license to estrange ordinary life and language. I also argue in this section that the anecdote's susceptibility to being repeated provides a rationale for the repetition of words, phrases, rhythms, and rhymes in *Lyrical Ballads.* The anecdote's constitutive iterability as a genre provides a rationale from within common speech for the verbal repetitions on which poetic language is founded.

"Anecdote for Fathers" appears to represent the first-person narrative of a father recalling a walk with his son around Liswyn Farm. Mulling over their earlier residence at the seaside village of Kilve, the narrator repeatedly asks his son Edward to specify which of the two places he prefers. We are told three times that the man takes the boy "by the arm" (*LB* l. 26, l. 30, l. 34, p. 72), all the while pressing him for an answer. The boy finally ventures "Kilve" as his answer, but the narrator, not satisfied with this, again sets about interrogating the boy, now requiring him to explain why he has nominated Kilve as his preferred spot. At a loss for an appropriate response, the boy casts his eyes upward and, seeing a weathervane, seizes on the object as a way of justifying his answer, telling his father he would rather be at Kilve since the house at Kilve lacks a weathervane. The poem ends with the father's exclamations of elation at this response. In a sudden turn from anecdotal narrative, he apostrophizes the lad as "My dearest, dearest boy!" and expresses a wish to be able to teach the boy "the hundredth part / Of what from thee I learn" (*LB* l. 57, ll. 59–60, p. 73). Don Bialostosky's description of "Anecdote for Fathers" as a "'kids say the darnest things' anecdote" is flippant but accurate.[4]

In its recounting of a story of the kind a father might tell about his son in verse, "Anecdote for Fathers" exemplifies Wordsworth's sense that poetry can emanate from the incidents of everyday life. But the poem also illustrates the plasticity of the relationship that Wordsworth posits between real life and poetry. In the 1798 Advertisement, for example, Wordsworth informs his readers that, with the exception of "Goody Blake and Harry Gill," a poem that he claimed was "founded on a well-authenticated fact which happened in Warwickshire," the poems in the collection are "either absolute inventions of the author, or facts which took place within his personal observation or that of his friends" (*PW* 1:117). A cursory reader of the Advertisement might come away with the impression that a direct relationship exists between the poems and the events that inspired them. But on closer inspection the sentence obscures this connection between the poems and the facts to which they supposedly refer. Most readers would have had no way of sifting the "absolute inventions" in the collection from those poems supposedly inspired by "facts." Nor would they have been able to distinguish the poems based on incidents that occurred under the author's "personal observation" from those poems based on incidents witnessed by "his friends." A seemingly straightforward assertion of the poems' factuality turns out to be a covert acknowledgment of their provenance in a mixture of fact and invention, of personally witnessed events, and communal gossip. One of the defining features of the anecdote as a genre is its claim to narrate a historical event, although the claim that its narrative corresponds to a preexisting event is simultaneously undercut by the anecdote's characteristic looseness of reference. The role of "Anecdote for Fathers" and poems of its kind in

Lyrical Ballads, then, is partly to suggest that the suspension between actuality and fictionality that characterizes the anecdote is also a defining feature of poetry as such.[5]

What we do know about the circumstances in which "Anecdote for Fathers" was written confirms the impression given in the Advertisement and the Preface that the relationship between the poems and the real-life incidents that apparently inspired them is fairly circuitous. In the remarks recorded by Isabella Fenwick in 1843, Wordsworth claimed that the poem was inspired by an actual incident that occurred on the grounds of Alfoxden House in Somerset, which William and Dorothy Wordsworth were leasing at the time when William Wordsworth was writing many of his contributions to the first incarnation of *Lyrical Ballads*. At this time, William and Dorothy were being paid fifty pounds per year to raise and educate Basil Caroline Montagu: the boy to whom the Edward of "Anecdote for Fathers" and "Lines Written in Early Spring" appears to correspond. In the poem, Edward substitutes for Basil, and the unnamed father substitutes for Wordsworth himself, echoing Wordsworth's real-life assumption of the role of substitute father. Wordsworth never lived at Kilve, an actual village in Somerset, although he and Dorothy had recently moved to Alfoxden from Racedown, a village that does lie near the Dorsetshire coast, a place that Kilve may stand for in the poem. People appear to be as just as fungible as places are in "Anecdote for Fathers." The speaker of the poem is associated with some biographical details that belong not to Wordsworth himself but to John Thelwall, his radical acquaintance and member of the London Corresponding Society, who lived at Llys Wen—an actual farm in Brecknockshire. Assuming that something like the incident of which "Anecdote for Fathers" narrates really did happen, the poem's core of truth has evidently been wrapped in a tissue of inventions and substitutions.

David Simpson has interpreted the poem's displacements of real places, people, and experiences in the manner of Freudian dream interpretation, seeing them as distortions of reality that serve to assuage Wordsworth's anxieties at the time that the poem was written. The anxieties he identifies include Wordsworth's remorse over his physical separation from his illegitimate daughter Caroline (whose first name is the same as Basil Montagu's middle name) and her mother Annette Vallon, as well as guilt over his failure to prevent the forced departure of his radical friend John Thelwall from Llys Wen.[6] But the poem's displacements of facts might be read, more fundamentally, as Wordsworth's way of marking, if only to himself and those who knew him, poetry's oblique relationship to lived experience.

The displacements of people and places in "Anecdote for Fathers" illustrate how both anecdotes and poems can pull themselves away from history, relocate events in time and space, and put words in the mouths of people who never said them. The identification of the wailing woman in "The Thorn" as "Martha Ray," a name that the figure in the poem shares with Basil Montagu's murdered grandmother, is the most notorious example of the pervasive phenomenon in *Lyrical Ballads* whereby real people are transformed into fictional avatars of themselves.

"Anecdote for Fathers" refuses, however, to place poetry securely either in the realm of absolute fact or absolute fiction, as in Sir Philip Sidney's *An Apology for Poetry* (1595), in which Sidney argues that the poet "never affirms, and therefore never lieth."[7] Rather, "Anecdote for Fathers" is concerned with what happens to language when subjected to the force of disorientating events. Edward's noticing and naming of the weathervane becomes in itself a perceptual and linguistic event produced under the pressure of his father's hands and words:

> His head he raised—there was in sight,
> It caught his eye, he saw it plain—
> Upon the house-top, glittering bright,
> A broad and gilded vane. (*LB* ll. 49–52, p. 73)

The boy's noticing of an object seen many times before but only singled out for attention under the force of circumstance might be compared to Wordsworth's account to Isabella Fenwick of the immediate impetus for "The Thorn," which, he claimed, "Arose out of my observing, on the ridge of Quantock Hill, on a stormy day a thorn which I had often past in calm and bright weather without noticing it." Looking at the thorn as if for the first time, Wordsworth recalls, "I said to myself, 'Cannot I by some invention do as much to make this thorn permanently an impressive object as the storm has made it to my eyes at this moment.'"[8] The work of poetry, on this account, is essentially one of reproducing experiences in which reality already appears strange. The attempt to do so obliges the poet to depart from strict historicity. For to try to narrate the encounter with the thorn, seen many times but hitherto never noticed, as it "really" happened, would be to lose the strangeness that made the thorn seem so striking in the first place. A poem's truth, then, for Wordsworth, is not to be found in its exact correspondence to previous experiences but rather in its capacity to bear the imprint of estranging events. Like anecdotes, the poems of

Lyrical Ballads are themselves linguistic events at least as much as they are records of preceding occurrences.

Perhaps in recognition of the necessarily oblique relationship between poetry and historical experience, the Preface that introduces the 1800 edition of *Lyrical Ballads* qualifies the 1798 Advertisement's claims for the factuality of the poems still further. In this version of the Preface, Wordsworth explains that the "truth" of the poems is to be found in their correspondence not to historical incidents but to the more general category of common life. "The principal object" of the poems, Wordsworth writes, "was to make the incidents of common life interesting by tracing in them, truly though not ostentatiously, the primary laws of our nature: chiefly as far as regards the manner in which we associate ideas in a state of excitement" (*PW* 1:122–24). This shifts the ground away from Wordsworth's claim in the Advertisement that at least some of the poems correspond to actual incidents. By the time Wordsworth comes to write the 1800 Preface, the poems' fidelity to preceding events is less important than their ability to indicate the workings of the universal laws of human nature behind the seemingly random transactions of everyday life. The identification of common life as the field in which the "primary laws of our nature" are to be sought out indicates the close relationship between Wordsworth's poetic project and the Enlightenment science of human nature. In both cases, anecdotes can serve both as evidence for theories of human nature and as correctives to the systematizing ambitions of those theories themselves.[9]

The dialogue that anecdotes create between incidents and ideas often defies easy summary. Notwithstanding this, the original headnote for "Anecdote for Fathers" did suggest a tidy principle could be extracted from the poem. It proclaimed in capital letters that the poem was an exemplary tale "SHEWING HOW THE ART OF LYING MAY BE TAUGHT" (*LB* p. 71). The subtitle invites readers to see the boy's seizing on the weathervane, a mental leap made under the excitement of duress, as an illustration of how the ability to lie is learned as children struggle to accommodate their own desires and thoughts to the arbitrary authority of their guardians. Commentators on "Anecdote for Fathers" have traced this account of the origin of lying to the educational theories of William Godwin and Jean-Jacques Rousseau.[10] The poem can be read as an anecdote linking a specific incident in lived experience to more general accounts of how children learn to fib. In spite of its subtitle, however, the poem also resists the original headnote's effort to draw a one-to-one relationship between the incident that it describes and a general precept about human nature. The bland suggestion that the poem illustrates "how the practice of lying may be taught" is in any case at odds with the poem's final apostrophe to the boy, which seems to intimate that there is more to be learned from the boy and from the poem that contains him than can be captured in a short subtitle. At the same time, of course, the unspecified nature of what exactly it is that the father learns about the boy or about himself opens the alternative possibility that little or nothing is really to be learned about the nature of children from the poem at all. We might easily surmise that what the poem really represents is either the father's or the poet's absurd overinvestment in a trivial incident. The anecdote's characteristic hovering between triviality and significance is also the condition of "Anecdote for Fathers" and poems like it in *Lyrical Ballads*—which are so easily parodied in part because they are already incipient parodies of themselves.

Wordsworth himself gestures towards the inadequacy of reading the poems in *Lyrical Ballads* as straightforward exemplifications of moral philosophical laws when he writes in the Preface that it is "truly though not ostentatiously" that he proposes to trace "the primary laws of our nature" in his contributions to the volume. Rather than encouraging readers to read the poems through a predetermined system of human nature, Wordsworth encourages his audience to approach the poems in much the same manner in which he and Dorothy Wordsworth approached the task of raising little Basil. Dorothy Wordsworth wrote to her friend Jane Marshall that "Basil is a charming boy, he affords us perpetual entertainment. Do not suppose from this that we make him our perpetual play-thing, far otherwise, I think that is one of the modes of treatment most likely to ruin a child's temper and character. But I do not think there is any Pleasure more delightful than that of marking the development of a child's faculties, and observing his little occupations."[11] "Anecdote for Fathers" models a similarly open-ended process of learning from children, anecdotes, and poems. Wordsworth enjoins the reader to read many of the poems in *Lyrical Ballads* with much the same exploratory spirit. Wordsworth claims in the Preface, for example, that every poem in the collection "has a worthy *purpose*" (*PW* 1:124). But he hastens to add that the purpose of any one poem is not to illustrate a preformulated principle of human nature. Instead, they are meant to enable an intuitive sense of the structure of human nature to emerge from the process of poetic composition. Wordsworth explains that he does not mean to imply that he always wrote "with a distinct purpose formally conceived," but that "habits of meditation have so formed my feelings, as that my descriptions of such objects as strongly excite those feelings, will be found to carry along with them a *purpose*" (*PW* 1:124–26). On this account, the poem's purpose—if it has one—appears only in and through the poem itself.

If anecdotes help show how poems are both inside and outside the Enlightenment science of man—with its search for the formal principles of human nature—they also model how poems are both inside and outside what Wordsworth calls "the real language of men." "Anecdote for Fathers" is in part an attempt to associate poetry with the common type of everyday language represented by the anecdote. But the anecdote itself helps model, in its formal compression and deracination, the separation of poetry from ordinary language. The small eddy opened by the anecdote within the flow of discourse helps model how poems may open spaces in which the rules underlying ordinary language may be twisted and bent. Wordsworth's gradual recognition that the language of poetry was not exactly coincident with the language of everyday life is reflected in the revisions he made to the critical material framing the poems in *Lyrical Ballads*. In the 1798 Advertisement, Wordsworth asks his readers to consider the poems as a series of "experiments . . . written chiefly with a view to ascertain how far the language of conversation in the middle and lower classes of society is adapted to the purposes of poetic pleasure" (*PW* 1:116). In the 1800 Preface, however, Wordsworth revises the Advertisement's description of the poems' ambitions to include the claim that the poems were written "to ascertain, how far, by fitting to metrical arrangement a selection of the real language of men in a state of vivid sensation, that sort of pleasure and that quantity of pleasure may be imparted, which a Poet may rationally endeavour to impart" (*PW* 1.118). Wordsworth now emphasizes the formal patterns that distinguish the poems from conversational language, the poet's work in selecting and fitting common words to the poetic line, and the intensity of the experiences staged within the poems that cause language to turn inward upon itself.

Wordsworth argues that the language of poetry is rooted in ordinary language, albeit ordinary language that deviates from regular forms of expression under the influence of intense feelings. Poems do not so much set out to depart from ordinary language as seize on particular moments in ordinary life that cause ordinary language to be shunted away from its usual tracks. In a passage added to the Preface in 1802, Wordsworth wrote that "if the Poet's subject be judiciously chosen, it will naturally, and upon fit occasion, lead him to passions the language of which, if selected truly and judiciously, must necessarily be dignified and variegated, and alive with metaphors and figures" (*PW* 1:137). The "turns" and "figures" of poetic language will thus

naturally emerge, in Wordsworth's view, from the encounter between ordinary language and events that cause language to twist back upon itself.
The anecdote helped Wordsworth reconsider the nature of poetry precisely
because it was a genre that did appear in everyday speech and yet could
be regarded as being autonomous from any particular conversation. This
capacity of the anecdote to suggest how poetic language is both bound to
and distinct from other forms of language is underlined when Wordsworth
turns, in the revised and expanded version of the Preface, to address the
"obvious question, namely, why, professing these opinions have I written in
verse?" (*PW* 1:144). In response to this anticipated objection, Wordsworth
appeals to the ability of rhythm and rhyme to contain and direct feelings.
He claims that, in Shakespeare, "the most pathetic scenes, never act upon
us as pathetic beyond the bounds of pleasure—an effect which is in a great
degree to be ascribed to small, but continual and regular impulses of pleasurable surprise from the metrical arrangement" (*PW* 1:146). Here again, the
anecdote helps contain the apparent exclusivity of poetry within everyday
forms of speech. The "continual and regular impulses of pleasurable surprise," to which Wordsworth refers, could describe the habitual exchange of
anecdotes in spontaneous conversation as much as they could refer to the
effect of rhyme and meter on the mind.

"Anecdote for Fathers" thus dramatizes how poetic language floats above
and yet is anchored in "the real language of men." The poem belongs to a
class of poems in *Lyrical Ballads* described by Bialostosky as "dialogic personal anecdotes," poems that seem to transcribe first-person stories told by
a dramatized speaker who may or may not be identifiable with Wordsworth
himself.[12] Yet the title also severs the poem from any actual conversation.
The poem's title presents the poem as a monitory anecdote for "Fathers"
and not any particular father. In fact, of course, the poem addresses anyone
that cares to read it. And yet the poem's obvious separation from any actual
speaking situation is also anticipated by the formal separation from context
that characterizes the anecdote as a genre. The anecdote's ability to move
between multiple contexts in print and in speech already points toward the
detached and deracinated state in which we read "Anecdote for Fathers" in
Lyrical Ballads.

"Anecdote for Fathers" sets in motion a push and pull dynamic between
conversational and poetic language that is played out in the progression of
the first stanza. The opening line, "I have a boy of five years old," exemplifies
Wordsworth's aspiration to capture the language of everyday speech. But

this impression of closeness to everyday language is promptly modified by the lines that follow:

His face is fair and fresh to see;
His limbs are cast in beauty's mould,
And dearly he loves me. (*LB* ll. 1–4, p. 71)

The archaic "to see" at the end of the second line signals that the poem has shifted toward the language of the ballad. Thomas Percy's *Reliques of Ancient English Poetry* (1765) offers many examples of the locution, including the Scots ballad "Edward, Edward," in which a mother asks her murderous son, whose sword drips with the blood of his father, "And quat wul ze doe wi' zour towirs and zour ha'/That were sae fair to see, O?" (And what will you do with your towers and your halls,/That were so fair to see, O?)[13] In addition, the description of the limbs of the Edward of "Anecdote for Fathers" as "cast in beauty's mould" echoes the description of the doomed little girl's limbs as "fram'd in beautyes mould" in the *Reliques'* "Children of the Wood," a ballad Wordsworth quotes in the revised Preface of 1802.[14] The shadow of violence that accompanies the father's repeated grasping at the arm of his child in "Anecdote for Fathers" is thus made explicit through the poem's linguistic and thematic links with these two ballads of child murder and patricide in the *Reliques*. The movement from the anonymous ballads "The Children of the Wood" and "Edward, Edward" to Wordsworth's "Anecdote for Fathers" is a passage from extraordinary to ordinary incident. But the intertextual links between Percy's *Reliques* and *Lyrical Ballads* suggest darker forces moving beneath the relationship between parent and child in Wordsworth's poem.

Lyrical Ballads' domestications of the traditional ballads' tales of love, war, and crime, its adaptations of conventional ballad meters, and its incorporations of idioms such as "fair to see" and "cast in beauty's mould" help associate poems like "Anecdote for Fathers" with popular orality, albeit a very different kind of orality than that of ordinary talk. At the same time, "Anecdote for Fathers" appears to locate itself in the oral culture of everyday conversation, rather than the (real or pretended) orality of the ballad.[15] Short narrative poems like "Anecdote for Fathers" in *Lyrical Ballads* are thus suspended over the generic space between ballads and anecdotes. These poems press domestic content into balladic form, attempting to invest ordinary incidents with the aura of popular tradition and to bring the folk ballad into rapprochement with contemporary domestic life. The result is a set of

poems that modulate, sometimes awkwardly, between the language of conversation and the language of the ballad.

One source of disjunction between these two registers that posed special
problems for Wordsworth's efforts to associate poetry with common speech
were the verbal repetitions characteristic of the ballad form. In his classic
study of the ballad, Francis B. Gummere identifies "incremental repetition"
as a key characteristic of the English and Scots ballad, in which variations
are spun upon a recurrent phrase.[16] This type of repetition affects the word
"think" in "Anecdote for Fathers," when the speaker is remembering the day
of which he is speaking as one:

> ... when I could bear
> To think, and think, and think again;
> With so much happiness to spare,
> I could not feel a pain. (*LB* ll. 13–16, p. 71)

In her reading of the poem, Cynthia Chase comments on the strangeness
with which the threefold repetition of "think" erupts into the poem, a repetition that, she suggests, "compounds the difficulty of imagining what sort
of reflection this line describes" since "To think again is to reverse a previous judgment, but to think again and again implies repetition rather than
reversal or progression. Triple repetition describes a form of thinking that
consists in repetition, and repetition is also what this line does. Hence the
activity of thinking becomes indistinguishable from the activity of repeat-
ing the words 'to think.'"[17] The line "To think, and think, and think again"
enacts, in Chase's reading, a collapse between the description of the act of
thinking and the process of thinking itself. I would add that the line bor-
rows the emphatic repetitions of key words and phrases in the traditional
ballad for the purpose of exploring the mutual interaction of words and
minds. But the line does so at the expense of appearing to deviate from the
conversational manner of the poem's opening line "I have a boy of five year's
old," which seems to assume an addressee standing in front of the speaker,
who is then progressively forgotten. The insistent repetitions characteristic
of ballads—and *Lyrical Ballads*—draw attention to themselves in a way that
marks their distance from conversational language. These verbal repetitions
point to one of the central problems that Wordsworth faces in the Preface:
how to justify the repetitions of phrases, words, and sounds that seem to
detach the collection's poems from the "real language of men."

Wordsworth goes some way to addressing this question when he claims
in the Preface that language under the pressure of affecting events will

inevitably exhibit some of the formal patterning of verse. In the note appended to "The Thorn" in the 1800 edition of *Lyrical Ballads*, he informs readers that the "loquacious narrator" of "The Thorn" is not to be confused with the poem's author and presents the poem as an attempt to inhabit the thoughts and feelings of someone recently retired from working life, "a Captain of a small trading vessel for example," who has gone to live in "some village or country town of which he was not a native, or in which he had not been accustomed to live" (*LB* p. 350). The poem's repetitious language, on this account, emerges from the alienated and obsessed state of the captain's mind. The note goes on, however, to suggest that a predilection for repetition is not simply a linguistic peculiarity of the character represented in "The Thorn" but may in fact be fundamental to poetic language in general. As Corrina Russell has shown, the note to "The Thorn" and "The Thorn" itself theorize and perform a poetics of repetition that implies that a compulsion to repeat is central to the nature of poetry. I would add that this poetics of repetition is itself rooted in the discursively iterative genre of the anecdote.[18]

Wordsworth turns to mount a defense of verbal repetitions in poetry in general when he objects to the opinion of "a numerous class of Readers who imagine that the same words cannot be repeated without tautology":

> Words, a Poet's words more particularly, ought to be weighed in the balance of feeling, and not measured by the space which they occupy upon paper. For the Reader cannot be too often reminded that Poetry is passion: it is the history or science of feelings: now every man must know that an attempt is rarely made to communicate impassioned feelings without something of an accompanying consciousness of the inadequateness of our own powers, or the deficiencies of language. During such efforts there will be a craving in the mind, and as long as it is unsatisfied the Speaker will cling to the same words, or words of the same character.

Wordsworth then immediately offers another apparently diametrically opposed explanation for verbal repetition in poetry. He claims that in moments of strong feeling, the mind seizes on words "not only as symbols of the passion, but as *things*, active and efficient, which are of themselves part of the passion" and "luxuriates in the repetition of words which appear successfully to communicate its feelings" (*LB* p. 351). Wordsworth explains repetition as a phenomenon that arises from feelings and words either being too distant or too close to one another. Words are either too far from the feelings they attempt to capture, so that the same inadequate words are spoken over and over again in the fruitless attempt to communicate them, or they are so close to the feelings that they merge with and come to sustain the feelings themselves, leading similarly to the endless repetition of the same words. The idea that words themselves are "part of the passion" opens the possibility that poems may be less representative of the feelings of individuals (whether those of the poet or some invented speaker) as engines of feeling in themselves.

The repetition that Wordsworth associates with poetic language can be related to the repetitious nature of anecdotes themselves, which solicit their own iteration in speech and in writing and are, by their very nature, detachable from any particular speaker, circulating as if on their own accord within a community of speakers and writers. The conjunction of poetry and anecdote in *Lyrical Ballads* thus helps associate the repetitions of poetry with a repetitious genre that seems to emerge spontaneously out of "the real language of men." A dialectic between singularity and repetition is played out in many of the volume's experimental poems at the level of content as well as form. In "The Thorn," for example, a singular incident of infanticide is reconstructed from the repeated motifs of thorn, pond, and moss. The bewildered question that emanates from a bewildered interlocutor or reader:

> "But what's the thorn? and what's the pond?
> "And what's the hill of moss to her?
> "And what's the creeping breeze that comes
> "The little pond to stir?" (*LB* ll. 210–13, p. 83)

receives the uncertain answer:

> I cannot tell; but some will say
> She hanged her baby on the tree,
> Some say she drowned it in the pond,
> Which is a little step beyond,
> But all and each agree,
> The little Babe was buried there,
> Beneath that hill of moss so fair. (*LB* ll. 214–20, p. 84)

This stanza suggests a relationship between the tales told about the circumstances in which Martha Ray supposedly killed and buried her baby—all of which represent variants on a single repeated story—and the prevalence of verbal repetition in the poem itself. The poem also hints that the obscure incident "The Thorn" entwines itself around may be more an effect of language itself than any preceding event occurring in the region around the thorn. "The Thorn" tells the story of an attempt to triangulate an act of infanticide from a matrix of repeated objects, words, and stories. Repetition is translated into singularity, but the possibility that the poem itself will be repeated allows singularity to be translated, once again, into repetition.

Similarly, in "Anecdote for Fathers" the father's repetition of the verb "think" is echoed by the various modes of repeated action in the poem: the father's and son's walking and talking around Liswyn Farm, the father's repetitious thoughts implied by the line "To think, and think, and think again," the threefold repetition of the father's gesture of holding his son by the arm. The sudden pleasure that the father expresses at Edward's choice of the absence of the weathervane as his justification for favoring Kilve over Liswyn derives in part from the way the jolt of the boy's answer releases him from the prison of repetition. The weathercock itself is an object character-ized by repeated movements—of circling around the same spot—and yet it is also a machine that bears witness to sudden changes in the direction of the wind. The weathercock is an emblem of the dialectic of repetition and event, which may be the poem's ultimate subject. The interruption that Edward's answer introduces into the poem's repetitions becomes occasion for another kind of repetition—the repeated telling and retelling of the an-ecdote itself—to which the title "Anecdote for Fathers" looks forward.

Other poems in the first edition of *Lyrical Ballads* play out the same drama between iteration and event. In "We are Seven," the poem with which "Anecdote for Fathers" is paired in the first edition, the girl who insists on counting her dead siblings among her brothers and sisters is described as having "many a curl / That cluster'd round her head" (*LB* ll. 7–8, p. 74). After her sister Jane dies—or as the girl puts it "went away"—she runs in cir-cles around Jane's grave: "Together round her grave we played, / My brother John and I" (*LB* l. 52, ll. 55–56, p. 75). "Simon Lee, the Old Huntsman" ends with the narrator's act of severing a tree root at which Lee had been laboring for hours and with his surprise at the old man's fulsome gratitude. In "The Last of the Flock" a shepherd encountered on the road informs the narrator that the dead lamb whose body he holds in his arms is the last remnant of his once thriving herd, in which the repeated losses of the animals on which his livelihood depends are seen to tragically converge on the single lamb he now cradles in his arms.

These poems all tell of small disruptions that occur when a narra-tor comes into contact with children, laborers, or itinerants, who disturb and startle him. The precipitation of an event from a matrix of repeated

actions and repeated words in "Anecdote for Fathers" and the other experimental poems in the collection connects the poems to the famous "spots
of time," which were soon to appear in the two-book *Prelude* written in
1799. "Spots of time" are, in the first instance, moments of past experience
that Wordsworth describes as persisting in the memory and "with distinct
pre-eminence retain / A fructifying virtue."[19] Many poems written over the
period between 1798 and 1805, in which Wordsworth drafted early versions
of *The Prelude*, link the repetitive return of the mind to its "spots of time"
with the repetitive telling and retelling of anecdotes, anecdotes that, as if to
anticipate their own future telling and retelling, include representations of
repetitive action within themselves. Several of these poems can be traced
back to prose anecdotes. Wordsworth's long poem *Peter Bell* (begun in 1798
but only published in 1819), for example, was inspired by an anecdote first
appearing in the newspaper *Aris's Birmingham Gazette*, which told of a donkey's continual return to the spot where its master drowned: "On Friday
morning a man by the name of Kirby, was found drowned in the Worcester
Canal, near this town. He is supposed to have been intoxicated, and to have
missed his road. His ass was the means of discovering him; as the animal,
though repeatedly driven from the bank of the canal, continually returned to
the spot, until the body was seen and taken out of the water."[20] The donkey
in the anecdote seems to be afflicted by a literal version of what Geoffrey
Hartman dubs Wordsworth's "spot syndrome": returning again and again to
the spot in which a singular event has occurred.[21]

In the 1799 *Prelude* the narratives explicitly identified as "spots of time"
are the episode in which Wordsworth comes across a declivity where a man
was hanged and exhibited in a gibbet and the episode in which he remembers waiting for horses to take him back to his father's house shortly before
his father died. Critics have nominated other "spots of time" in the 1799 *Prelude*, including the passages in which the poet remembers himself as a boy
stealing a boat for a midnight excursion, pausing while skating on the ice
and seeing the world appear to spin around him, and observing a drowned
man being dredged out of a lake. Later versions of the *Prelude*, written before the poem's eventual publication in 1850, added more passages that have
been, in turn, counted as additional "spots of time." In a classic essay on
the *Prelude*, Jonathan Bishop has remarked on the way the passages typically
identified by critics as "spots of time" often begin with crowds, from which
emerges a solitary figure, or with repeated actions, from which emerges a
single event. "Just as, at the climax of a 'spot,'" Bishop writes, "the protagonist detaches himself from his companions, so the rhythm of motion, rising

to a height, often receives a check, a breaking in of new experience."[22] The "spot of time," then, is a movement from collectivity to individuation and from iteration to rupture. But the "spot of time," like the anecdote, also demands to be told again and again. Both the poetic "spot of time" and the anecdote as a genre, then, are forms in which singularities emerge from collectivities and continuities—but the poetic "spot of time" and the anecdote also make the singularities they produce available for collective reception and repetition. Both the "spot of time" and the anecdote, then, help model how poetry in general is constantly emerging from within the "real language of men" and moving back into it.

I have been arguing that the connection Wordsworth establishes between anecdotes and poems in *Lyrical Ballads* underwrites Wordsworth's major claims in the Preface for the nature of poetry itself: that poetry emanates from the actualities of human experience, that it lays bare the "primary laws of our nature," and that its language is continuous to the language of conversation. The anecdote allowed Wordsworth both to illustrate and to qualify these claims. Poems, like anecdotes, are no simple retellings of preexisting incidents. Rather, both anecdotes and poems are treated in *Lyrical Ballads* as linguistic events that deflect and distort both ordinary life and language. Key formal characteristics of the anecdote—its deracination from context and its capacity for indefinite iteration—already pointed in the direction of the self-enclosedness and incantatory pull of poetry. The anecdote allowed Wordsworth to both anchor poetry in real life and language and to give it license to roam from those domains. In what follows, I argue that the anecdote is also implicated in another major claim that Wordsworth makes for poetry: the claim that poetry constitutes a science of human feelings.

THE SCIENCE OF FEELINGS

Wordsworth proposed in the Preface that poetry could define itself against yet also remain in dialogue with the specialized researches of the Man of Science. Here the word "Science" denotes, of course, any specialized kind of inquiry, whether into the physical or the human world. Poetry's relationship to contemporary experimental inquiries into the processes underlying life in general are, however, very much a concern of Wordsworth's Preface. The two Men of Science I discuss in this section are Erasmus Darwin and Thomas Beddoes. In *Zoonomia; or, the Laws of Organic Life* (1794–96), Darwin ambitiously sought to develop a theory of the underlying workings of living things that would "bind together the scattered facts of medical knowledge, and converge into one point of view the laws of organic life"

(*Z* 1:2). Wordsworth consulted Darwin's work while he was writing his contributions to the first edition of *Lyrical Ballads.* Thomas Beddoes, a friend and correspondent of Darwin's, was the author of several tracts on chemistry, practical and theoretical medicine, and mathematics, as well as a series of radical pamphlets.[23] In 1799 he founded the Bristol Pneumatic Institution for researching the effects of inhaling chemical gasses, where he employed the young Humphry Davy as an assistant. Joseph Cottle, the original publisher of *Lyrical Ballads,* later remembered how Beddoes had performed early experiments with nitrous oxide on his friends, asking them "to breathe this innocent, but exhilarating nitrous oxide, while they described, and he recorded their sensations."[24] Coleridge and Robert Southey were among those who made themselves Beddoes's willing experimental subjects.

The poems of *Lyrical Ballads* were also offered to readers as a set of experiments in poetic language that were analogous to Beddoes's experiments with facetious airs: poetic experiments whose purpose is to test "in what manner language and the human mind act and react on each other" (*PW* 1:120). In versions of the Preface published after 1802, Wordsworth once again suggested that poems were textual events akin to chemical experiments, describing the poet's task as one of considering "man and the objects that surround him as acting and re-acting upon each other, so as to produce an infinite complexity of pain and pleasure" (*PW* 1:140). As Wordsworth describes it in the Preface to *Lyrical Ballads,* the crucial difference between "Poet" and the "Man of Science" lay not in the methods they used or the objects of their inquiries. Rather, the difference hinged on the Poet's ability to take pleasure with humanity as a whole in the contemplation of life, with the Man of Science being restricted to sharing his pleasure in a body of knowledge with only a small coterie of fellow specialists.

Beddoes's and Darwin's immersion in the specialized languages of medicine and chemistry do qualify them as "Men of Science" in the expansive sense that "Science" carries in the Preface to *Lyrical Ballads.* But both Beddoes and Darwin would have resisted the idea that, as Men of Science, they were interested in reaching only a small number of expert readers. In his preface to *Zoonomia,* for example, Darwin expressed his belief that his theory "would enable every one of literary acquirements to distinguish the genuine disciples of medicine from those of boastful effrontery, or of wily address; and would teach mankind in some important situations the *knowledge of themselves*" (*Z* 1:2). *Zoonomia* is scattered with conversational anecdotes that argue for the relevance of Darwin's abstract theories to human experience. As we will see, Wordsworth's most obvious borrowing from *Zoonomia* in *Lyrical Ballads* is, in fact, an anecdote. Beddoes also saw anecdotes as fruitful sources of evidence for the advancement of medical knowledge. He published pamphlets aimed at the wider reading public such as *A Guide for Self Preservation and Parental Affection* (1793), which dispensed advice on raising children in salubrious conditions. These pamphlets are, in the words of Beddoes's early biographer John Edmond Stock, written "in the most familiar manner, and are illustrated by a variety of apt illustration and anecdote."[25]

If both Beddoes and Darwin were drawn to anecdotes as part of their medical inquiries, they were also, like Wordsworth, writers of poetry. Darwin sought to explain the contemporary sciences of life in long poems written in heroic couplets, such as *The Loves of The Plants* (1789). Beddoes showed a particular talent for poetic imitation and parody: mimicking Darwin's poetry in *Alexander's Expedition* and Wordsworth's and Coleridge's in "Domiciliary Verses." The dichotomy posited in the Preface between the "Man of Science" and the "Poet" is complicated by the personal and intellectual connections among Darwin, Beddoes, Coleridge, and Wordsworth: writers who worked on and over the lines between poetry and prose and between popular and philosophical discourse. The personal and intellectual links between Darwin and Beddoes and Coleridge and Wordsworth have been well discussed in recent scholarship.[26] Here, however, I focus on the affinity Beddoes, Darwin, and Wordsworth share as users of anecdotes.

The Poet and the Man of Science turn out to have more in common for Wordsworth than we might expect. Both, as we have seen, are understood in the Preface to pursue knowledge as a source of pleasure. Indeed, Wordsworth argues, "we have no knowledge, no general principles drawn from the contemplation of particular facts, but what has been built up by pleasure, and exists in pleasure alone." Wordsworth suggests in the 1802 Preface that the Poet and the Man of Science depart from each other only in that

> the knowledge of the one cleaves to us as a necessary part of our existence, our natural and unalienable inheritance; the other is a personal and individual acquisition, slow to come to us, and by no habitual and direct sympathy connecting us with our fellow-beings. The Man of Science seeks truth as a remote and unknown benefactor; he cherishes and loves it in his solitude: the Poet, singing a song in which all human beings join with him, rejoices in the presence of truth

as our visible friend and hourly companion. Poetry is the breath and
finer spirit of all knowledge; it is the impassioned expression which is
in the countenance of all Science. (*PW* 1:141)

Whereas the Man of Science withdraws from other people into his own
specialized researches, the Poet reaches out to humanity as a whole. As
Rowan Boyson has argued, Wordsworth's counterintuitive association of
both the Man of Science and the Poet with the pursuit of pleasure reflects
his sense that both of them pursue the same object of knowledge, albeit
the Poet takes the easier path to a true apprehension of nature: "the Poet,
'prompted' by pleasure, 'converses' with nature, with 'affections' similar to
those of the Man of Science, but the scientist has taken longer and laboured
harder to achieve the same epistemological joy."[27] In Wordsworth's utopian
vision, the poet creates a new pleasure-based community through poetry. At
a time when intellectual specialization was becoming the precondition for
the production of new knowledge, however, Wordsworth's aspiration to address and embrace all of humanity put in doubt his claim that poetry could
serve as a "history or science of feelings"—a field with a delimited object of
study and a specialized language and distinctive set of procedures like any
other intellectual discipline.[28] Wordsworth's response to this dilemma was
to shift between the claim that poetry is a specialized branch of knowledge ("the science of feelings") and the claim that poetry is an emanation of
knowledge in general ("the breath and finer spirit of all knowledge").[29] Here
Wordsworth presents poetry, like the anecdote, as a genre with the potential
to reconcile popular wisdom with the specialized researches of the Man
of Science.

Wordsworth does not distinguish poetry from science by arguing that
poetry is anecdotal whereas science is not. Rather, he suggests that Men of
Science begin to resemble poets when they turn to anecdotes for evidence
and inspiration. The anecdote thus could serve as a methodological point
of connection between poetry and contemporary investigations into human
sensation and the human mind, which frequently inserted anecdotes into
their disquisitions on human thought, feeling, and perception. The year
after the appearance of the first edition of *Lyrical Ballads*, for example, Beddoes published a compilation of observations, experimental reports, and
medical case studies, entitled *Contributions to Physical and Medical Knowledge, Principally from the West of England* (1799) with Cottle. As a collection
of anecdotes, many of which refer to England's West Country, the volume
bears comparison to *Lyrical Ballads*. Like *Lyrical Ballads*, *Contributions to*

Physical and Medical Knowledge came prefaced with a theoretical introduction, in which Beddoes makes similar claims as Wordsworth does for the unity of the human sciences. Beddoes holds that "The science of human nature is altogether incapable of division into independent branches." But he proposes that it is physiology (rather than poetry) that ought to become the foundation for the science of man. Where Wordsworth identifies poetry as "the history or science of feelings," Beddoes claims for physiology the ability to open "a comprehensive view of the laws that regulate feeling" and to ground the "science of human nature" in the moving, thinking, and sensing body (*CPM* Intro., 3). In the passage recorded by the *Oxford English Dictionary* as the first use of "biology" in its modern sense, Beddoes writes "Physiology therefore—or more strictly *biology*—by which I mean *the doctrine of the living system in all its states,* appears to be the foundation of ethics and pneumatology" (*CPM* Intro., 4).[30] Physiology is to Beddoes what poetry is to Wordsworth: at once a specific branch of knowledge and the ultimate foundation of human knowledge in general.

Like Wordsworth, Beddoes sees an important role for anecdotes as sources of empirical evidence for the study of human beings. He celebrates "the invention of printing" for allowing the expansion of the available fund of accounts of incidents that would previously have been lost to science. In particular, Beddoes suggests that it is thanks to "Periodical publications for preserving and embodying short and otherwise fugitive pieces" that "we owe much of the superiority of the modern over antient medicine" (*CPM* Intro., 6). His book is dedicated to compiling just such "fugitive pieces," which include among them a letter containing a self-described "anecdote" sent to him by the blind doctor Robert Hamilton. Hamilton tells of a case of catarrh that was cured when the sufferer, a servant boy in his household, spent a frosty night wandering the streets for fear of being punished for returning home late. Hamilton tells Beddoes that the event seemed to him so "uncommon" that he wrote it down on the same night that it happened, beginning it on the night of the February 27, 1797, and finishing it in the early hours of the next day (*CPM* 313). The account comes complete with a detailed table of readings from the thermometers Hamilton had already set up in the garden for the purpose of measuring the air temperature at fixed times during the day, which shows that over the period between February 19 and February 27 the mercury fell as low as 28 degrees Fahrenheit at midnight. (Readings are absent from the night of February 27, presumably because Hamilton was out trying to find the boy.) Hamilton closes his letter with another anecdote about a time he donated clothes to a vagrant, who later became sick, threw off the new garments, and put on his rags again, "swearing that the warm clothes had killed him." Hamilton's letter ends with some sage medical advice for treating cases of catarrh based on these events: "We cannot send our patients, when they apply to us under this complaint, to walk abroad in frosty weather; but we can forbid them their warm drinks, warm rooms, increased quantity of bed-cloathes, &c. &c." (*CPM* 320). If only he could get them to take his advice, however, Hamilton would presumably advise patients to walk out in cold weather whenever they felt the catarrh coming on.

Hamilton's anecdotes are concerned with much the same thematic territory as Wordsworth's poetry, with its young children who wander off into the night ("The Idiot Boy" and the boat-stealing episode from the *Prelude*) and its gallery of vagrants ("The Female Vagrant," "The Old Cumberland Beggar," and many others). Hamilton's letter also shares with Wordsworth's poetry a confidence in the capacity of the accidental event to provide useful insights into human beings. The blind doctor calls his story an "anecdote" in the first place because the event of which it tells was unforeseen and uncontrolled: it marks an occasion when his boy servant escaped his jurisdiction both as a master and as a physician. Hamilton seems to consider these kinds of events as valuable precisely because of their accidental and unplanned nature, precious for the potential they hold for challenging conventional medical wisdom. The anecdote provides a source of practical knowledge for physicians, a form of storytelling that enables them to derive medical insights from the lives of ordinary people.

Although most accounts in the book are written by doctors like Hamilton, Beddoes does hold that the wider public can play a role in contributing to the stock of medical knowledge, writing optimistically that "if whole communities could but relinquish petty interests to join in the great work of forwarding the knowledge, and by consequence diminishing the sufferings, of human nature, the treasure of physiological facts would be easily doubled in less than twenty years." Beddoes suggests that any useful medical facts be reported by the "medical functionaries" of hospitals every month or so in public meetings, with a special attention to any case that seems "instructive or singular" (*CPM* Intro., 8). When it happens that one of these meetings turns up a case that seems "uncommonly interesting," Beddoes proposes that a "commissioner or committee of verification should be appointed to examine the circumstances." While doctors and medical staff would be the primary sources of stories in Beddoes's proposal for the advancement of medical knowledge, he does set aside a place for the public in determining which stories may be of most use to medical science. The meetings are to be held in public because a large audience increases the chances that someone will see the importance of an account, even if "the very same particulars, for want of necessary associations, should be utterly lost upon the reporters themselves; just as sparks fail to kindle a blaze when they fall upon incombustible materials." As Beddoes writes, "So intimate likewise has science rendered the connection between the organic and inorganic kingdoms of nature, that the unprofessional philosopher, well apprized of the desiderata of medicine, may be sometimes more in a capacity to supply them, than the unphilosophical practitioner" (*CPM* Intro., 9). Beddoes writes as someone learned in technical sciences ranging from geology to chemistry to medicine. But, at least in theory, he still sees a role for nonprofessionals in the production of medical knowledge through the sharing and evaluation of anecdotal stories.

Beddoes's "unprofessional philosopher" resembles nobody so much as Wordsworth's Poet: a figure who specializes in the discovery of human significance in events that would pass others by.[31] Beddoes's faith in the capacity of the unusual anecdote to yoke a wide audience into the practice of physiology echoes Wordsworth's faith in poetry's ability to act as a form of inquiring into human nature that gives ordinary people a stake in the making of knowledge. Both Wordsworth and Beddoes take care to give a special role to physicians and poets vis-à-vis the wider public. The physician has more training and expertise than the layperson. But the poet is also distinguished from ordinary members of the public. The poet is, as Wordsworth writes in a passage added to the Preface in 1802, "a man speaking to man," though with the crucial qualification that the poet is one "with more lively sensibility, more enthusiasm and tenderness, who has a greater knowledge of human nature, and a more comprehensive soul, than are supposed to be common among mankind" (*PW* 1:138). But Wordsworth and Beddoes both see the anecdote as a crossroads where two types of professionals—physicians and poets—can converse not only with each other but also with the wider communities in which they are embedded.

The closeness of a physician like Beddoes and a poet like Wordsworth is underlined by the fact that Beddoes himself, as we have already seen, dabbled in verse. Beddoes is distinguished in particular for creating what may be the first parody of *Lyrical Ballads*, a poem he entitled "Domiciliary Verses." Beddoes had a printed version of this poem bound into his copy of *Lyrical Ballads*, where it appears as if it were any other poem in the collection, apparently as a joke at Coleridge's and Wordsworth's expense:

I knew an Irishman; to England he
Came every spring a hay-making; and much
Would praise his cabin. By a bog it stood,
And he had store of peats. Without a chimney,
Stood the little cabin. Full of warmth and smoke,
It cherished its owner. The smoke he loved,
Loved for the warmth's sake, though it bleared his eyes

Now when the North-East pinches, I bethink me
Of this poor Irishman; and think "how sweet
It were to house with him, and pat his cur,
And peel potatoes mid his cabin's smoke."[32]

When Beddoes later published this poem in Robert Southey's *Annual Anthology* (1799), Cottle wrote to Wordsworth to reassure him about this parody: "Pray give yourself no uneasiness about Dr Beddoes's verses—in truth it is a very harmless performance."[33] Beddoes may not have had Wordsworth's poetry in mind, however, so much as Coleridge's poem "Reflections on Having Left a Place of Retirement," first published as "Reflections on Entering into Active Life" in the October 1796 issue of the *Monthly Magazine*. In the same issue, Beddoes himself contributed another poem, "On the occasion of an interrupted Voyage from Ross to Chepstow, September 1796," which reflects on the geological forces that have created the landscape around the same region of the River Wye where Tintern Abbey is located.[34] Even though the poem that Beddoes inserted into his copy of *Lyrical Ballads* may not have had Wordsworth as its primary target, the poem in context still works to underline how *Lyrical Ballads'* poetic "experiments" constantly court the failure to contribute to the "history and science of human feelings." Rather than throw light into the recesses of human nature, all that Beddoes's poem seems to do, it appears, is generate smoke. It tells an anecdote that turns out to be a failed experiment that goes nowhere.[35]

If Beddoes makes fun of the verse anecdotes of *Lyrical Ballads*, he nevertheless put his faith in the possibility that medical anecdotes might reveal undiscovered truths. For his part, Wordsworth thought that anecdotes in verse might also uncover something about human nature, even if exactly what they uncovered might be difficult to articulate. He made use of anecdotes from his reading in the works of Men of Science as well as anecdotes drawn from his own observations of people. "Goody Blake and Harry Gill," which appeared in the first edition of *Lyrical Ballads*, was based on an anecdote that he had found in Darwin's *Zoonomia.* Wordsworth had asked Cottle to send him Darwin's work *"by the first carrier"* in a letter written in early 1798, while he was beginning to prepare his contributions to the project.[36] In *Zoonomia,* Darwin proposes that everything that living beings do, think, or feel can be explained by the vibrations of bodily tissues. He uses this assumption to construct a common explanatory framework for analyzing both the body and the mind. *Zoonomia* classifies all the motions of the body and the mind under four "modes": "irritation," "sensations of pleasure and pain," "volition," and "association." People suffer mental and physical afflictions when any one of these "modes" becomes unbalanced. Alongside his disquisitions on the four modes, Darwin fills the pages of *Zoonomia* with anecdotes that he claims to have taken from his own experience, people he has talked to, and his reading of newspapers, histories, and travel literature. He uses the anecdotes not only to show how the modes can go awry but also to illuminate how the modes normally work. *Zoonomia* illustrates the persistence of anecdotal practices in "serious" contributions to the human sciences through the late eighteenth century. Darwin seizes on anomalous cases as the cases that best reveal the laws of the body and of the mind. One of them is the prose anecdote that Wordsworth would rewrite as "Goody Blake and Harry Gill."

Like Hamilton's anecdote of the sick boy who wandered off into a chilly night, Darwin's anecdote is presented as a record of an actual historical event. Darwin vouches for the truth of the anecdote that would inspire "Goody Blake and Harry Gill," claiming that he had good information of its truth and that it was "published a few years ago in the newspapers." He tells the story to illustrate the effects of excessive "volition," which Darwin describes as bearing "the same analogy to desire and aversion, which sensation does to pleasure and pain," and explains that "when desire or aversion produces any action of the muscular fibres, or of the organs of sense, it is termed volition; and the actions produced in consequence are termed voluntary actions" (Z 1:524–25). But voluntary actions are not necessarily "voluntary" in the sense of being consciously willed. A case in point is the unfortunate farmer in *Zoonomia* that Wordsworth would later christen "Harry Gill." Darwin diagnoses this farmer as suffering from *mania mutabilis,* whose victims subordinate their mental processes to one "mistaken or imaginary idea," to which they obsessively return again and again. The farmer's case reveals how a disturbance of mental volition can show up as disturbances of the body and its senses:

A young farmer in Warwickshire, finding his hedges broke, and the sticks carried away during a frosty season, determined to watch for the thief. He lay many cold hours under a hay-stack, and at length an old woman, like a witch in a play, approached, and began to pull up the hedge; he waited till she had tied up her bottle of sticks, and was carrying them off, that he might convict her of the theft, and then springing from his concealment, he seized his prey with violent threats. After some altercation, in which her load was left upon the ground, she kneeled upon her bundle of sticks, and raising her arms to heaven beneath the bright moon then at the full, spoke to the farmer already shivering with cold, "Heaven grant, that thou never mayest know again the blessing to be warm." He complained of cold all the next day, and wore an upper coat, and in a few days another, and in a fortnight took to his bed, always saying nothing made him warm, he covered himself with many blankets, and had a sieve over his face, as he lay; and from this one insane idea he kept his bed above twenty years for fear of the cold air, till at length he died. (Z 2.239)

I have not been able to discover any newspaper including a story resembling the one that Darwin tells in *Zoonomia*. If it does turn out that the story had indeed been published "a few years" before Darwin published *Zoonomia*, as Darwin claimed, then even in that case it would have been an old story, since, according to the report, the Warwickshire farmer lingered in his hypochondriac hypothermia "above twenty years." Even in Darwin's original anecdote, the story is open to being read as a piece of folkloric storytelling, an "old wives' tale," a fantastic story telling of a witch's curse on a farmer foolish enough to meddle with her. The description of the old woman approaching "like a witch in a play" serves to acknowledge the possibility of the supernatural reading, even as Darwin accounts for everything that happens in terms of natural processes.

Wordsworth's verse version of the story in *Lyrical Ballads* reroutes the narrative back into a simulated oral tradition, though one in which the story is handed down in song rather than in conversation.[37] By turning Darwin's anecdote into a ballad, Wordsworth understands himself to be giving the story a new life in both written and oral culture. He writes in the introductory note to the poem, "I have the satisfaction of knowing that it has been communicated to many hundreds of people who would never have heard of it, had it not been narrated as a Ballad" (*PW* 1:150). Wordsworth's hope is that his adaptation of Darwin's anecdote into verse will allow the story to enter into popular consciousness in the manner of a traditional ballad. In Wordsworth's poem, Harry Gill's constantly chattering teeth tell the constantly reiterated story of his own imagined curse:

> No word to any man he utters,
> A-bed or up, to young or old;
> But ever to himself he mutters,
> "Poor Harry Gill is very cold."
> A-bed or up, by night or day;
> His teeth they chatter, chatter still.
> Now think, ye farmers all, I pray,
> Of Goody Blake and Harry Gill. (*LB* 121–28, p. 62)

Like "Anecdote for Fathers," "Goody Blake and Harry Gill" presents itself as a poem containing useful wisdom for a particular social group but seeks to hold the attention of the widest possible audience. The two poems are natural companions. As several critics have noted, the father figure in "Anecdote for Fathers" and Harry Gill in "Goody Blake and Harry Gill" both seize apparently weaker people by the arm, though the tables are turned on the antagonists in both poems.[38] Both are readily recognizable as poetic anecdotes told in the style of the ballad. Indeed "Goody Blake and Harry Gill" might equally well have been titled "Anecdote for Farmers."

Wordsworth's decision to rewrite Darwin's physiological report in the style of a popular ballad reflects a desire to find connections among poetry and the specialized researches of Men of Science and a popular tradition of storytelling represented in part by the genres of anecdote and ballad. The result is a poem riven by mixed generic signals. Pulled between medical case study and popular ballad, the strain the poem puts on Wordsworth's poetic theory is palpable in the subtitle of the poem ("A True Story") and the explanation for it in the Preface, where Wordsworth states that in writing the poem, "I wished to draw attention to the truth that the power of the human imagination is sufficient to produce such changes even in our physical nature as might almost appear miraculous. The truth is an important one; the fact (for it is a *fact*) is a valuable illustration of it" (*PW* 1:150). The insistence on the factuality both of the story itself and the mental phenomena it is supposed to exemplify seems to be a response to the ease with which the story can be read as pure fiction. Indeed, Wordsworth failed to convince the anonymous reviewer in the *British Critic* of the poem's factuality, who concluded "it is a miracle; and modern miracles can seldom be admitted, without some degree of credulity, or a very uncommon weight of evidence."[39]

To cast Darwin's anecdote into poetry is to emphasize its magical dimensions, connecting the story to a tradition of oral storytelling that promiscuously mixes presumed facts with fiction and fable. In "Goody Blake and Harry Gill," the poem's attraction toward the supernatural is reflected in its attraction to language that deviates from the "real language of men." The poem is, after all, one of the most obsessively repetitive of *Lyrical Ballads,* as if Harry's condition had also afflicted the speech of the poem's narrator:

> Oh! what's the matter? what's the matter?
> What is't that ails young Harry Gill?
> That evermore his teeth they chatter,
> Chatter, chatter, chatter still. (*LB* ll. 1–4, p. 59)

If Harry Gill's story stretches the limits of credibility (despite the 1798 subtitle "A True Story"), then it also stretches the limits of the "real language of men" to near breaking point. The poem itself appears to be afflicted with Harry Gill's condition, with its stuttering repetitions ("Chatter, chatter, chatter") and its games with meter, as when in the fourth line of the poem the unvarying iambic scheme is suddenly broken by the trochees of Harry's rattling teeth.[40]

Just as "Goody Blake and Harry Gill" is torn between the desire for fidelity to the "real language of men" and the possibilities of poetry as sound, it is torn between the impulse to claim the authority of physiological fact and expert knowledge and the desire to revel in the pleasures of fiction and popular storytelling. "Goody Blake and Harry Gill" shows that the methods of poetry and physiology could still overlap in their use of anecdotes as sources of insight into the human. But Wordsworth's rewriting of Darwin's anecdote as a ballad is also, despite itself, a critique of the use of anecdotes as records of facts on which a precise science might be constructed. The anecdote emerges, in poems like "Goody Blake and Harry Gill," as a genre that opens up a kind of licensed play, in which claims to factuality and general application are partially suspended without being disavowed completely. By drawing attention to the anecdote's representational instability and making a poetic virtue of it, Wordsworth makes an implicit argument in *Lyrical Ballads* that the anecdote might most convincingly create new knowledge in poetry. The poet may follow the same anecdotal procedures of investigating human nature as Men of Science like Beddoes and Darwin do. But the Poet's verse productions ultimately supersede the prose disquisitions of the Man of Science on the nature of consciousness, which stand more at a remove from the mind than the Poet's explorations, which attempt to reproduce the turns of the mind in turns of verse.

WORDSWORTH AND COLERIDGE

Up until this point I have been discussing Wordsworth's poetic theory and Wordsworth's poetry almost exclusively. But *Lyrical Ballads* was, of course, the product of Wordsworth's collaboration with Coleridge, and not the work of a single writer. As is well known, Wordsworth wrote the Preface in close dialogue with Coleridge, who would later claim in an 1802 letter to Southey that it was "half a child of my own Brain," although he also wrote in the same letter of his suspicions that there existed "a radical Difference in our theoretical opinions regarding Poetry."[41] The story of how Coleridge and Wordsworth drew further apart both personally and on questions of poetics is a familiar one. In revisiting this story, I emphasize the question of the anecdote as a kind of theoretical hinge that allowed Coleridge to distinguish his own ideas about poetry from Wordsworth's. At first, the anecdote provided a point of commonality between Coleridge's and Wordsworth's sense of poetry. Only later did the anecdote become a point from which their ideas about poetry would diverge. The anecdote thus helped Coleridge define the difference between his own poetic theory and what he saw as Wordsworth's.

The contrast between Coleridge's and Wordsworth's ideas about poetry as Coleridge presents them in the *Biographia Literaria* rests in no small part on Wordsworth's articulation of an anecdotal poetics in *Lyrical Ballads*. The cleft between the two is especially visible in their treatment of the anecdote's relationship to poetry. Whereas Wordsworth in the Preface to *Lyrical Ballads* frames the anecdote as a genre that points in the direction of poetry, Coleridge in the *Biographia Literaria* insists on the anecdote's distance from poetry. Coleridge indicts those poems of Wordsworth's that most closely resemble prose anecdotes as exhibiting what he considers one of the worst tendencies of Wordsworth's poetry. These include "a *matter-of-factness* in certain poems," which appears in "the insertion of accidental circumstances" of the kind that "might be necessary to establish the probability of a statement in real life, where nothing is taken for granted by the hearer, but appear superfluous in poetry, where the reader is willing to believe for his own sake" (*BL* 2:126). Coleridge underlines the differences that divide the speech of illiterate rustics from the speech of a literate middle class, the differences that divide speech from writing, and the differences that divide prose from poetry. He takes issue in particular with Wordsworth's apparent disregard for the differences between poetry and prose, making Wordsworth's account of the complicated relations between poetry and spoken language and poetry and written prose into a straw man argument for collapsing all three. Against the naive position that he ascribes to Wordsworth, Coleridge contends that "prose itself, at least, in all argumentative and consecutive works, differs, and ought to differ, from the language of conversation; even as reading ought to differ from talking" (*BL* 2:60–61).[42] An even wider chasm divides poetry and prose, in Coleridge's view, than the one that divides written prose from conversational speech.

Coleridge is therefore especially critical of Wordsworth's more obviously "anecdotal" poetry. The idea that an anecdote could be made poetic simply by putting it into verse is, in Coleridge's view, fundamentally mistaken. Although he does not define poetry in contradiction to prose, Coleridge does hold that metrical composition implies forms of language that deviate from ordinary language. "I write in metre," Coleridge writes, "because I am about to use a language different from that of prose" (*BL* 2:69). Coleridge accuses Wordsworth of making a generic category mistake in writing his anecdotes in verse. He lists Wordsworth's "Anecdote for Fathers," "Simon Lee, the Old Huntsman," "Alice Fell; or Poverty," "Beggars," and "The Sailor's Mother" as poems that "notwithstanding the beauties which are to be found in each of them where the poet interposes the music of his own thoughts, would have been more delightful to me in prose, told and managed, as by Mr. Wordsworth they would have been, in a moral essay, or pedestrian tour" (*BL* 2:68–69). These are all markedly "anecdotal" poems, and it is precisely their proximity to the prose anecdote that earns them Coleridge's censure. For Coleridge, poems and anecdotes have their own specific uses and powers, the former being suited to recording "the music of thoughts," the latter to recounting the small incidents of everyday life.

As it is now well known, Coleridge misrepresents the circumstances of his collaboration with Wordsworth in the *Biographia Literaria*, describing an orderly plan for the two poets to divide their poetic labors that is belied by the much messier history of how *Lyrical Ballads* was actually put together.[43] Yet Coleridge's account of the origins of *Lyrical Ballads* is worth looking at again for the light it throws on how he sought to distinguish his own poetics from Wordsworth's. Coleridge writes in the *Biographia Literaria*:

> It was agreed, that my endeavours should be directed to persons and characters supernatural, or at least romantic; yet so as to transfer

from our inward nature a human interest and a semblance of truth sufficient to procure for these shadows of imagination that willing suspension of disbelief for the moment that constitutes poetic faith. Mr. Wordsworth, on the other hand, was to propose himself as his object, to give a charm of novelty to things of every day, and to excite a feeling analogous to the supernatural, by awakening the mind's attention from the lethargy of custom, and directing it to the loveliness and the wonders of the world before us. (*BL* 2:6–7)

This story of Coleridge choosing to write poetry of the supernatural and Wordsworth the poetry of the everyday maps onto the distinction Coleridge draws between himself and Wordsworth as theorists of poetry, with Coleridge distinguishing the language of poetry from that of everyday life and Wordsworth confounding the two. The story also helps Coleridge pinpoint the source of Wordsworth's failings both as a poet and as a theorist of poetry. Wordsworth's poetic theory, for Coleridge, cannot account for Wordsworth's best poems, but it accounts for his worst poems only too well, with their air of naively parlaying matters of fact and blithe neglect of the distinction between verse and prose.

The divergence between Wordsworth's and Coleridge's poetics that opens up in the *Biographia Literaria* thus rests on an opposition between prose and verse—two words whose etymologies are closely related. The *Oxford English Dictionary* traces "prose" back to the Latin adjective *prosus* "straightforward," which in turn derives from the past participle *proversus* "turned forwards." "Verse" derives from the Latin *versus* meaning "a line" or "row" and, in particular, "a line of writing." "Prose" thus suggests writing that moves in a straight line, and "verse" suggests writing that turns or twists away from linearity. By Wordsworth's time, however, "prose" had come to suggest not simply truthfulness but also a dull literalism. This connotation is most visible in the adjective "prosaic," which, when applied to language, according to the *Oxford English Dictionary*, at the end of the seventeenth century acquires the meaning of "having the character, style, or diction of prose as opposed to poetry; plainly or simply worded; lacking in poetic expression, feeling, or imagination."[44]

In the *Lectures on Fine Art*, delivered over the course of the 1820s, Georg Wilhelm Friedrich Hegel drew on the similar connotations of the German noun *Prosa* when he described "the prose of the world" as a state in which the individual "stands in dependence on external influences, laws, political institutions, civil relationships" and is "entangled in many-sided particular circumstances, conditions, obstacles, and relative matters."[45] In an essay applying the opposition between poetry and prose to the novel tradition, Michal Peled Ginsburg and Lorri G. Nandrea observe, "The world of prose is one where poetry is lacking; the world of poetry is inhibited, destroyed, or produced as a fantasmatic other by the world of prose."[46] This description of poetry pushed aside by prose aligns perfectly with Coleridge's story of his and Wordsworth's poetic collaboration. Coleridge would, in the aftermath of the *Lyrical Ballads* project, represent his own contributions to *Lyrical Ballads* as the "fantasmatic other" of Wordsworth's world of prose.

Although Coleridge's "Rime of the Ancyent Marinere" was not originally intended as a fantastic foil to Wordsworth's poetry of everyday life, Coleridge would reinterpret the poem as such in the *Biographia Literaria*. I use the "Rime of the Ancyent Marinere" here to show the usefulness of the anecdote as a way of thinking about Coleridge's and Wordsworth's sociotextual relationship. First, the origins of the poem itself remind us that the "Rime of the Ancyent Marinere" grew out of a shared practice of transforming prose anecdotes into poetry. Second, the early publication history of the poem suggests an attempt to bring the "Rime of the Ancyent Marinere" closer to Wordsworth's poems in the collection by making the poem more "anecdotal." And third, Coleridge later came to associate anecdotes not only with Wordsworth's poetry but his own failures as a poet.

"The Rime of the Ancyent Marinere" contains accounts of events that stretch the boundaries of possibility much farther than most of the anecdotes recounted in Wordsworth's contributions to *Lyrical Ballads*. It recounts the sighting of a ship commandeered by dice-playing ghouls, a dead crew coming to life and throwing themselves to work, and a blessing of sea snakes that brings rain and partial redemption for the mariner. More than four decades after the first publication of *Lyrical Ballads*, however, Wordsworth would locate the wellsprings of the poem in less miraculous occurrences. The Reverend Alexander Dyce, a friend of Wordsworth's in his later years, recorded a conversation in which Wordsworth had claimed that the inspiration for the "Rime" was a dream of Coleridge's friend John Cruickshank, who had seen a "skeleton ship, with figures in it."[47] In his conversations with Isabella Fenwick in the 1840s, Wordsworth also claimed that the ancient mariner's transgression came from his reading of George Shelvocke's *Voyage round the World by the Way of the Great South Sea* (1726).[48] In his account of the voyage, Shelvocke records the shooting of an actual albatross:

we had continual squals of sleet, snow and rain, and the heavens were perpetually hid from us by gloomy dismal clouds. In short, one would think it impossible that any thing living could subsist in so rigid a climate; and, indeed, we all observed, that we had not had the sight of one fish of any kind, since we were come to the Southward of the streights of *le Mair,* nor one sea-bird, except a disconsolate black *Albitross,* who accompanied us for several days, hovering about us as if he had lost himself, till *Hatley,* (my second Captain) observing, in one of his melancholy fits, that this bird was always hovering near us, imagin'd, from his colour, that it might be some ill omen. That which, I suppose, induced him the more to encourage his superstition, was the continued series of contrary tempestuous winds, which had opress'd us ever since we had got into this sea. But be that as it would, he, after some fruitless attempts, at length, shot the *Albitross,* not doubting (perhaps) that we should have a fair wind after it.[49]

The sources to which Wordsworth traced Coleridge's "Rime of the Ancyent Marinere" in his conversations with Isabella Fenwick retrospectively smooth over some of the disjuncture between the Preface's claim that the poems in the collection present the "events of real life" and the presence of the "Rime of the Ancyent Marinere." The documented and oral history of the making of the "Rime of the Ancyent Marinere" suggests that even a poem as incredible as this one could have its wellsprings in real events: or at least, in anecdotes of events that were creditable as actual occurrences. Neither the dream nor the shooting of the albatross were experienced firsthand by Wordsworth or Coleridge. These events were told first as anecdotal narratives—a written one in Shelvocke's case and presumably an oral one in Cruickshank's—before they entered into the making of the "Rime of the Ancyent Marinere." Anecdotes, then, provided important narrative seeds from which Coleridge's poem grew.

Despite the anecdotal origins it shared with many other poems in *Lyrical Ballads,* Wordsworth's sense of the place the "Rime of the Ancyent Marinere" occupied in the collection as a whole seems to have changed between the first and the second editions. Wordsworth acknowledged in the Advertisement that some poems in the collection were "absolute inventions of the author." In the first edition of *Lyrical Ballads,* then, the "Rime of the Ancyent Marinere" can be understood as an "absolute invention" by contrast to apparently more factual poems such as "Anecdote for Fathers." But in the 1800 edition of *Lyrical Ballads,* Wordsworth was less willing to countenance poems appearing less tethered to actual events in the collection than he had been in the first edition. As we have seen, he replaced the Advertisement's claim that at least a portion of the poems adhere to literal fact with a more global statement that his "principal object" in his own poems in the volume is to create a poetry that would take "the incidents of common life" as its primary source of inspiration. Just as "The Rime of the Ancyent Marinere" soon leaves the natural for the supernatural, its consciously archaic language draws attention to its distance from anything resembling "the language of common life," despite Wordsworth's insistence in the Preface that its language was still "intelligible" to contemporary readership. Given Wordsworth's framing of the collection as an attempt to put poetry in touch with the incidents and language of common life, "The Rime of the Ancyent Marinere" could only look like an anomaly, especially in the expanded second edition of *Lyrical Ballads,* which added a second volume of poems, all of them by Wordsworth. As Wordsworth wrote later, "it seems that The Ancyent Mariner has upon the whole been an injury to the volume, I mean that the old words and the strangeness of it have deterred readers from going on. If the volume should come to a second Edition I would put in its place some little things which would be more likely to suit the common taste."[50] In the event, the "Rime of the Ancyent Marinere" remained in the collection, though in a form that would bring it closer in line with the theory of poetry outlined in Wordsworth's Preface.

In the second edition the "Rime of the Ancyent Marinere" was removed from its original place as the opening of *Lyrical Ballads* and relegated to the penultimate position in the first volume of the collection. The poem was also renamed "The Ancient Mariner: A Poet's Reverie," apparently in an attempt to tether the poem more securely to reality, if only to a reverie that a poet might plausibly have had. The Argument that prefaced the poem was rewritten to emphasize the centrality of the shooting of the albatross, an event that could at least plausibly be claimed to fall into the domain of common life. The first edition's Argument read: "How a Ship having passed the Line was driven by Storms to the cold Country towards the South Pole; and how from thence she made her course to the tropical Latitude of the Great Pacific Ocean; and of the strange things that befell; and in what manner the Ancyent Marinere came back to his own Country."[51] In the first edition it is the "strange things that befell" the ancient mariner that are emphasized, and the shooting of the albatross is not mentioned at all. In the second edition, however, the subtitle was rewritten so that the shooting is placed at the very center of the narrative. Readers are directed to see the poem as revolving around one of the more probable events, to which the strange events that later befall the mariner are subordinated. The subtitle reads, in the second edition, "How a Ship, having first sailed to the Equator, was driven by Storms, to the cold Country towards the South Pole; how the Ancient Mariner cruelly, and in contempt of the laws of hospitality, killed a Sea-bird; and how he was followed by many and strange Judgements; and in what manner he came back to his own Country."[52] The first sub-title describes a poem seemingly unmoored from common life, but the second describes one that, despite its apparent strangeness, is ultimately anchored in a credible narrative of a single incident. The text of the "Rime of the Ancyent Marinere" was revised in the second edition to remove some of its archaisms, thus bringing it closer to Wordsworth's "real language of men." As Jerome McGann observes, the effect of these revisions "was to make the 'Rime' appear less a literary ballad and more a lyrical ballad," bringing the poem more in line with narrative verses such as "Anecdote for Fathers" and "Simon Lee, the Old Huntsman." The shift is also reflected in the style of the 1800 Argument, which, as McGann notes, unlike the 1798 version, "remains in a contemporary idiom that perfectly marries with the new, self-conscious title."[53]

Given that Coleridge associated the Wordsworthian anecdote-poem with poetic failure, as well as the displacement of his own poetry by Wordsworth's, it is not surprising that in Coleridge's writings of the 1810s, prose anecdotes often herald a bathetic fall from poetic sublimity. In describing chapter 10 of the *Biographia Literaria* as "A chapter of digression and anecdotes, as an interlude preceding that on the nature and genesis of the imagination or plastic power" (*BL* 1:168), for example, Coleridge frames anecdotes as distractions that detain his progress toward the transcendent imagination: the ultimate destination of Book One.[54] The same association of the anecdote, in Coleridge, with obstruction and failure appears in the note appended to the first published version of "Kubla Khan" in 1816:

On awaking he appeared to himself to have a distinct recollection of the whole, and taking his pen, ink, and paper, instantly and eagerly wrote down the lines that are here preserved. At this moment he was unfortunately called out by a person on business from Porlock, and detained by him above an hour, and on his return to his room, found to his no small surprise and mortification, that though he still retained some vague and dim recollection of the general purport of the vision, yet, with the exception of some eight or ten scattered lines and images, all the rest had passed away like the images on the surface of a stream into which a stone has been cast, but, alas! without the after restoration of the latter.[55]

Coleridge's own anecdote of the person from Porlock, which prefaced the 1797 poem in 1816, is thus understandable as a story of one genre (the anecdote) guillotining another (poetry). In *Lyrical Ballads*, however, Wordsworth—and to a significant extent Coleridge as well—saw the possibility for a reciprocal relationship between anecdotes and poems.

In this vision, prose and poetry could meet in the genre of the anecdote, a genre that illustrated Wordsworth's argument in the Preface that poetry "can boast of no celestial Ichor that distinguishes her vital juices from those of prose; the same human blood circulates through the veins of them both" (*PW* 1:134). Wordsworth's metaphor of "the same human blood" circulating between prose and poetry has been read by Lucy Newlyn as a covert acknowledgment of the close collaboration between Dorothy Wordsworth and William Wordsworth, in which the linguistic relationship between poetry and prose was intertwined with the filial relationship between sister and brother.[56] A prose anecdote in Dorothy Wordsworth's *Alfoxden Journal* (1798) describing the appearance of the moon during a nocturnal walk, for example, has a poetic counterpart in William Wordsworth's "A Night-Piece," a poem written in 1798 but only published in Wordsworth's 1815 *Poems*. Whether Dorothy's journal inspired William's poem or the other way around is still unclear, although, as Newlyn observes, "Using exact verbal correspondences to establish priority is beside the point when we can instead think in terms of shared perceptions, shared vocabulary, even shared oral composition."[57] If the close relationship posited between prose and poetry in the Preface to *Lyrical Ballads* is reflected in William and Dorothy Wordsworth's literary and filial relationship, then the increasing distance that opened up between William Wordsworth and Coleridge as theorists of poetry was also reflected in the fraying of their friendship after their collaboration in *Lyrical Ballads*. By separating poetry from anecdote in the *Biographia Literaria*, Coleridge was also marking his personal estrangement from Wordsworth.

LYRICAL ANECDOTES

I end this chapter by arguing that Wordsworth's lyric poems in *Lyrical Ballads* do not derive from a turning away from or abandonment of the narrative impulse but instead develop lyric resources that are already present in the anecdote as a genre.[58] To write of Wordsworth's lyric poetry in *Lyrical Ballads* is complicated, of course, by the fact that Wordsworth did not use the word "lyric" in the way modern critics usually use the term. The current tendency to oppose lyric to narrative, for example, emerged from a long development in critical terminology over the nineteenth and twentieth centuries. Wordsworth's own description in the "Essay, Supplementary to the Preface" (1815) of "lyrical" poems as those in which "for the production of their *full* effect, an accompaniment of music is indispensable" (*PW* 3:27) suggests that Wordsworth understood the term "lyric" primarily in its musical sense as words intended to be sung to the accompaniment of the lyre. My understanding of "lyric" in this section is guided more by Jonathan Culler's argument that the lyric is "not the description and interpretation of a past event but the iterative and iterable performance of an event in the lyric present, in the special 'now,' of lyric articulation."[59] I would add that the anecdote is also an "iterative and iterable performance of an event," in addition to being a recounting of an event, which may or may not have actually happened. Indeed, the anecdote's capacity to become itself a linguistic event, even in the absence of any "real" event preceding it, was what allowed it to become a conduit in Wordsworth's poetry from the "real language of men" to the special type of linguistic event—staged in a timeless present tense—with which Culler associates the lyric.

Wordsworth's "The Complaint of a Forsaken Indian Woman," for example, generates a type of "lyric articulation" by means of a narrative anecdote. The short headnote that prefaces the poem refers readers to Samuel Hearne's posthumously published *A Journey from Prince of Wales's Fort in Hudson's Bay, to the Northern Ocean* (1795), which details Hearne's three attempts to reach the Arctic Ocean from Hudson's Bay between 1769 and 1772. Hearne did indeed succeed in reaching the Arctic Ocean on the third journey. But he failed to find the fabled Northwest Passage from the Atlantic to the Pacific oceans, which he had been searching for on behalf of the Hudson's Bay Company, and died of dropsy soon after his return from his travels. In his narrative of the third successful journey, Hearne frequently turns his attention to the party of Chipewyan people who led him across the continent, one of whom was abandoned by the party after falling too ill to keep up with them: "One of the Indian's wives, who for some time had been in a consumption, had for a few days past become so weak as to be incapable of traveling, which, among those people, is the most deplorable state to which a human being can possibly be brought. Whether she had been given over by the doctors, or that it was for want of friends among them, I cannot tell, but certain it is, that no expedients were taken for her recovery; so that, without much ceremony, she was left unassisted, to perish above-ground."[60] In fact, Hearne adds later that the woman was deserted several times, since she recovered and caught up with the party several times before being finally left to die.[61] Hearne writes as a distanced observer of the desertion, although, of course, he becomes implicated in the abandonment of the woman as a fellow traveler.

In an attempt to get a sense of what happened, and why, Hearne reinterprets the woman's abandonment as an example of a common practice among the people guiding him across the continent, writing, "Though this was the first instance of the kind I had seen, it is the common, and indeed the constant practice of those Indians; for when a grown person is so ill, especially in the Summer, as not to be able to walk, and too heavy to be carried, they say it is better to leave one who is past recovery, than for the whole family to sit down by them and starve to death; well knowing that they cannot be of any service to the afflicted."[62] He then pivots from the "custom" of one tribe to the universal directives of human nature that force the tribe to abandon members too sick to carry on: "A custom apparently so unnatural is perhaps not to be found among any other of the human race: if properly considered, however, it may with justice be ascribed to necessity and self-preservation, rather than to the want of humanity and social feeling, which ought to be the characteristic of men, as the noblest part of creation."[63] Hearne shifts from seeing the abandonment as a wholly singular event to seeing it as the singular custom of a particular people, to, finally, seeing it as an expression of the duty of self-preservation that is intrinsic to human nature.

Whereas Hearne looks at the incident from the point of view of himself and the tribe, Wordsworth looks at the incident from the perspective of the abandoned woman. But both Hearne and Wordsworth share the same impulse to imbue the story with universal significance. In the Preface, for example, Wordsworth describes the poem as an attempt to render "the last struggles of a human being at the approach of death, cleaving in solitude to life and society" (*PW* 1:126). As Maureen N. McLane points out, there is a contradiction between the Preface's explanation of the poem and the headnote: "In the *Preface*, this character serves as a figure for the human; in the note the character is more precisely restricted to the figure of the Indian."[64] The poem turns, then, on the generative contradiction between particularity and universality that has emerged in this book as one of the fundamental characteristics of the Enlightenment anecdote.

"The Complaint of a Forsaken Indian Woman" also turns formally on the disjunction between the narrative temporality of its source anecdote and the atemporality of articulation with which Jonathan Culler associates the lyric. Indeed, the turns from particularity to universality and temporality to atemporality are related movements toward abstraction. Wordsworth's "The Complaint of a Forsaken Indian Woman" thus shows how a prose anecdote situated in time can generate apostrophic speech in which absent figures may be addressed as if they were present. The Indian woman addresses her absent party, for example, by exclaiming, "Alas! you might have dragged me on / Another day, a single one!" (*LB* ll. 21–22, p. 112), and her absent child with "My Child! they gave thee to another, / A woman who was not thy mother" (*LB* ll. 31–32, p. 112). Apostrophe may be an atypical form of language that addresses absent things, but it is framed in the poem as a natural response to the extreme circumstances it depicts.

This poem might seem quite far from the generic conventions of the anecdote, with its usual focus on external actions. Indeed, Culler has even argued for an opposition between lyric apostrophe and anecdotal narrative: "If one brings together in a poem a boy, some birds, a few blessed creatures, and some mountains, hills, and groves, one tends to place them in a narrative where one thing leads to another, events demand to be temporally located. . . . But if one puts into a poem 'thou shepherd boy,' 'ye birds,' 'ye blessed creatures,' etc. they are immediately associated with what might be called a timeless present but is better seen as a temporality of lyric articulation or enunciation."[65] Culler argues that boys, creatures, and birds are denarrativized when they become the objects of apostrophe. "The Complaint of the Indian Woman" does, however, include narrative elements: the woman's abandonment by her tribe, the passing of her child to another woman, and the loss of the food the tribe left behind for her when a wolf makes away with it while she is asleep. If the voice that speaks in "The Complaint of the Indian Woman" appears isolated and disembodied, this is a result of the very specific narrative conditions described in the poem and its headnote. Thus, Culler's generalization that Wordsworth shunned apostrophe, instead creating "lyrical ballads: anecdotes which signify," has to be qualified.[66] In poems such as "The Complaint of the Indian Woman" and "Anecdote for Fathers" Wordsworth does indeed employ the rhetorical figure of apostrophe. But he takes care to show the trail that leads back to the original anecdote that helps gives rise to the lyric voice. When juxtaposed with its anecdotal source, then, "The Complaint of a Forsaken Indian

Woman" suggests that lyric and anecdote are intertwined with each other in Wordsworth's poetry. Both genres constitute complementary and connected methods of tracing universal knowledge of human beings from the evidence of singular events.

A similar connection between anecdote and lyric can be found in "Lucy Gray," a poem that first appeared in the 1800 edition of *Lyrical Ballads*. Wordsworth told Isabella Fenwick that the poem was based on, "a circumstance told me by my Sister, of a little girl, who not far from Halifax in Yorkshire was bewildered in a snow-storm. Her footsteps were traced by her parents to the middle of a lock of a canal, and no other vestige of her, backward or forward, could be traced. The body however was found in the canal."[67] Because the poem's subject is a child who never reaches maturity, "Lucy Gray" is not usually classed as one of Wordsworth's "Lucy" poems. The poem nonetheless shows the same depersonalization and abstraction that characterize the poems that critics have traditionally included among the "Lucy" poems. These processes depend upon the deliberate avoidance of narrative specificity. "Lucy Gray" ends with the search for the lost girl, which, unlike the search described in the original anecdote, fails to find anything. The search party trace the footprints until they find themselves at a bridge. At this point, the syntax becomes ambiguous. The "they" in the last stanza can be read as referring both to the search party or the footprints themselves:

> They follow'd from the snowy bank
> The foot-marks, one by one,
> Into the middle of the plank
> —And further there were none. (*LB* ll. 53–56, p. 172)

Jay Clayton has described this poem as modulating from anecdotal narrative to lyric transcendence. Whereas the anecdote that inspired the poem specifies that Lucy's body was later found in the river, the poem omits this detail. Instead, it is as if Lucy's body disappeared into the ether. "In her pure, wordless singing, a sound that can be heard in the whistling wind, we encounter the life of lyricism itself," writes Clayton, adding, "Through the death of narrative, Wordsworth hopes to keep his lyric alive."[68] But another reading of the poem by analogy to the footprints that lead nowhere is also possible. We can also consider the poem as a bridge leading from the stories exchanged in common life to lyric.

The poems typically identified as Wordsworth's "Lucy" poems exhibit the same symbiosis between narrative and lyric. "Strange fits of passion I have known," for example, ends with a similarly arrested narrative, in which the speaker, making his way toward another Lucy, has a sudden premonition of her death:

> My horse mov'd on; hoof after hoof
> He rais'd and never stopp'd:
> When down behind the cottage roof
> At once the planet dropp'd.
>
> What fond and wayward thoughts will slide
> Into a Lover's head—
> "O mercy!" to myself I cried,
> "If Lucy should be dead!" (*LB* ll. 21–28, p. 162)

This lyric is more obviously "anecdotal" in a manuscript version, which originally ended with a living Lucy being told of the journey and the strange thoughts it had engendered:

> I told her this; her laughter light
> Is ringing in my ears;
> And when I think upon that night
> My eyes are dim with tears. (*LB* ll. 25–28, p. 294)

Much as the original anecdote on which "Lucy Gray" was based disambiguates the fate of the girl who wandered off into the night, so too does this draft version of "Strange fits of passion I have known" make clear that Lucy has not, in fact, died, or at least not that night. But the effect of these poems is still traceable to the actual or implied anecdotes that lie behind them: an effect that is intensified by Wordsworth's refusal to supply the sense of an ending that is usually expected of the anecdote.

The poem appearing in the 1800 *Lyrical Ballads* that is known as "A slumber did my spirit seal," in which the name "Lucy" does not appear at all, goes further still in nearly eliminating narrative altogether:

> A slumber did my spirit seal,
> I had no human fears:
> She seem'd a thing that could not feel
> The touch of earthly years.
>
> No motion has she now, no force;
> She neither hears nor sees;
> Roll'd round in earth's diurnal course
> With rocks and stones and trees! (*LB* ll. 1–8, p. 164)

I would argue that "A slumber did my sprit seal" is an anecdote, albeit one in which the narrative minimalism of the genre has been pushed as far as it can possibly go, with the result that narrative has almost completely evaporated from the poem. What remains is only a bare narrative of a realization that a "she" (which could be read either as a beloved female who has died or as the poet's own spirit) had once been full of motion but now is said to have none. But the "she" of the poem is nevertheless still seen to be under the influence of what Darwin in *Zoonomia* called "gravitating motions." Darwin describes these "gravitating motions" as movements that encompass "the annual and diurnal rotations of the earth and planets, the flux and reflux of the ocean, the descent of heavy bodies, and other phænomena of gravitation" (*Z* 1:6).[69] These "gravitating motions," along with the motions of chemistry and the motions of life, form the three kinds of "primary" motion in Darwin's *Zoonomia*. The motions of the minds and bodies of human beings obey their own laws, though they are not regarded as ontologically different from the motions of the Earth. By contrast to Darwin, the philosopher Donald Davidson draws a fundamental distinction between the unwilled motion of the planets and the intentional acts of human beings. He opens one lecture on the nature of intentional action by pointing out that "Not all human motion is behavior," for "Each of us in this room is moving eastward at about 700 miles an hour, carried by the diurnal rotation of the earth, but this is not a fact about our behaviour."[70] Much of the effect of "A slumber did my spirit seal" derives, however, from its refusal to acknowledge any fundamental distinction between the motion of the Earth and the motions of the human body (reading the "she" as the beloved) or of the mind (reading the "she" as the poet's spirit).[71] The price of enlightenment in the "A slumber did my spirit seal" is the loss of the idea of human nature as something independent of the forces that shape and reshape the natural world.

"A slumber did my spirit seal" reduces the anecdote to its basic elements: the opening state of equilibrium, the swerve that disrupts it, and the consequent readjustment of beginning assumptions. What is gained from this process of depersonalization is knowledge of human nature itself, understood as a set of incompletely apprehended forces, which bend the mind as ineluctably as the gravitational forces that operate on rocks and stones and trees. The "I" and the "she" of the poem become physical and mental trajectories that merge, finally, with the formal and figurative turns of poetry itself. The process of abstraction through which Wordsworth appears to have arrived at "A slumber did my spirit seal" suggests something important about the anecdote as a genre. As much as they seem to provide points of contact with the details of human experience, anecdotes just as often seem to lead away from human experience toward the invisible laws to which all human beings are subject. "A slumber did my spirit seal" is an anecdote that makes visible the void over which the human beings are suspended, spun around by unseen forces profoundly indifferent to their lives, loves, and deaths.

Coda

The anecdote was a central genre in the Enlightenment science of human nature. Anecdotes imbued the essays of John Locke, Joseph Addison, Richard Steele, and Eliza Haywood with their questioning energies. They acted as intermediaries between the common life and philosophy in the writings of David Hume. They became focal points for debates over the value of the information gleaned by the *Endeavour* voyage for the study of human nature. And they underlay Wordsworth's poetic practice and poetic theory in *Lyrical Ballads,* not only inspiring many poems in the collection but helping shape Wordsworth's theory of poetry. I have argued that Enlightenment anecdotes and the Enlightenment as a whole illuminate one another. To examine the uses that Enlightenment writers made of anecdotes is to see how a genre often regarded as a trivial indulgence was, at a specific moment in its history, widely valued for the glimpses it appeared to open onto the universal nature of human beings. By the same token, to recover the anecdotes that permeated the literature and philosophy of the eighteenth century is to discover an anecdotal waywardness and eccentricity at the very heart of Enlightenment thought on the human. To close this book, I would like to show that the central tension I have been exploring—the tension between the singular anecdote and the universal laws of human nature— also animates two other Enlightenment texts: Montesquieu's *Spirit of the Laws* and Laurence Sterne's *Tristram Shandy.* My aim in juxtaposing these texts is to suggest how the small genre of the anecdote might allow us to make connections between writings that may otherwise seem quite dissimilar—as well as to suggest how an attention to anecdotes might illuminate other Enlightenment writings beyond the particular constellation of texts I have chosen to concentrate on in this book.

The *Spirit of the Laws* is Montesquieu's ambitious attempt to lay bare the general principles behind the various written and unwritten laws that govern societies around the globe. From the beginning, Montesquieu sees no sharp distinction between laws of nature and laws that are created by human beings to organize their collective lives. Laws are, Montesquieu writes, "the necessary relations deriving from the nature of things; and in this sense, all beings have their laws: the divinity has its laws, the material world has its laws, the intelligences superior to man have their laws, the beasts have their laws, man has his laws" (*M* 3). Indeed, these laws are all seen as depending on one another in Montesquieu's book. God creates the unchanging laws of nature that prevail over the natural world, and the natural world, in its turn, determines the shape of human societies that establish themselves within it. According to Montesquieu's climactic theory, for example, the human societies of the East, whose climates are marked by sharp swings of temperature between the summer and winter months, and whose countries border on other countries with very different climates, are predisposed by nature to despotic government. The milder climate of the West, by contrast to the East, produces a predilection for monarchical and republican government. The distinction between natural and human-made laws, for Montesquieu, lies in the fact that "the intelligent world is far from being as well governed as the physical world." While Montesquieu thinks that "the intelligent world also has laws that are invariable by their nature," he notes that "unlike the physical world, it does not follow its laws consistently." This is because "particular intelligent beings are limited by their nature and are consequently subject to error; furthermore, it is in their nature to act by themselves" (*M* 4). Montesquieu's object is to look beyond the multiplicity of human laws and conventions—and behind the peculiarities of particular rulers and officials—and identify the invariable principles that underpin the diversity of human societies. Montesquieu seeks to set out the universal laws that produce the vast variety of human-made laws that, in turn, rule the human world.

The method by which Montesquieu came to write his book, in his own description, involved a mental oscillation between particular cases and general principles. "I began by examining men," Montesquieu explains, "and I believed that, amidst the infinite diversity of laws and mores, they were not led by their fancies alone. I have set down the principles, and I have seen particular cases conform to them as if by themselves, the histories of all nations being but their consequences, and each particular law connecting with another law or dependent on a more general one" (*M* xliii). This circle of interpretation that moves from individual human beings to principles and back again suggests the anecdote's centrality to Montesquieu's book, both as a vehicle for examining individual human beings and a means of verifying the general laws he discerns behind the societies in which those individuals exist. Just as the anecdote may help isolate the general principles that subtend the laws that govern particular societies, so too do these principles, once discovered, cause a vast number of anecdotal cases suddenly to line up with the principles like iron filings in a magnetic field.

Montesquieu borrowed one of the many anecdotes that he tells in the *Spirit of the Laws* from Izaäk Commelin's compilation of accounts written by travelers employed by the Dutch East India Company to discover new trading routes, which was first translated from the Dutch 1645 original into French as the *Recueil des voyages qui ont servi à l'éstablissement & aux progrés de la Compagnie des Indes Orientales* in 1702. The anecdote is used to illustrate the principle that despotic government, by contrast to monarchical government, has no laws to constrain the single person who governs: "in despotic government, one alone, without law and without rule, draws everything along by his will and his caprices" (*M* 10).[1] Where laws do exist in despotic governments, they are capricious and cruel. Montesquieu identifies Japan, where the "laws upset all ideas of human reason," as an embodiment of despotic government and gives as an example of this irrationality one anecdote from the *Recueil des voyages.* Compressing the original anecdote into one curt sentence, Montesquieu writes: "An account tells of two young women who were shut up in a box studded with nails until they died; the one, for having had some intrigue of gallantry; the other, for not having revealed it" (*M* 202). Montesquieu appears to see the punishment of the women as contrary to reason not simply because of its extreme cruelty but also because the crime of covering up the initial crime is punished in exactly the same way as the initial crime itself. The story originally told by Henry Hagenaar, as it appears in the 1725 edition of *Recueil des voyages,* mentions that it has not been "long since" that the "Seigneur de Firando" decreed the sentence to which Monesquieu refers, though Hagenaar specifies that three women were punished this way, rather than two.[2] Montesquieu's vagueness about the provenance of the account dispenses with the need to specify that Hagenaar may not have actually witnessed the event but had presumably been told of its occurrence shortly before his arrival in Firando (present-day Hirado) in September 1626. Much as Montesquieu deliberately simplifies the chain of hearsay leading back to the putative event, he also simplifies the event itself by reducing the three women whose dreadful fate Hagenaar describes (the one who had the affair and the two who failed to report it) to only two. The loss of the third woman allows the anecdote to appear to map more cleanly onto the general principle that punishments are applied indiscriminately in "despotic" systems of government to lawbreakers and accomplices alike.

The irrationality with which Montesquieu associates despotism is partly contained through anecdotes that suggest an underlying logic even behind the most brutal punishments. Montesquieu also explains despotic irrationality by tracing it back to the climatic conditions that apparently produce it. But the relationship between anecdotal cases and general principles in the *Spirit of the Laws* is not always as straightforward as Montesquieu's initial explanation would seem to suggest. As Ernst Cassirer remarks in his *Philosophy of the Enlightenment* (1932), Montesquieu's "delight in particulars is so great that at times his illustrative anecdotes overshadow the main lines of thought and threaten to make them unrecognizable."[3] One way that the anecdotal cases create a sense of disorder in the very structure of the *Spirit of the Laws* is by blurring Montesquieu's distinction between monarchial and despotic governments. The anecdotes that proliferate in the *Spirit of the Laws* do not always line up neatly with Montesquieu's attempt to find the master principles underlying the laws that hold in particular societies and the links between these principles and the physical environments in which those societies are placed. As Sharon Krause has observed, "despotism permeates, or threatens to permeate, the West as well as the East."[4] The tendency of despotism to invade the more apparently rational systems that order human societies in the West is most visible in the anecdotes Montesquieu tells.

Although Montesquieu claims that the despotic ruler is distinguished from a monarch because the despot's power is untrammeled by law, he also argues that despotic rulers are, in practice, so addled by the abject obsequiousness of those around them that they are unable to rule effectively. "Such a prince," writes Montesquieu, "has so many faults that one must fear exposing his natural foolishness to the light of day. He is hidden, and one remains in ignorance of his condition. Fortunately, men in these countries are such that they need only a name to govern them." The despotic ruler withdraws to the pleasures of the harem—or its equivalent depending on the despotic society the ruler happens to be in—and hands over the actual business of governing to a deputy. To illustrate the tendency of the despotic ruler to become a cypher, a mere figment of the imagination, Montesquieu reproduces an anecdote that he had found in Voltaire's *Histoire du Charles XII* (1731). In this early historical work, Voltaire tells the story of what happened after the sister of Charles XII of Sweden, during the king's exile in Turkey, had written to her brother informing him that the Swedish senate had tried to convince her to take the regency in his absence and then to make her agree to a peace treaty with the Russian czar and the king of Denmark. In response, Voltaire reports, Charles wrote a letter to the senate informing them that if they would not be ruled by him, then he would send one of his boots to rule in his stead. In Voltaire's anecdote, Charles's letter appears to be intended both as a gesture of contempt and a reminder that the senate can do nothing without his will. Montesquieu, however, takes the story quite literally, remarking that if Charles had actually carried out the plan, then "The boot would have governed like a despotic king" (*M* 59). The anecdote is certainly memorable. But it also has the effect of complicating the link between government and geography that underpins the *Spirit of the Laws*. Charles writes his letter from Turkey, one of Montesquieu's primary examples of despotism, but Voltaire observes immediately before he tells the boot anecdote that Charles had picked up his despotic tendencies not from the Turks but from his upbringing in Sweden: "The despotism that he had imbibed with his mother's milk made him forget that in times past Sweden was free, and that the senate formerly governed the kingdom in conjunction with the kings."[5] A predilection to despotism, then, is to be found even in an apparently enlightened European monarch. Montesquieu's use of Voltaire's anecdote, moreover, implies that monarchical government, quite as much as despotic government, rests on a collective fantasy that allows the whole machinery of government to function.

Another anecdote that Montesquieu tells in the *Spirit of the Laws* enables a similar invasion of the West by the specter of Eastern despotism. Without naming his source, Montesquieu tells us:

> It is said that a certain pope, upon his election, overcome with his inadequacy, at first made infinite difficulties. Finally, he agreed to turn all matters of business over to his nephew. He was awestruck and said, "I would never have believed that it could be so easy." It is the same for the princes of the East. When, from that prison where eunuchs have weakened their hearts and spirits and have often left them ignorant even of their estate, these princes are withdrawn to be put on the throne, they are stunned at first; but when they have appointed a vizir, when in their seraglio they have given themselves up to the most

brutal passions, when in the midst of a downtrodden court they have followed their most foolish caprices, they would never have believed that it could be so easy. (*M* 20)

The anecdote of the pope creates a topsy-turvy effect, in which the familiar institution of the Catholic Church is suddenly viewed through Western stereotypes of Eastern despotism. Much as the pope "never believed that it could be so easy" to relegate all the actual work to his nephew, the reader of the *Spirit of the Laws* is left astonished that it could be so easy for Montesquieu to compare a pope with an Eastern despot.

As these three anecdotes suggest, Montesquieu especially associates despotism with strange logics of substitution and repetition that enable one thing or person to take the place of or receive the same treatment as another: the woman who covers up the affair is punished the same way as the woman who had the affair, the boot substitutes for a king, the nephew exercises the power of his uncle, the vizier exercises the power of the sultan. If the West is always in danger of falling into despotism, then Montesquieu's *Spirit of the Laws* itself is always in danger of falling into the substitutive illogic of despotism. What is at issue throughout the *Spirit of the Laws* is the very capacity of anecdotes to stand in for the normal operations of government Montesquieu identifies as despotic, monarchical, and republican. In practice, Montesquieu's anecdotes tend to disarrange Montesquieu's geographical distinctions and trouble the opposition between a despotic East and enlightened West. The anecdotes also highlight a form of arbitrariness and irrationality in intellectual method that underpins the *Spirit of the Laws*, which Montesquieu describes as a matter of setting down principles and seeing individual cases exhibit those principles "as if by themselves." What Montesquieu leaves unanswered is whether the principles themselves are rational—for the teeming multiplicity of human life is always apt to supply cases that may appear to confirm a hypothesis. Montesquieu appears to be quite aware of this source of arbitrariness and irrationality in his own method of investigating the general laws behind the diversity of human laws: midway through the *Spirit of the Laws* he interrupts his own discussion to interpolate an "Invocation to the Muses" to inspire him to complete his system: "Virgins of the Pierian Mount, do you hear the name I give you? Inspire me. I have run a long course. I am crushed by pain, fatigue, and worry. Give my spirit the calm and the gentleness that now flee from me. You are never as divine as when you lead to wisdom and truth through pleasure" (*M* 337). Although the "Invocation" is obviously in jest, it still implies that Montesquieu's system may be more a product of poetic enthusiasm than rational inquiry, and that Montesquieu, far from standing back as a distanced observer of human affairs, may share in the cruel pleasures afforded by his own anecdotes. The Montesquieu who writes the *Spirit of the Laws* is a figure easily overwhelmed not only by the number of "particular cases" that occur to him in light of his principles, but by his own thoughts on the general laws underpinning human laws that "crowd upon" him (*M* 80) and threaten to derange his ideas.[6]

An attention to how anecdotes work (or fail to work) in the *Spirit of the Laws* thus uncovers an illogic that is intrinsic to Enlightenment thought on human nature. Montesquieu's encyclopedic work, from this perspective, comes close to Walter Shandy's "*TRISTRA-pædia*": the unfinished encyclopedia that Tristram says his father compiled as a complete "system of education for me; collecting first for that purpose his own scattered thoughts, counsels, and notions; and binding them together, so as to form an INSTITUTE for the government of my childhood and adolescence" (*LS* 1:445). Judith Hawley has surveyed *Tristram Shandy*'s satire of Enlightenment theories of human nature (most prominently John Locke's account of the association of the ideas) that attempted to reduce human existence to a small number of mechanical principles.[7] Human life in *Tristram Shandy* keeps frustrating the theories and systems designed to explain and order it. In poking fun at the contemporary tendency to derive theories of human nature from anecdotes, however, Sterne also imaginatively inhabits the same process of reasoning about human nature through anecdotes that is one of the characteristic resources of the Enlightenment science of human nature. A work such as the *Spirit of the Laws* and a work such as *Tristram Shandy* can both be read as expressions of the Enlightenment's affinity for anecdotal thinking.

Tristram begins *Tristram Shandy* with a narrative that he explicitly describes as an "anecdote" and attributes to Uncle Toby: the story of how Tristram's own conception was botched when his mother asked "*have you not forgot to wind up the clock?*" when his father was on the point of ejaculation (*LS* 1.2). The resulting confusion of the "animal spirits" that are supposed to guide the "HOMONCULUS" on its way to the womb has contributed to the general disorder that reigns in both Tristram's mind and *Tristram Shandy* itself. *Tristram Shandy* is, among other things, a satire on the use of anecdotes to understand the nature of human beings.[8] Tristram writes of his father, Walter, that "he was all uniformity;—he was systematical, and, like all systematick reasoners, he would move both heaven and earth, and twist and torture every thing in nature to support his hypothesis" (*LS* 1:61). But Walter's systems do have room for anecdotes of unaccountable instances of human behavior, and indeed they are founded upon them. Walter endlessly retells the scandal of Tristram's great aunt Dinah marrying a coachman, because he finds in it a confirmation of his theory that one's Christian name determines one's character. As Tristram writes of his father, "my aunt *Dinah's* affair was a matter of as much consequence to him, as the retrogradation of the planets to *Copernicus:*—The backslidings of *Venus* in her orbit fortified the *Copernican* system, call'd so after his name; and the backslidings of my aunt *Dinah* in her orbit, did the same service in establishing my father's system, which, I trust, will for ever hereafter be call'd the *Shandean System,* after his" (*LS* 1:76). This is why Tristram is only partially correct when he writes that his father was consigned to be "baffled and overthrown in all his little systems and wishes; to behold a train of events perpetually falling out against him, and in so critical and cruel a way, as if they had purposedly been plann'd and pointed against him, merely to insult his speculations" (*LS* 1:64). The accidents of Tristram's conception, delivery, naming, and circumcision may bring pain to Walter, but these retrograde events nevertheless bolster his belief in the determining influence of such things as noses and names on the course of one's life.

The search for the general causes of painful events was a very personal problem for Sterne. In the journal Sterne addressed to Elizabeth Draper, for example, he discussed a painful experience in one of his diary entries that he said "w[ould] make no bad anecdote in T. Shandy's Life." In the letter, as in *Tristram Shandy,* the act of relating anecdotes inevitably leads both the attention of teller and listener toward taboo parts of the body. Sterne relates his discovery of an ailment afflicting "the most painful, & most dangerous of any in the human Body," which a physician informs him is a "venereal Case," a diagnosis that Sterne disputes: "'tis impossible at least to be that, replied I—for I have had no commerce whatever with the Sex—not even with my wife, added I, these 15 Years." After being informed that "these taints of the blood laid dormant 20 Years," however, Sterne understands that he may be "suffering the Chastisement of the grossest Sensualist" for his own backslidings decades before (*LS* 6:178).

The process of finding an explanation for Sterne's diseased member is similar to the process by which characters in *Tristram Shandy* attempt to make sense of the disruptive incidents that break into their world. When a hot chestnut drops into a gap in Phutatorius's breeches and scalds his penis, for example, Phutatorius searches for a reason for the calamity that has befallen him, for, as Tristram observes, "When great or unexpected events fall out upon the stage of this sublunary world—the mind of man, which is an inquisitive kind of a substance, naturally takes a flight, behind the scenes, to see what is the cause and first spring of them." Phutatorius's conjecture as to the reason the chestnut fell into his breeches becomes the general consensus on the matter: namely that Yorick had deliberately thrown the chestnut there in order to make a "sarcastical fling" at a book, written by Phutatorius twenty years before the chestnut incident, entitled *De concubinis retinendis* (*On the Keeping of Concubines*), "the doctrines of which, they said, had inflamed many an honest man in the same place" (*LS* 1:384). The disasters that befall Sterne's and Phutatorius's private parts are both hypothesized to have their causes in events that took place approximately twenty years prior. Both Sterne and Phutatorius also perform the same type of reasoning from present anecdotes to causes that lie far back in the past, both discovering an odd species of causality underlying their injuries, in which prior events are seen to produce effects long after they have happened. The anecdotes provide a way of looking at the world that reveals, or seems to reveal, an underlying order beneath the apparently contingent events falling out into the human world. Unfortunately, *Tristram Shandy* also implies that the search for some order lying behind the welter of anecdotal incidents may be a kind of insanity in itself.

Tristram Shandy thus identifies a form of madness lurking at the very center of the Enlightenment science of human nature. Sterne's work frequently points out the absurdities of trying to establish a system of human nature on the basis of anecdotes. But *Tristram Shandy* is also animated by the ability of anecdotes to generate new ways of thinking about human beings. If Tristram and his family are odd, then perhaps their oddness does in fact reveal something about the nature of human nature. Like Tristram and his father, writers from Locke to Wordsworth were drawn to theorizing about human nature through anecdotal stories. They turned anecdotes into engines for thinking on the nature of human nature, in the process turning the very idea of the human itself into something elusive and strange. I have set out to show in this book that it was the very friction between anecdotal stories and the larger intellectual systems that purport to explain them that helped galvanize new conceptions of human nature over the long eighteenth century. In his inability to stop telling anecdotes or cease thinking about them, Tristram is a true child of the Enlightenment.

Notes

INTRODUCTION

1. "The Speech of Miss Polly Baker," *General Advertiser*, 1.

2. Ibid., 2.

3. Helen Deutsch coins the phrase "anecdotal immortality" to describe the after-life of Samuel Johnson in anecdotes in *Loving Dr. Johnson*, 15, 67. On the eighteenth-century shift from poetry to prose as the medium for attaining literary immortality see Jost, *Prose Immortality*.

4. See "The Speech of Miss Polly Baker," *Boston Weekly Post-Boy*, 1.

5. For a detailed study of the Polly Baker story and the changes it underwent on its travels, see Hall, *Benjamin Franklin and Polly Baker*. On the general phenomenon of "transatlantic stories" see Bannet, *Transatlantic Stories*.

6. See "To the Editor of the Covent-Garden Magazine." This appearance of the Polly Baker story is not mentioned in Hall's study.

7. *Eccentric Biography*, iii-iv. For the telling of the Polly Baker story, see *Eccentric Biography*, 11–14.

8. Annet, *Social Bliss Considered*, 99. For the Polly Baker anecdote, see idem., 99–108.

9. See Raynal, *Histoire philosophique et politique*, 6:257–62. Raynal wrote this work in collaboration with Denis Diderot and others.

10. Diderot, *Political Writings*, 59.

11. Thomas Jefferson to Robert Walsh, 4 December 1818 in Jefferson, *Writings of Thomas Jefferson*, 10:121. Jefferson's anecdote contains at least one misstatement of fact (though whether it is Jefferson's or Franklin's cannot, of course, be determined): the Polly Baker story did not appear in Franklin's *Pennsylvania Gazette* at all. See Hall, *Benjamin Franklin and Polly Baker*, 39.

12. For an overview of the distinctive shape the Enlightenment took in Britain, see Porter, *Enlightenment*.

13. Polly Baker's phrase closely resembles "the laws of nature and of nature's God" invoked in the Declaration of Independence. See Jefferson, *Political Writings*,

102. I. Bernard Cohen considers the possibility that Polly Baker's phrase may have been at the back of Jefferson's mind when he wrote the Declaration of Independence in his *Science and the Founding Fathers*, 302–4. Allen Jayne discusses the deistical implications of the Declaration of Independence's invocation of "the laws of nature and of nature's God," arguing that the phrase "does not refer to the God of revelation or the Bible but to 'Nature's God,' or Bolingbroke's deistic God of natural religion" in *Jefferson's Declaration of Independence*, 38.

14. "Interesting Reflections," 291. Hall writes in his *Benjamin Franklin and Polly Baker* that this article "shows signs of being from some undiscovered London periodical" (173), a periodical neither Hall nor I have been able to track down.

15. Jolles, *Simple Forms*, 153. James Chandler also comments on the connection between Jolles's "case" and the anecdote in his *England in 1819*, 209.

16. Derrida, "Before the Law," 187.

17. *Oxford English Dictionary Online*, s.v. "anecdote."

18. The possibility that the anecdote may have no ties to any surrounding narrative context distinguishes it from the episode that is, as Matthew Garrett writes, "an *integral* but also *extractable* unit of any narrative." See his *Episodic Poetics*, 3. Anecdotes can certainly appear in longer works, such as James Boswell's *Life of Johnson*, but they are also able to stand alone.

19. Novalis, *Philosophical Writings*, 69.

20. For an influential articulation of this thesis see Gallagher, "Rise of Fictionality."

21. For an account of the emergence of the novel as a distinctive genre in the early nineteenth century see H. O. Brown, *Institutions of the English Novel*.

22. Labov emphasizes oral stories as discursive events in his "Speech Actions and Reactions," 219–47.

23. My thanks to Jenny Davidson for pointing this out to me.

24. Genette, *Narrative Discourse*, 116.

25. Genette writes illuminatingly on the conjunction of iteration and singularity that characterizes a favorite anecdote told repeatedly by Françoise the cook in Proust's *À la recherche du temps perdu* (1913–27). The anecdote is about a visitor who, complaining about the early hour the family had lunch, was given the bewildering explanation by Marcel's father that it was a Saturday. The visitor was not to know that the family regularly had lunch an hour early on Saturdays, so as to allow Françoise to make it to the Roussainville market. Genette writes on Proust's treatment of this anecdote in the world of the novel: "All that is left is for the narrator to treat that element of the Sabbath ritual like the others, that is, in the iterative mode, in order to 'iteratize,' as it were, the deviant event in its turn, in accord with this irresistible process: singular event—repetitive narrating—iterative narrative (of that narrating). Marcel tells (at) one time how Françoise told often what happened undoubtedly only once: or how to turn a unique event into the subject of an iterative narrative." Genette, *Narrative Discourse*, 127.

26. Linné [Linnaeus], *Nemesis Divina*, 104.

27. On Stendhal's use of anecdotes as seeds for novels see Coe, "Anecdote and the Novel."

28. See, for example, Bent, "Illuminating Power of Anecdote."

29. D'Israeli, *Dissertation on Anecdotes*, 16. For discussions of D'Israeli as a theorist of subliterary genres such as the anecdote see Connell, "Bibliomania"; Ferris, "Antiquarian Authorship"; and London, *Literary History Writing*, 81–110.

30. Croce, *History as the Story*, 119.

31. Todorov, *In Defense*, 7. The brackets are included in the text of the English translation.

32. Pocock, *Barbarism and Religion*, 1:9.

33. See, for example, the various chapters in Roy S. Porter and Mikuláš Teich's collection *The Enlightenment in National Context*.

34. See Sorkin, *Religious Enlightenment*.

35. M. Brown, *Irish Enlightenment*, 23.

36. On the interplay between individualist and communitarian concepts of the human in the long eighteenth century see Yousef, *Isolated Cases*.

37. Habermas, *Structural Transformation*.

38. Siskin and Warner, "This Is Enlightenment," 11.

39. Dan Edelstein criticizes Siskin and Warner on this point in his short book *The Enlightenment*, arguing "To locate the singularity of the Enlightenment, we must also consider *what* was mediated, not just *how* it was" (11).

40. Fludernik, *Towards a "Natural" Narratology*, 81.

41. Habermas, *Structural Transformation*, 28.

42. For a study of how the eighteenth-century novel, like the anecdote, discovers strangeness and wonder in the everyday, see Kareem, *Eighteenth-Century Fiction*.

43. For a discussion of the room as a metaphor for the mind in Locke's *Essay*, see Silver, *Mind Is a Collection*, 31–32. For a wide-ranging account of the room as a metaphor for the mind across the long eighteenth century, see Pasanek, *Metaphors of Mind*, 205–26.

44. On the importance of gentlemanly conduct to the production of scientific truth see Shapin, *Social History of Truth*.

45. Blair, *Lectures on Rhetoric*, 405.

46. For a useful table setting variants of the anecdote of Newton and the apple, as told by William Stuckley, Voltaire, Isaac D'Israeli, and others, see Martínez, *Science Secrets*, 64. For the anecdote of Johnson kicking the stone to refute Berkeley see Boswell, *Life of Samuel Johnson*, 248.

47. For a recent study of the role "systems" play in the modern intellectual disciplines see Siskin, *System*.

48. D'Israeli, *Dissertation on Anecdotes*, 3.

49. For a discussion of the close connections between anecdotes and the ethos of conversation—which requires any conclusions about the matter under discussion

to remain provisional and subject to further discussion and debate—see Simpson, *Academic Postmodern*, 53–71. Simpson associates the anecdote in both contemporary cultural criticism and in the literary cultures with the long eighteenth century with a provisional conclusion that allows for a sense of progress in conversations that might otherwise seem circuitous and interminable: "when it is well deployed, the anecdote serves to bring to temporary closure or summation the otherwise infinite possible series of interpretations that come with participation in the culture of conversation. It provides a temporary clincher, or landing place, which we know to be only provisional, and very much a function of the skill and tact of the teller, and hence itself dramatic, within the orbit of the voice" (53).

50. Fineman, "History of the Anecdote," 61.

51. I have found the following accounts of the development of the word "anecdote" from its origins in secret history especially helpful: Annabel Patterson's account of the history of the word in *Early Modern Liberalism*, 156–59, and Lionel Gossman's in "Anecdote and History," 151–55.

52. *Greek-English Lexicon*, s.v. "ἀνέκδοτος."

53. For studies of secret history see McKeon, *Secret History of Domesticity*, 469–620, and Bullard, *Politics of Disclosure*. On the circulation of the scandalous "anecdotes" of secret history in both oral and written circuits in eighteenth-century Paris see Darnton, *Devil in the Holy Water*, 99–108.

54. Chambers, *Cyclopaedia* (1728), s.v. "Anecdotes, anecdota."

55. Swift, *Gulliver's Travels*, 299–300.

56. Johnson, *Dictionary of the English Language* (1773), s.v. "anecdote."

57. *Dictionnaire de l'Académie Française* (1694), s.v. "anecdotes." For both the quotations from the *Dictionnaire de l'Académie Française* I am using Virginia Scott's translations of the same entries in *Women on the Stage in Early Modern France*, 12.

58. *Dictionnaire de l'Académie Française* (1740), s.v. "anecdotes."

59. On Hume's distinction between an authentic, "manly" history and a set of feminized pseudo-historical genres including the anecdote see K. Temple, "'Manly Composition,'" 263–82.

60. Tierney-Hynes, "Hume, Romance," 645.

61. Christensen, *Practicing Enlightenment*, 109.

62. Although Hume is attempting to draw a clear distinction between history and "novels and romances," the title pages for early eighteenth-century works of fiction in fact used all three of these terms interchangeably, as Leah Orr shows in detail in *Novel Ventures*, 16–20. Orr finds that the term "secret history," however, had clearer generic implications, denoting a work uncovering the scandalous doings of public figures through either an allegorical or a "straight" historical narrative.

63. For the original French see the preface to Varillas, *Les Anecdotes de Florence*, n.p. For the translation see Varillas, *Anecdota Heterotiaka*, n.p.

64. My translation. The original text reads "Les anecdotes sont un champ resserré où l'on glane après la vaste moisson de l'histoire" (*V* 13C:1).

65. Junod, *"Writing the Lives of Painters,"* 59–62.

66. Chambers, *Cyclopaedia* (1778–88), s.v. "Anecdotes, anecdota."

67. Edgeworth, *Castle Rackrent, Irish Bulls, Ennui,* 5.

68. D'Israeli, *Dissertation on Anecdotes,* vi, 3.

69. R. Smith, "Language of Human Nature," 89, qtd. in J. Davidson, *Breeding,* 2. On the wide variety of genres implicated in the study of human nature, from the novel to works we now think as primarily philosophical, see Frasca-Spada, "Science and Conversation."

70. Locke closely follows Ménage's original French text, which reads as follows: "Quand cet Abbé de saint Martin vint au monde, il avoit si peu la figure d'un homme qu'il ressembloit plûtôt à un monstre. On fut quelque tems à délibérer si on le batiseroit. Cependant il fut batisé & on le déclara homme par provision. Il étoit si disgracié de la nature, qu'on l'a apellé toute sa vie l'*Abbé Malotru.*" Ménage, *Menagiana,* 1:278.

71. For a study of how three Enlightenment writers negotiated the observed diversity of human behavior, see D. Carey, *Locke, Shaftesbury, and Hutcheson.*

72. Croce, *History as the Story,* 119–20.

73. In emphasizing the historical specificity of the Enlightenment idea of human nature, this project shares the same impulse motivating Peter de Bolla's recent book *The Architecture of Concepts,* which emphasizes the noncommensurability between the eighteenth-century concept of "human rights" and our own. However, where de Bolla's method is based on keyword searches of *Eighteenth-Century Collections Online* to discover the words that are typically associated with rights in the period, my book rests much more on more traditional practices of close reading.

74. J. E. H. Smith, *Nature, Human Nature,* 7–8.

75. Outram, *Enlightenment,* 78.

76. De Quincey, "Last Days of Immanuel Kant," 139. I cite the anecdote as it originally appeared in *Blackwood's Edinburgh Magazine.* Deleuze and Guattari cite David Masson's 1890 edition of De Quincey's *Collected Writings* (*What Is Philosophy?* 222n8).

77. Deleuze and Guattari, *What Is Philosophy?,* 72.

78. Ibid., 73.

79. See Nussbaum, *Limits of the Human,* 1.

80. Nash, *Wild Enlightenment,* 3.

81. J. Davidson, *Breeding,* 1.

82. For a study of recent criticism attentive to form, as well as an argument that the idea of form cannot be defined apart from the particular disciplines and to particular kinds of inquiry from which it emerges, see Kramnick and Nersessian, "Form and Explanation."

83. Shklovsky, *Theory of Prose,* 206–9.

84. See Hayot, *Hypothetical Mandarin,* 42.

85. Agamben, *Homo Sacer*, 21. Agamben's discussion of belonging and inclusion is inspired by Alain Badiou's use of set theory for thinking about ontological and political questions in *Being and Event*, in particular Badiou's concept of the "event" as "a multiple whose belonging to the situation [both a mathematical set and a state of affairs] is undecidable" (201). Only the basics of set theory are needed to get a grasp on what Agamben means by "belonging" and "inclusion," which have specific meanings in set theory. As Agamben briefly explains, belonging and inclusion are separate concepts in set theory: to say that "*x* belongs to set *y*" is to say that *x* is an element of *y*, and "*a* is included in set *b*" is to say that all the elements of set *a* are also elements of set *b*. An element can belong to a set and not be included in it. Conversely, a set can be included in another set and not belong to it.

86. Agamben, *Homo Sacer*, 21–22.

87. Helen Deutsch uses the phrase "Exemplary Eccentricity" to describe Samuel Johnson and the anecdotes about him, which nicely captures the way anecdotes hang between the example and the exception. See Deutsch, *Loving Dr. Johnson*, 24.

88. See Fludernik, *Towards a "Natural" Narratology*, 85–86, On the *exemplum*, see Lyons, *Exemplum*, and on exemplary figures in humanist writing see Hampton, *Writing from History*.

89. On the dissonance between example and precept, see the essays in Gelley, *Unruly Examples*.

90. For a reflection on and defense of the use of anecdotes in literary theory see Gallop, *Anecdotal Theory*.

91. A prominent exception is Alan Liu's careful reflections on New Historicism in his *Local Transcendence*, a phrase that Liu uses to describe the sense often produced in New Historicism and related forms of cultural criticism that an anecdotal detail has unlocked a larger cultural law. Liu observes that recent critics outwardly committed to the local and the particular often "recognize this witching moment of local transcendence in their works. In some of their most meditative passages, they pause on the threshold of transcendence aware that Keatsian magic casements of detail are about to open on a foam of perilous seas, in faery lands forlorn" (129).

92. Gallagher and Greenblatt, *Practicing New Historicism*, 51.

93. Jacques Derrida's remarks on the tension between the singularity of any individual performative speech act and its repeatability in any number of different contexts apply equally well to the anecdote as a report of an event as well as a linguistic event in itself: "We should first be clear on what constitutes the status of 'occurrence' or the eventhood of an event that entails in its allegedly present and singular emergence the intervention of an utterance [*énoncé*] that in itself can be only repetitive or citational in its structure, or rather, since those two words may lead to confusion: iterable." Derrida, "Signature Event Context," 17–18.

94. Gallagher and Greenblatt, *Practicing New Historicism*, 19.

95. My book obviously goes against Jesse Molesworth's argument in *Chance and the Eighteenth-Century Novel* that "narrative, by its very nature, is an exceptionally

poor medium for enlightening" (3). In this revisionist book, Molesworth draws attention to the way narrative, with its attraction to the anomalous case that departs from the norm and its teleological bias, is at cross-purposes with the turn toward probabilistic thinking in the Enlightenment. My understanding of the Enlightenment, however, emphasizes the tendency toward naturalistic explanations of phenomena in both the human and natural worlds. Narrative was an important means of "enlightening" in this sense, for anecdotal narratives of human behavior could be mined for insights much as reports of animal behavior or experiments in the laboratory could. However, I have found Molesworth's book useful for its emphasis on the magical dimensions of "realist" fictions and stories that pass as "real."

ONE. ANECDOTAL EXPERIMENTS

1. D'Israeli, *Dissertation on Anecdotes*, 27–28.

2. My translation. The original French reads "Parmi nous combien de livres ne sont fondés que sur des bruits de ville, ainsi que la physique ne fut fondée que sur des chimères répétées de siècle en siècle, jusqu'à notre temps!" (*V* 38:281).

3. For an argument that experimental practice helped shape the early novel as a genre see Bender, *Ends of Enlightenment*, 23–37.

4. Auerbach, *Mimesis*, 292.

5. Black, *Of Essays and Reading*, 67–85. On the commonplace book tradition in the Renaissance and its relation to classical rhetoric see Moss, *Printed Commonplace Books*.

6. I have de-italicized the original text as reproduced in the Nidditch edition of *An Essay Concerning Human Understanding* as the introduction is italicized as a whole.

7. Quoted in Black, *Of Essays and Reading*, 93.

8. Tyers, *Historical Essay on Mr. Addison*, 18. Tyers tells the story on the authority of Jacob Tonson, who apparently always said he saw the *Dictionnaire* open on Addison's desk when he came to visit him—although the intervening years between Tonson's death in 1736 and the publication of *An Historical Essay on Mr. Addison* in 1783 makes one wonder about the reliability of Tyers's account. Even so, Donald F. Bond, in his notes to his edition of the *Spectator*, observes, "Many of the historical anecdotes in the *Spectator* can in fact be traced to the [Bayle's] *Dictionary*" (*S* 1:380).

9. On the continuity between alchemy and the emergent discipline of chemistry see W. R. Newman, *Atoms and Alchemy*.

10. Dear, *Discipline and Experience*, 19–20.

11. Dear himself in the title to one of his essays describes these narratives of natural philosophical experiments as "anecdotes"—underlying the resemblance between the report of the premeditated experiment and the anecdote's narrative of a spontaneous event in human life in his "Narratives, Anecdotes, and Experiments." On the practice of "virtual witnessing" through textual accounts of

experimental events as a solution to the limitation on the number of people who could witness an experiment directly, see Shapin and Schaffer, *Leviathan and the Air-Pump,* 60–65.

12. Chico, *Experimental Imagination,* 17–43.

13. Quoted in Bender, *Ends of Enlightenment,* 27.

14. Wotton, *Reflections,* 15–16.

15. Bacon, *New Organon,* 147–48.

16. On Locke's interest in natural philosophy and involvement in Royal Society circles see Anstey, *John Locke and Natural Philosophy;* Walmsley, *Locke's* Essay; and Forde, *Locke, Science, and Politics.*

17. For a study of the Locke-Molyneux correspondence and the revisions to the *Essay Concerning Human Understanding* it occasioned, see Kramnick, "Locke's Desire." For an account of the Molyneux-Locke epistolary relationship focused on Molyneux's end of the correspondence, see my own "William Molyneux."

18. William Molyneux to John Locke, 2 March 1693, in Locke, *Correspondence of John Locke,* 4:651.

19. Cheselden, "Account of some Observations," 447.

20. For an account of the surgical technique of "couching" see Degenaar, *Molyneux's Problem,* 58. Degenaar notes that although the operation might initially succeed, the "couched" eye often became infected, blinding the patient once again. In addition, the clouded lens could easily return to its original position, rendering the operation useless.

21. Cheselden, "Account of some Observations," 448.

22. Tunstall, *Blindness and Enlightenment,* 5.

23. Riskin, *Science,* 20.

24. My translation. The original text reads: "Ou on n'a pas donné le tems à l'organe dioptrique ébranlé, de se remettre dans son affiéte naturelle; ou à force de tourmenter le nouveau voyant, on lui a fait dire ce qu'on étoit bien aise qu'il dît." La Mettrie, *Histoire naturelle de l'âme,* 352–53.

25. Gendler, *Thought Experiment,* 12.

26. Ross Hamilton sees Locke's anecdote of the Indian Philosopher—and the *Essay* as a whole—as a crucial moment in the long-term shift from a notion of "accident" as a phenomenon secondary to "substance" to a notion of accidents as the primary sources of information through which human beings make sense of the world. See his *Accident,* 118–20.

27. For examples of other tellings of the king of Siam anecdote in the context of the eighteenth-century debate on miracles see Bitzer, "'Indian Prince' in Miracle Arguments."

28. Shapin, *Social History of Truth,* 244.

29. For a study of Locke's use of travel literature in general as evidence for the science of man see D. Carey, *Locke, Shaftesbury, and Hutcheson,* 69–97.

30. W. Temple, *Memoirs of what Past,* 57–58.

31. Keenleyside, *Animals and Other People*, 128.

32. L. Brown, *Fables of Modernity*, 249.

33. Quoted in ibid., 250.

34. W. Temple, *Memoirs of what Past*, 57. Temple reports Prince Maurice's eagerness to die on the authority of the Prince of Orange, who would become William III of England.

35. Patterson, *Early Modern Liberalism*, 173.

36. For Addison's original oration, see the University of Oxford, *Theatri Oxoniensis Encaenia*.

37. See L. Stewart, *Rise of Public Science*, 92. For studies of the relationship between the *Spectator* and the new science see Picciotto, *Labors of Innocence*, 566–83, and Cowan, "Curious Mr. Spectator."

38. Addison, *Interesting Anecdotes*, 2:158.

39. For a reading of *Spectator* 46 as a self-reflective commentary on the *Spectator* project itself see Knight, "Bibliography and the Shape," 244–48.

40. Adam Smith would later describe the fear of death as "one of the most important principles in human nature." See Smith, *Theory of Moral Sentiments*, 16.

41. *Spy upon the Spectator*, iv. The original lines are in italics but as the whole preface is in italics I have de-italicized the lines.

42. Broughton, *Mottoes of the Spectators*, 7.

43. For Petronius's telling of the story see Petronius, *Satyricon*, 101–4. Helen Deutsch discusses Petronius's story in the context of the long line of attempts to exhume Samuel Johnson, literally in the case of his autopsy, and figuratively in the telling of anecdotes about him in *Loving Dr. Johnson*, 155–94.

44. Ligon, *True & Exact History*, 55.

45. Ibid., 65.

46. Some of the many retellings and adaptations of the Inkle and Yarico story are collected in Felsenstein, *English Trader, Indian Maid*.

47. Peter Hulme discusses the resemblance between Inkle and Yarico and the Dido and Aeneas story in *Colonial Encounters*, 249–55. Heidi Hutner notes the story's resemblance to the Pocahontas myth in *Colonial Women*, 107–8.

48. *Oxford English Dictionary Online*, see s.v. "counterpart, *n*" and s.v. "indenture, *n*."

49. Horejsi, "'Counterpart to the Ephesian Matron,'" 204.

50. Steele himself directly profited from the slave trade as he inherited a Barbados slave plantation from his first wife, Margaret Ford Stretch, when she died in 1707. See Blanchard, "Richard Steele's West Indian Plantation."

51. See Felsenstein, *English Trader, Indian Maid*, 81.

52. Baucom, *Specters of the Atlantic*, 11.

53. See also Sophie Gee's reading of the tears of joy that Mr. Spectator weeps in the Royal Exchange in *Spectator* 60 at seeing the bustling commerce before him: "Though they appear to mimic the superabundance of the economy he describes,

in actual fact they disrupt it. While they are symbolically uncontaminated, they have no value: they are pure surplus—and this is what makes them conspicuous in an economy of equivalence." Gee, *Making Waste*, 140. In his *Spectacular Suffering*, Ramesh Mallipeddi draws attention to how Mr. Spectator's tear helps create a community between himself and Arietta (and presumably the *Spectator*'s readers as well): "His sympathetic tear for Yarico's distress reveals his imaginary relation to the object of suffering and works to produce a good society . . . Arietta and Mr. Spectator are brought together via their inarticulate compassion for Yarico" (59).

54. Wylie Sypher suggests that Addison may have picked up the story from "someone returned to London coffee-houses from the West Indies." See Sypher, *Guinea's Captive Kings*, 139. Both the anecdote of Inkle and Yarico and the anecdote of the two slaves in love with the same woman were subsequently incorporated into Raynal's *Histoire philosophique et politique*.

55. For a reading of this number of the *Spectator* in conjunction with *Spectator* 11 see Brycchan Carey, "Accounts of Savage Nations." Wylie Sypher in *Guinea's Captive Kings* also compares the two numbers, commenting that "whereas one is wistful, the other is violent" (138).

56. For a reading of the Enlightenment concept of aesthetic taste as underpinned by the repressed knowledge of slavery as an institution that produced luxuries to be consumed and an example of human abjection against which men and women of taste could define themselves, see Gikandi, *Slavery and the Culture*. My own sense is that an awareness of the culture of taste's imbrication in slavery is not as repressed to the extent that Gikandi suggests across the long eighteenth century. At least an inchoate awareness of the link between slavery and taste is implied by the way miscellaneous projects like the *Spectator* shuttled between anecdotes of slaves in the New World and anecdotes of fashionable London.

57. For a reading of the *Female Spectator*'s revision of the *Spectator* see Bannet, "Haywood's Spectator." For a study of how periodicals over the long eighteenth century created spaces for women's learning see my own "Periodicals and the Problem."

58. Erin Mackie discusses the extensive attention given to the hoop petticoat in the *Spectator* in *Market à la Mode*, 104–43.

59. Picciotto, *Labors of Innocence*, 573.

60. On the *Female Spectator*'s encouragement of women to study natural history, see Girten, "Unsexed Souls."

61. On the centrality of gender difference to the early periodical, see Shevelow, *Women and Print Culture*, and Maurer, *Proposing Men*.

62. Anthony Pollock in *Gender and the Fictions* writes of Haywood's anecdote of the outsized sword, "it is precisely in Haywood's attempt to 'outdo' the spectatorial mechanisms at work in Addison and Steele—through a process of excess, exacerbation, and parodic juxtaposition—that she foregrounds the gendered partiality and violence obscured by her predecessor's claims to benign neutrality" (155).

63. Manushag N. Powell shows how Haywood uses the parrot eidolon to reclaim and reframe misogynistic associations of women's speech with the idle and unthinking speech of the parrot in *Performing Authorship*, 131–92.

TWO. HUME AND THE LAWS OF ANECDOTE

1. Mossner, *Life of David Hume*, 28.

2. Forbes, *Hume's Philosophical Politics*, 127.

3. Richetti, *Philosophical Writing*, 42.

4. Livingston, *Hume's Philosophy of Common Life*.

5. Annette Baier writes in *Progress of Sentiments*: "The 'real connexion' that Book One and the 'Appendix' despaired of finding is not to be found by fragmenting a person-history into separate perceptions, out of physical or social space, but by seeing persons as other persons see them, as living (really connected) bodies, with real biological connections to other persons, in a common social space, depending on them for much of our knowledge, depending on them for the sustaining of our pleasures and for the comfort in our pain, depending on them also for what independence and autonomy we come to acquire" (141).

6. See James Caulfeild, 1st Earl of Charlemont, "Anecdotes of Hume," RIA, MS 12/R/7, f.497. This manuscript was written by Caulfeild for his sons, Francis (1775–1863), James (1776–1793), and Henry (1779–1862), whom he addresses as "My dear Boys." He does, however, forbid them from publishing the manuscript, telling them "it may be necessary that I should demand of you, and of your Posterity, that your filial Partiality shou'd never induce you to make them public." See "Anecdotes of Hume," f.3.

7. Ibid., f.527.

8. Ibid., f.511.

9. Ibid., f.507. My translation (following Charlemont's original punctuation) is as follows: "Ah, Madame—Madame—I am suffocating *with* love! and then again He groaned—Dear—Dear Lady—I am alone—lost—annihilated!—Oh, as to being annihilated, said she, that is nothing but a very natural operation of your system— But raise yourself for goodness sake—I do not want to see you suffer any more in this posture—come—raise yourself, I beg you—I order you—."

10. Here I am summarizing the overarching argument of Livingston's *Hume's Philosophy of Common Life*.

11. Baier, *Progress of Sentiments*, 119.

12. On the frequent targeting of disabled and deformed people in the comic literature of the eighteenth century see Dickie, *Cruelty and Laughter*, 45–110. On the place of "defects" in Enlightenment ideas of the human more generally see Nussbaum, *Limits of the Human*, and the essays in Deutsch and Nussbaum, *Defects*.

13. *Oxford English Dictionary Online*, s.v. "bubble, *n*." For a useful overview of the metaphorical possibilities of the "bubble" see Kareem, "Enlightenment Bubbles, Romantic Worlds."

14. Caulfield, "Anecdotes of Hume," RIA, MS 12/R/7, f.500. Quoted in Coventry and Mazza, "Humeaneyes," 9.

15. See Coventry and Mazza, "Humeaneyes."

16. This quotation appears in a collection of manuscript documents, in the possession of William Zachs, by Alexander Stenhouse, Hume's nephew (also named David), and others, that seem to have been prepared for a projected Hume biography that was never published. The description is prefaced by a note that describes two portraits of Hume by Allan Ramsay and suggests that the comments may be based on Hume's appearance in the Ramsay portraits. See Zachs, *David Hume,* 60. I have omitted the note in brackets noting that a word has been deleted between "it" and "became" in the original manuscript. Quoted in Coventry and Mazza, "Humeaneyes," 8.

17. For the story of the falling-out between Hume and Rousseau see Zaretsky and Scott, *Philosophers' Quarrel.*

18. Jean-Jacques Rousseau to David Hume, 10 July 1766, in Hume, *Concise and Genuine Account,* 52–53. Quoted in Coventry and Mazza, "Humeaneyes," 10.

19. Mossner, *Life of Hume,* 214.

20. Duncan, *Scott's Shadow,* 119.

21. Livingston describes Hume as a writer apt to play "the *fool*" in *Philosophical Melancholy and Delirium,* 39, and quotes the lines from the *Enquiry Concerning Human Understanding* on the same page.

22. Ibid., 23.

23. This description comes from Samuel Richardson's letter to Lady Bradshaigh, 9 October 1756, in S. Richardson, *Selected Letters of Samuel Richardson,* 329.

24. Christina Lupton remarks on the way that the story of the porter's letter helps Hume draw attention to the ways our sense of reality is mediated by technologies of writing. See her *Knowing Books,* 78–80.

25. D'Épinay, *Memoirs and Correspondence,* 3:295. Quoted in Mossner, *Life of Hume,* 444.

26. Deleuze, "He Stuttered," 28.

27. In conversation with Claire Parnet, Deleuze remarked that an empiricist might analyze a "Blue-eyed boy" into "a boy, some blue, and eyes—an assemblage. AND . . . AND . . . AND, stammering. Empiricism is nothing other than this." See Deleuze and Parnet, *Dialogues II,* 59. Quoted (with a slightly different translation) in Coventry and Mazza, "Humeaneyes," 3. For a wide-ranging discussion of representations of stuttering and stammering, see Shell, *Stutter.*

28. Baier, *Progress of Sentiments,* 30.

29. On Hume as an early theorist of narrative see Valenza, "Editing the Self." I have drawn on Valenza's reading of Hume's application of the relations of resemblance, contiguity, and cause and effect to the analysis of narrative in the discussion that follows.

30. See Jakobson, "Two Types of Language," 111.

31. This is not the same thing as arguing that there is no such thing as a cause or suggesting that people can get by without an intuition of cause and effect. For the argument that Hume accepted the reality of causation see Strawson, *Secret Connexion*, which argues that most commentators on Hume have confused the epistemological argument that the nature of causation cannot be known with the ontological argument that causal relationships do not exist (10–11).

32. Valenza, "Editing the Self," 140.

33. I have de-italicized the original quotation.

34. Richetti, *Philosophical Writing*, 209. Quoted in Potkay, *Fate of Eloquence*, 183.

35. See Potkay, *Fate of Eloquence*, 181–85.

36. Catherine Gallagher and Stephen Greenblatt note that the anecdote is a generator of *energia*, although they deny that the vividness the anecdote produces is "only a matter of rhetoric." See their *Practicing New Historicism*, 29.

37. For an overview of how Hume responded to the widening of the sense of history, beyond the study of great political events, to embrace social history and the history of the arts and sciences in the *History of England*, see M. S. Phillips, *Society and Sentiment*, 31–78.

38. Novalis, *Philosophical Writings*, 69.

39. Pocock, *Barbarism and Religion*, 2:184.

40. Noggle, "Literary Taste as Counter-Enlightenment," 624.

41. The material from which Hume created his anecdote appears in Melville, *Memoires of Sir James Melvil*, 50–53. In the original narrative, Melville does not report his thoughts on leaving Elizabeth but informs Mary Queen of Scots of his belief that Elizabeth means no good to her after a longer discussion.

42. Smollett, "*History of Great Britain*," 394.

43. Puttenham, *Art of English Poesy*, 323.

44. Johnson, *Dictionary of the English Language* (1755), s.v. "preposterous."

45. Blackwell, "Preposterous Hume," 95.

46. Warburton, *Remarks on Mr. David Hume's Essay*, 9. In this book, Warburton pretends that someone else well read in his own works has sent him the remarks on Hume's work without making his identity known. Richard Hurd tells the story of how Warburton sent his collected remarks on Hume's *Natural History of Religion* to him so that he could prepare them for publication in his *A Discourse by way of General Preface to the Quarto Edition of Bishop Warburton's Works*, 81. Warburton's quip is quoted in Potkay, *Fate of Eloquence*, 162.

47. Gigante, *Taste*, 58.

48. "*Mr. Hume's Dissertations continued*," 214.

THREE. ANECDOTES IN THE WAKE OF THE *ENDEAVOUR*

1. Boswell, "Boswelliana," MS Hyde 51 Case 9 (5), f.88. Houghton Library, Harvard University. I have slightly modified this quotation for clarity: in the original the

word "All" appears before the word "Everything." A very freely edited version of the anecdote appears in Boswell, *Boswelliana*, 271.

2. Kippis, *Life of Captain James Cook,* 497.

3. Burke, *Selected Letters of Edmund Burke,* 102.

4. See Kerr, *Census of Alexander Shaw's Catalogue,* 3.

5. Shaw, *Catalogue of the Different Specimens,* 8.

6. Kerr, *Census of Alexander Shaw's Catalogue,* 4.

7. Banks recorded another instance of barkcloth being unraveled. For Anne Salmond's explanation of the ceremony's significance, see note 51 below.

8. Lamb, *Preserving the Self,* 113. On the "minute particular" in eighteenth-century accounts of South Sea voyages see also Lamb, "Minute Particulars." Like Lamb, Simon Schaffer questions the common identification of James Cook's voyages of the discovery with the advent of a new "scientific" approach to the observation of the South Pacific in his "'On Seeing Me Write.'"

9. Greene, "Island Logic," 141.

10. Daston, "Description by Omission," 13.

11. Linné [Linnaeus], *Linnaeus' Philosophia Botanica,* 220.

12. Linné [Linnaeus], *Nemesis Divina,* 136–37.

13. On Linneaus's use of the anecdote form see Fleming, "Perfect Story."

14. See Green and Cook, "Observations made."

15. David Paxman discusses how Europeans in the Pacific interpreted unfamiliar gestures like Terapo's self-wounding in "'Distance Getting Close.'"

16. V. Smith, *Intimate Strangers,* 153.

17. Pratt, *Imperial Eyes,* 62.

18. See Williamson, *Social and Political Systems,* 3:81–82.

19. Rennie, "Point Venus 'Scene,'" 240.

20. Anne Salmond in *Aphrodite's Island* identifies the "Scene" as part of a ceremony performed by the Tahitian *Ariori* sect. Nicholas Thomas in *Discoveries,* on the other hand, interprets the performance as a parody of the visitors' own proclivity for having sex in public (159). Salmond's and Thomas's divergent interpretations show that the "true" meaning of the events that the voyagers witnessed and recorded in the form of anecdotes is by no means settled now. For a study focused on the role similar accounts of Polynesian sexuality played in helping Europeans define themselves in a rapidly globalizing age see Cheek, *Sexual Antipodes.*

21. Thomas, *Discoveries,* 71.

22. Obeyesekere, *Cannibal Talk,* 53.

23. Boswell, *Boswell: The Ominous Years,* 341.

24. Two unauthorized histories also told versions of the story of the *Endeavour* voyage: the anonymous *Journal of a Voyage Round the World in His Majesty's* Endeavour (1771) and Sydney Parkinson's *A Journal of a Voyage to the South Seas* (1773), but these did not achieve the same circulation or cultural cachet as Hawkesworth's book.

25. See Kaufmann, *Borrowings from the Bristol Library,* 113.

26. Rennie, "Point Venus 'Scene,'" 234.

27. "Review of New Publications," 28.

28. "Histories of the Tête à Tête annexed," 457.

29. "Heroic Epistle from the Injured Harriet," 42.

30. Dening, *Mr Bligh's Bad Language*, 262.

31. Pindar, *Peter's Prophecy*, 27.

32. On this network see G. Russell, "'Entertainment of Oddities.'"

33. C.H., "Banksiana written at the request of my Friend Dawson Turner Esq of Great Yarmouth," RP 5146 British Library, London, ff.2–3. This manuscript was prepared for Dawson Turner, who was gathering materials for a projected biography of Joseph Banks, which never came to fruition. This manuscript is now in private hands, having been sold in a Southeby's auction, but a photocopy exists in the British Library, from which I quote.

34. *"Bozzy and Piozzi,"* 411.

35. C.H., "Banksiana," ff.24–25.

36. John Gascoigne provides an extensive survey of Banks's close involvement in colonial projects in *Science in the Service*.

37. W. H. R., "Anecdotes and Bons Mots," 345.

38. Thomas, "Licensed Curiosity," 123.

39. For Latour's account of the "center of calculation" see Bruno Latour, *Science in Action*, 215–58. David Philip Miller argues that Banks's botanical and imperial activities constitute an example of one of Latour's "centers of calculation," in "Joseph Banks, Empire." For a further development of Miller's argument see Fulford, Lee, and Kitson, *Literature, Science and Exploration*, 33–45.

40. W. H. R., "Anecdotes and Bons Mots," 345.

41. *Authentic Narrative of the Dissensions*, 65.

42. Ibid., 66.

43. On the dispute see Heilbron, "Mathematician's Mutiny, with Morals."

44. Pindar, *Peter's Prophecy*, 11.

45. Charles Blagden to Sir Joseph Banks, 27 December 1783, in Banks, *Scientific Correspondence*, 2:3.

46. These are the titles to chapters 3 and 4 of Gascoigne, *Joseph Banks*.

47. Sir Joseph Banks to Sir Everard Home, 30 September 1783, in *Scientific Correspondence*, 3:43.

48. Dunbar, *Essays on the History*, 26.

49. For a general discussion of the use of voyages to the Pacific in the Enlightenment science of man see Withers, *Placing the Enlightenment*, 136–63.

50. Millar, *Origin of the Distinction*, 94.

51. Ibid., 99.

52. In *Aphrodite's Island*, Salmond writes that ceremony was, for the Tahitians, "a way of at once acknowledging and containing their *mana* (ancestral power) . . . unwrapping bark cloth from a person or thing released their *mana*, and when a

woman was unwrapped in this way, this was a ceremonial act rather than a gesture of sexual enticement" (166–67).

53. Home, *Sketches of the History of Man*, 1:42.

54. Dampier, *New Voyage Around the World*, 464.

55. For a study of the development of the concept of "race" in the eighteenth century, see Hudson, "From 'Nation' to 'Race.'" Roxann Wheeler argues that stadial theories helped generate later biological theories of human difference in *Complexion of Race*, 176–233. As Wheeler notes, Kames "hedged" on the question of whether the perceived disparity in social progress between peoples inhabiting different areas of the world "resulted from the stimulus of a people's nature or from the influence of climate" (187).

56. "Sketches of the History of Man," 464.

57. Boswell, *Boswell's Journal*, 96.

58. For a discussion of the encounter between Monboddo and Johnson see Nash, *Wild Enlightenment*, chapter 5. For accounts of the extent to which Boswell and Johnson's tour of Scotland was imaginatively intertwined with James Cook's first voyage to the Pacific see Rogers, *Johnson and Boswell*, and Henare, *Museums, Anthropology and Imperial Exchange*, 49–73.

59. See L. Brown, *Homeless Dogs and Melancholy Apes*, 28.

60. Monboddo, *On the Origin and Progress*, 1:289. For a discussion of the significance of Monboddo's ideas for eighteenth-century conceptions of the human/animal distinction more generally, see L. Brown, *Homeless Dogs and Melancholy Apes*, 55–58. Brown frames Monboddo's theories as a natural extension of prior arguments for the innate sensibility of the great apes and observes that his theory is built, like so many eighteenth-century writings on the "Orang Outang," on a "redaction and collation of prior anecdotes and observations" (55).

61. Monboddo, *On the Origin and Progress*, 1:262.

62. Boswell, *Boswell for the Defence*, 146.

63. Monboddo, *Antient Metaphysics*, 4:58. For an account of Johnson's knowledge of and views on the Scottish Enlightenment in general see O'Brien, "Johnson's View of the Scottish Enlightenment."

64. Boswell, *Boswell for the Defence*, 68–69.

65. Poovey, *History of the Modern Fact*, 250.

66. Johnson, *Dictionary of the English Language* (1755), s.v. "system."

FOUR. ANECDOTAL POETICS IN *LYRICAL BALLADS*

1. Novalis's comment is from his *Philosophical Writings*, 69. Don H. Bialostosky offers a Bakhtinian analysis of Wordsworth's narrative verse in *Making Tales*. See pages 104–59 of his book for a discussion of Wordsworth's first-person "Dialogic Personal Anecdotes" in *Lyrical Ballads* and pages 160–84 for an account of how Wordsworth transformed what was originally a freestanding poetic anecdote of an encounter with a discharged soldier into an episode in the *Prelude*. James Chandler discusses the role

of anecdotes in generating a new sense of history in second-generation Romanticism in *England in 1819*, 203–66, drawing extensively on André Jolles's concept of the "case" as he does so. Kevis Goodman argues that Wordsworth's *Excursion* mobilizes the anecdote as a means of gaining a mediated access to a history that always exceeds total comprehension or representation in *Georgic Modernity and British Romanticism*, 127–39, although she also suggests that Wordsworth's poetry deliberately refuses to give the readers the pleasure they might expect from anecdotes.

2. For a discussion of the interplay between lyric poetry and the prose novel in Wordsworth's poetry and poetics see Starr, *Lyric Generations*, 159–202.

3. For a study on how Wordsworth's poetry drew on the Enlightenment science of human nature see Bewell, *Wordsworth and the Enlightenment*.

4. Bialostosky, "Genres from Life," 115.

5. Peter Hühn argues that anecdotes with lyric poetry are genres that mix fictional and factual codes and can be understood, alternately, as both fictional and factual in his essay "Problem of Fictionality and Factuality."

6. See Simpson, "Public Virtues, Private Vices."

7. Sidney, *Apology for Poetry*, 103.

8. Wordsworth, *Fenwick Notes of William Wordsworth*, 64.

9. Alan Bewell argues in *Wordsworth and the Enlightenment* that Wordsworth departs from Enlightenment moral philosophy in that his poems usually avoid making marginal figures, in particular "the 'idiots,' 'wild children,' blind, deaf, and mute people whose case histories formed a vital part of moral philosophical speculation," yield up easily understandable universal truths (39–40). I find, however, that the moral philosophical tradition that Bewell sees Wordsworth as simultaneously indebted to and critical of was itself often aware of the gap between anecdotes of marginal people and any universalizing conclusion that might be drawn from them.

10. See, for example, Simpson, "Public Virtues, Private Vices," 169–71, and Pfau, *Wordsworth's Profession*, 202.

11. Dorothy Wordsworth to Jane Marshall, 30 November 1795, in Wordsworth and Wordsworth, *Letters of William and Dorothy Wordsworth*, 160.

12. See Bialostosky, *Making Tales*, 104–59. For a discussion of the conflicted relationship between Wordsworth's poetry and the ideal of conversation, see Mee, *Conversable Worlds*, 192–200.

13. Percy, *Percy's Reliques of Ancient English Poetry*, 1:55, 2.35–36. These citations are to the volume and page numbers of the three-volume original edition.

14. Ibid., 3:172, l.20.

15. Although as Brennan O'Donnell points out, "None of the various four-line stanzas employed by Wordsworth in *Lyrical Ballads* may properly be labeled 'ballad stanzas,' though many bear outward resemblance to the 'simple ballad strain'" in *Passion of Meter*, 137.

16. Gummere, *Popular Ballad*, 117–34.

17. Chase, "'Anecdote for Fathers,'" 204–5.

18. C. Russell, "Defence of Tautology."

19. Wordsworth, *Prelude*, 50, ll.289–90.

20. *Aris's Birmingham Gazette*, 3. For further details on this anecdote, which to my knowledge has not been discussed before by critics, see my own "Peter Bell's Founding Anecdote."

21. See Hartman, *Wordsworth's Poetry*, 212.

22. Bishop, "Wordsworth and the 'Spots of Time,'" 47.

23. For general studies of Beddoes's medical and scientific researches see Jay, *Atmosphere of Heaven,* and Porter, *Doctor of Society.*

24. Cottle, *Early Recollections*, 2:36.

25. Stock, *Memoirs of the Life of Thomas Beddoes*, 102.

26. See, for example, A. Richardson, *British Romanticism;* Jackson, *Science and Sensation;* Vickers, *Coleridge and the Doctors;* and Ruston, *Creating Romanticism.*

27. Boyson, *Wordsworth and the Enlightenment Idea*, 116.

28. Robin Valenza explores this distinction in her last chapter of *Literature, Language, and the Rise of the Intellectual Disciplines in Britain,* in which she concludes that Wordsworth redefined poetry's function as the "practice whose specialized role was the creation of common language and universal experience" (142).

29. On this distinction, see Bennett, "Wordsworth's Poetic Ignorance."

30. Quoted in Jackson, *Science and Sensation,* 5.

31. For accounts of Wordsworth's relationship to professionalism, see Goldberg, *Lake Poets and Professional Identity,* and Pfau, *Wordsworth's Profession.*

32. Beddoes's copy of Wordsworth and Coleridge, *Lyrical Ballads* (1798), British Library. The poem appears immediately between pages 62 and 63 in Beddoes's copy of *Lyrical Ballads.* For the likely explanation that Beddoes inserted the poem as a joke at Wordsworth's and Coleridge's expense see Wu, *"Lyrical Ballads."*

33. Joseph Cottle to William Wordsworth, 2 September 1799, in Butler, "Wordsworth, Cottle, and the *Lyrical Ballads,*" 150.

34. Dorothy A. Stansfield notes the resemblance between Beddoes's parody and "Reflections on having left a place of Retirement" in *Thomas Beddoes,* 135–36.

35. Jack Stillinger has compared the narrative verse of *Lyrical Ballads* to the comic genre of the "shaggy dog" story, which depends for its comic effect on deliberately letting down its listeners at the end. See "Wordsworth, Coleridge, and the Shaggy Dog." On the staging of disappointment in "Simon Lee" see Freer, "Wordsworth and the Poetics of Disappointment."

36. William Wordsworth to Joseph Cottle, in Wordsworth and Wordsworth, *Letters of William and Dorothy Wordsworth,* 218.

37. Since the publication of Thomas Percy's *Relics of English Poetry* in 1769, of course, the ballad had been a popular form for conferring an aura of traditional orality on lyrics of the poet's own invention belonging to the culture of print. On this phenomenon see Harker, *Fakesong,* and the chapters "Notes on Distressed Genres" and "Scandals of the Ballad" in S. Stewart, *Crimes of Writing.* For recent discussions

of Wordsworth and the ballad tradition see Newman, *Ballad Collection, Lyric*, and McLane, *Balladeering, Minstrelsy*.

38. David Simpson observes, "The taking by the arm is but a muted version of the violence which Harry Gill exerts upon Goody Blake," in *Irony and Authority*, 40. Susan Wolfson similarly notes that the father in "Anecdote for Fathers" "persists" in his questioning, "almost becoming Harry Gill to Edward's Goody Blake" in *Questioning Presence*, 47.

39. "*Lyrical Ballads, with a few other Poems*," 367.

40. For more on Wordsworth's metrical experiments in "Goody Blake and Harry Gill" and their relation to the gender politics of the poem see Pinch, *Strange Fits of Passion*, 88–97.

41. Samuel Taylor Coleridge to Robert Southey, 29 July 1802, in Coleridge, *Collected Letters of Samuel Taylor Coleridge*, 2:449.

42. On the oversimplifications of Coleridge's presentation of Wordsworth's poetic theory in the *Biographia Literaria* see Bialotosky, "Coleridge's Interpretation of Wordsworth's Preface."

43. For an overview of the evidence of the circumstances in which the *Lyrical Ballads* were put together, see James Butler and Karen Green's introduction to the Cornell edition of Wordsworth, *Lyrical Ballads* (*LB* pp. 3–33).

44. *Oxford English Dictionary Online*, See s.v. "prose, *n*" and s.v. "verse, *n*."

45. Hegel, *Aesthetics*, 1.149.

46. Ginsburg and Nandrea, "Prose of the World," 246.

47. Quoted in Coleridge, *Poetical Works*, 361.

48. See also Wordsworth's account of the circumstances of the poem's composition in the notes he dictated to Fenwick in Wordsworth, *Fenwick Notes*, 2–3.

49. Shelvocke, *Voyage round the World*, 72–73.

50. William Wordsworth to Joseph Cottle, 24 June 1799, in Wordsworth and Wordsworth, *Letters of William and Dorothy Wordsworth*, 264.

51. Wordsworth and Coleridge, *Lyrical Ballads* (1798), 3.

52. Wordsworth and Coleridge, *Lyrical Ballads* (1800), 1:153.

53. McGann, "Meaning of the Ancient Mariner," 40.

54. I have de-italicized Coleridge's chapter heading.

55. Coleridge, "Of the Fragment of Kubla Khan," 52–53.

56. Newlyn, *William and Dorothy Wordsworth*, 57–60.

57. Ibid., 59. On the social-textual relationship between Dorothy and William Wordsworth in "A Night Piece" see also Wolfson, *Romantic Interactions*, 173–75.

58. My reading of the collection between narrative and lyric in *Lyrical Ballads* differs from that of Brian McGrath, who writes of "Simon Lee," for example, "Generated by the tension Wordsworth perceived between narrative and lyric poetry, 'Simon Lee' moves the reader from the ballad, with its emphasis on narrative action, to the lyric, with its emphasis on emotional intensity." See McGrath, *Poetics of Unremembered Acts*, 78–79. I see a less antagonistic relationship between narrative and

lyric in Wordsworth's contributions to *Lyrical Ballads*, which reveal "lyric" potentialities residing in anecdotal narratives themselves.

59. Culler, *Theory of the Lyric*, 226.

60. Hearne, *Journey from Prince of Wales's Fort*, 202.

61. Ibid., 203.

62. Ibid., 202.

63. Ibid., 203.

64. McLane, *Romanticism and the Human Sciences*, 45.

65. Culler, *Theory of the Lyric*, 225–26.

66. Ibid., 226.

67. Wordsworth, *Fenwick Notes of William Wordsworth*, 38.

68. Clayton, *Romantic Vision and the Novel*, 120.

69. Desmond King-Hele notes that Wordsworth may be recalling Erasmus Darwin's use of the word "diurnal" in the line "Watch with nice eye the Earth's diurnal way" in *The Loves of the Plants*, the second part to *The Botanic Garden* (1789–91). See King-Hele, *Erasmus Darwin*, 81.

70. D. Davidson, *Essays on Actions and Events*, 229.

71. For an extended discussion of how this distinction could be collapsed or put in question in seventeenth- and eighteenth-century literature, see Kramnick, *Actions and Objects*.

CODA

1. I have de-italicized this quotation.

2. The original text reads, "Il n'y a pas longtems que le Seigneur de Firando fit enfermer toutes vives dans un cofre hériffé de pointes de clou tout-autour, trois des Demoiselles de l'apartement de ses femmes, & les y laisse expirer." Commelin, *Recueil des voyages*, 5:347.

3. Cassirer, *Philosophy of the Enlightenment*, 210.

4. Krause, "Despotism," 253. Quoted in Sullivan, *Montesquieu & the Despotic Ideas*, 7, a book that makes Krause's observation the basis for an entire reading of the *Spirit of the Laws*.

5. My translation. The original text reads "Le depotisme qu'il avait sucé en naissant lui faisait oblier qu'autrefois la Suède avait été libre, et que le sénat gouvernait anciennement le royaume conjointement avec les rois" (*V* 4:483).

6. For a study of how "distraction" was revalued in the Enlightenment as a source of mental liveliness, see N. M. Phillips, *Distraction*.

7. Hawley, "*Tristram Shandy*," 34–48.

8. For an account of how the anecdotes of *Tristram Shandy* look both backward to the "anecdote" in its residual sense as a component of secret history and forward to the anecdote in its emergent sense as a way of understanding historical individuals and their times, see London, "Secret History and Anecdote." 174–82.

Bibliography

MANUSCRIPTS AND SPECIAL COLLECTIONS

British Library, London

C. H. [Charles Hatchett], "Banksiana written at the request of my Friend Dawson Turner Esq of Great Yarmouth," RP 5146.

Wordsworth, William, and Samuel Taylor Coleridge, *Lyrical Ballads* (Bristol, 1798). Thomas Beddoes's copy. Shelfmark Ashley 2250.

Houghton Library, Harvard University

Boswell, James, "Boswelliana." MS Hyde 51 Case 9.

Royal Irish Academy, Dublin

Caulfield, James, 1st Earl of Charlemont, "Anecdotes of Hume," RIA, MS 12/R/7.

PRIMARY SOURCES

Addison, Joseph, and Richard Steele. *The Spectator.* Edited by Donald F. Bond. 5 vols. Oxford: Oxford University Press, 1965.

Addison, Mr. *Interesting Anecdotes, Memoirs, Allegories, Essays, and Poetical Fragments Tending to Amuse the Fancy and Inculcate Morality.* 12 vols. London, 1794–97.

Annet, Peter ["Gideon Archer"]. *Social Bliss Considered: In Marriage and Divorce; Cohabiting Unmarried, and Public Whoring.* London, 1749.

Aris's Birmingham Gazette 55 (October 10, 1796).

An Authentic Narrative of the Dissensions and Debates in the Royal Society. London, 1784.

Bacon, Francis. *The New Organon.* Edited by Lisa Jardine and Michael Silverthorne. Translated by Michael Silverthorne. Cambridge: Cambridge University Press, 2000.

Banks, Joseph. *The Endeavour Journal of Joseph Banks, 1768–1771.* Edited by J. C. Beaglehole. 2nd ed. 2 vols. Sydney: Angus & Robertson, 1963.

———. *The Scientific Correspondence of Sir Joseph Banks, 1765–1820.* Edited by Neil Chambers. 6 vols. London: Pickering & Chatto, 2007.

Beddoes, Thomas. *Contributions to Physical and Medical Knowledge, Principally from the West of England.* Bristol, 1799.

Blair, Hugh. *Lectures on Rhetoric and Belles Lettres.* Edited by Linda Ferreira-Buckley and S. Michael Halloran. Carbondale: Southern Illinois University Press, 2005.

Boswell, James. *Boswell: The Ominous Years, 1774–1776.* Edited by Charles Ryskamp and Frederick A. Pottle. Melbourne: William Heinemann, 1963.

———. *Boswell for the Defence, 1769–1774.* Edited by William K. Wimsatt Jr. and Frederick A. Pottle. Melbourne: William Heinemann, 1960.

———. *Boswelliana: The Commonplace Book of James Boswell.* Edited by Charles Rogers. London: Printed for the Grampian Club, 1874.

———. *Boswell's Journal of a Tour to the Hebrides with Samuel Johnson, LL.D., Illustrated.* Edited by Robert Carruthers. 2nd ed. London, 1851.

———. *Boswell's Journal of a Tour to the Hebrides with Samuel Johnson, LL.D., 1773.* Edited by Frederick A. Pottle and Charles H. Bennett. Melbourne: William Heinemann, 1963.

———. *The Life of Samuel Johnson.* Edited by David Womersley. London: Penguin, 2008.

"Bozzy and Piozzi, or the British Biographers, a Town Eclogue." *English Review, or, An Abstract of English and Foreign Literature* 7 (1786): 411–13.

Broughton, Thomas. *The Mottoes of the Spectators, Tatlers, and Guardians. Translated into English.* London, 1735.

Burke, Edmund. *Selected Letters of Edmund Burke.* Edited by Harvey C. Mansfield Jr. Chicago: University of Chicago Press, 1984.

Chambers, Ephraim. *Cyclopaedia: or, an Universal Dictionary of the Arts and Sciences.* 2 vols. London, 1728.

———. *Cyclopaedia: or, an Universal Dictionary of the Arts and Sciences.* 5 vols. London, 1778–88.

Cheselden, William. "An Account of some Observations made by a Young Gentleman, who was born Blind, or lost his Sight so early, that he had no Remembrance of ever having seen, and was couched between 13 and 14 Years of Age." *Philosophical Transactions of the Royal Society* 35, no. 402 (1728): 447–48.

Coleridge, Samuel Taylor. *Biographia Literaria.* Edited by James Engell and W. Jackson Bate. 2 vols. Princeton, NJ: Princeton University Press, 1983.

———. *The Collected Letters of Samuel Taylor Coleridge.* Edited by Earl Leslie Griggs. 6 vols. Oxford: Oxford University Press, 1956–71.

———. *Poetical Works.* Vol. 1, *Poems.* Edited by J. C. C. Mays. Princeton, NJ: Princeton University Press, 2001.

Commelin, Izaäk. *Recueil des voyages qui ont servi à l'éstablissement & aux progrés de la Compagnie des Indes orientale.* Translated by René Augustin de Constantin Rennevlle. 10 vols. Amsterdam, 1725.

Cook, James. *Journal of the Voyage of the* Endeavour, *1768–71.* Edited by J. C. Beaglehole. Cambridge: Hakluyt Society and Cambridge University Press, 1955.

Cottle, Joseph. *Early Recollections, Chiefly Relating to the Late Samuel Taylor Coleridge during his Long Residence in Bristol.* 2 vols. London, 1837.

Dampier, William. *A New Voyage Around the World.* London, 1697.

Darwin, Erasmus. *Zoonomia; or, the Laws of Organic Life.* 2 vols. London, 1794–96.

D'Épinay, Louise. *The Memoirs and Correspondence of Madame D'Épinay.* Translated by J. H. Freese. 3 vols. London: H. S. Nichols, 1897.

De Quincey, Thomas. "The Last Days of Immanuel Kant." *Blackwood's Edinburgh Magazine* 21, no. 122 (February 1827): 136–58.

Dictionnaire de l'Acadèmie Française. Paris, 1694.

Dictionnaire de l'Acadèmie Française. 4th ed. Paris, 1740.

Diderot, Denis. *Political Writings.* Translated and edited by John Hope Mason and Robert Wokler. Cambridge: Cambridge University Press, 1992.

D'Israeli, Isaac. *A Dissertation on Anecdotes.* London, 1793.

Dunbar, James. *Essays on the History of Mankind in Rude and Cultivated Ages.* London, 1780.

Eccentric Biography; or, Memoirs of Remarkable Female Characters, Ancient and Modern. London, 1803.

Edgeworth, Maria. *Castle Rackrent, Irish Bulls, Ennui.* Edited by Jane Desmararis, Tim McLoughlin, and Marilyn Butler. London: Pickering & Chatto, 1999.

Green, Charles, and James Cook. "Observations made, by appointment of the Royal Society, at King George's Island in the South Sea." *Philosophical Transactions of the Royal Society* 61 (1771): 397–421.

Hawkesworth, John. *An Account of the Voyages Undertaken by the Order of his Present Majesty for making Discoveries in the Southern Hemisphere, and successively performed by Commodore Byron, Captain Wallis, Captain Carteret, Captain Wallis, and Captain Cook, in the Dolphin, the Swallow, and the Endeavour.* 3 vols. London, 1773.

Haywood, Eliza. *Selected Works of Eliza Haywood.* Edited by Alexander Pettit et al. 6 vols. London: Pickering & Chatto, 2000.

Hearne, Samuel. *A Journey from Prince of Wales's Fort in Hudson's Bay, to the Northern Ocean. Undertaken by Order of the Hudson's Bay Company, for the Discovery of Copper Mines, a North West Passage, &c. In the Years 1769, 1770, 1771, & 1772.* London, 1795.

Hegel, Georg Wilhelm Friedrich. *Aesthetics: Lectures on Fine Art.* Translated by T. M. Knox. 2 vols. Oxford: Oxford University Press, 1975.

"An Heroic Epistle from the Injured Harriet, Mistress to Mr. Banks, to Oberea, Queen of Otaheite." *Westminster Magazine* 2 (January 1774): 42–43.

"Histories of the Tête à Tête annexed; or, Memoirs of the Circumnavigator and Miss B—n." *Town and Country Magazine* 5 (September 1773): 457–59.

Home, Henry, Lord Kames. *Sketches of the History of Man.* Edited by James A. Harris. 3 vols. Indianapolis: Liberty Fund, 2007.

Hume, David. *A Concise and Genuine Account of the Dispute between Mr. Hume and Mr. Rousseau: With the letters that passed between them during their Controversy. As also the Letters of the Hon. Mr. Walpole, and Mr. D'Alembert, relative to this extraor-dinary Affair.* London, 1766.

———. *A Dissertation on the Passions; The Natural History of Religion: A Critical Edition.* Edited by Tom L. Beauchamp. Oxford: Oxford University Press, 2007.

———. *An Enquiry Concerning Human Understanding: A Critical Edition.* Edited by Tom L. Beauchamp. Oxford: Clarendon Press, 2000.

———. *Essays Moral, Political, and Literary.* Edited by Eugene F. Miller. Rev. ed. Indianapolis: Liberty Classics, 1994.

———. *The History of England from the Invasion of Julius Caesar to The Revolution in 1688.* 6 vols. Edited by William B. Todd. Indianapolis: Liberty Classics, 1983.

———. *The Letters of David Hume.* Edited by J. Y. T. Greig. 2 vols. Oxford: Clarendon Press, 1932.

———. *A Treatise of Human Nature: A Critical Edition.* Edited by David Fate Norton and Mary J. Norton. 2 vols. Oxford: Oxford University Press, 2007.

Hurd, Richard. *A Discourse by Way of General Preface to the Quarto Edition of Bishop Warburton's Works, containing some Account of the Life, Writings and Character of the Author.* London, 1794.

"Interesting Reflections on the Life of Miss Polly Baker." *Edinburgh Magazine, or Literary Miscellany* 3 (April 1794): 288–94.

Jefferson, Thomas. *Political Writings.* Edited by Joyce Appleby and Terence Ball. Cambridge: Cambridge University Press, 1999.

———. *The Writings of Thomas Jefferson.* Edited by Paul Leicester Ford. 10 vols. New York: G.P. Putnam's Sons, 1892–99.

Johnson, Samuel. *A Dictionary of the English Language.* 2 vols. London, 1755.

———. *A Dictionary of the English Language,* 4th ed. 2 vols. London, 1773.

Kippis, Andrew. *The Life of Captain James Cook.* London, 1788.

La Mettrie, Julien Offray de. *Histoire naturelle de l'âme, traduite de l'Anglois de M. Charp.* Paris, 1745.

Ligon, Richard. *A True & Exact History of the Island of Barbados.* London, 1657.

Linné, Carl von [Carl Linnaeus]. *Linnaeus' Philosophia Botanica.* Translated by Stephen Freer. Oxford: Oxford University Press, 2003.

———. *Nemesis Divina.* Edited and translated by M. J. Petry. Dordrect: Kluwer Academic, 2001.

Locke, John. *The Correspondence of John Locke.* Edited by E. S. de Beer. 8 Vols. Oxford: Clarendon Press, 1976–89.

———. *An Essay Concerning Human Understanding.* Edited by Peter H. Nidditch. Oxford: Clarendon Press, 1975.

"*Lyrical Ballads, with a few other Poems.*" *British Critic* 14 (1799): 364–69.

Melville, Sir James. *The Memoires of Sir James Melvil of Hal-hill: Containing an Impartial Account of the most Remarkable Affairs of State during the last Age, not mention'd by other Historians: more particularly relating to the Kingdoms of England and Scotland, under the Reigns of Queen Elizabeth, Mary Queen of Scots, and King James, in which all Transactions the Author was Personally and Publickly concern'd, now published from the Original Manuscripts.* Edited by George Scott. London, 1683.

Ménage, Gilles. *Menagiana, ou bons mots, rencontres agreables, pensées judicieuses, et observations curieuses.* 2nd ed. 4 vols. Amsterdam, 1694.

Millar, James. *The Origin of the Distinction of Ranks, or, An Inquiry into the Circumstances Which Give Rise to Influence and Authority in the Different Members of Society.* Edited by Aaron Garrett. Indianapolis: Liberty Fund, 2006.

Monboddo, Lord (James Burnett). *Antient Metaphysics, Or, The Science of Universals,* 6 vols. Edinburgh: 1779–99.

———. *On the Origin and Progress of Language.* 2nd ed. 6 vols. Edinburgh, 1774–92.

Montesquieu, Charles de Secondat. *The Spirit of the Laws.* Edited by Anne M. Cohler, Basia Carolyn Miller, and Harold Samuel Stone. Cambridge: Cambridge University Press, 1989.

"Mr. Hume's *Dissertations continued.*" *Critical Review, or, Annals of Literature* 3 (1757): 209–16.

Novalis. *Philosophical Writings.* Translated and edited by Margaret Mahoney Stoljar. Albany: State University of New York Press, 1997.

Percy, Thomas. *Percy's Reliques of Ancient English Poetry.* 3 vols. London, 1765.

Petronius. *The Satyricon.* Translated by P. G. Walsh. Oxford: Oxford World's Classics, 1997.

Pindar, Peter [John Wolcot]. *Peter's Prophecy, or, the President and Poet. Or, An Important Epistle to Sir J. Banks, on the Approaching Election of a President of the Royal Society.* 2nd ed. London, 1788.

Puttenham, George. *The Art of English Poesy: A Critical Edition.* Edited by Frank Whigham and Wayne A. Rebhorn. Ithaca, NY: Cornell University Press, 2007.

Raynal, Guillaume-Thomas-François. *Histoire philosophique et politique des établissemens et du commerce des Européens dans les deux Indes.* 6 vols. The Hague, 1770.

"Review of New Publications." *Edinburgh Magazine and Review* 1 (November 1773): 28–48.

Richardson, Samuel. *The Selected Letters of Samuel Richardson.* Edited by John Carroll. Oxford: Clarendon Press, 1964.

Shaw, Alexander. *A Catalogue of the Different Specimens of Cloth Collected in the Three Voyages of Captain Cook; with a Particular Account of the Manner of the Manufacturing the Same in the Various Islands of the South Seas; Partly Extracted from Mr. Anderson and Reinhold Forster's Observations, and the Verbal Account of Some of the Most Knowing of the Navigators: with some Anecdotes that happened to them among the Natives.* London, 1787.

Shelvocke, George. *Voyage round the World by the Way of the Great South Sea.* London, 1726.

Sidney, Sir Philip. *An Apology for Poetry (or The Defence of Poesy).* Edited by Geoffrey Shepherd. Rev. ed. Edited by R. W. Maslen. Manchester: Manchester University Press, 2002.

"Sketches of the History of Man." *Critical Review* 37 (June 1774): 454–59.

Smith, Adam. *The Theory of Moral Sentiments.* Edited by Knud Haakonssen. Cambridge: Cambridge University Press, 2002.

Smollett, Tobias. "*The History of Great Britain,* Vol. II. Containing the Commonwealth, and the Reigns of Charles II. And James II. By David Hume, Esq." Critical Review 2 (December 1756): 385–404.

"The Speech of Miss Polly Baker." *General Advertiser,* no. 3889 (April 15, 1747): 1–2.

"The Speech of Miss Polly Baker." *Boston Weekly Post-Boy,* no. 661 (July 20, 1747), 1.

A Spy upon the Spectator. Part I. London, 1711.

Sterne, Laurence. *The Florida Edition of the Works of Laurence Sterne.* Edited by W. G. Day, Joan New, Melvyn New, and Peter de Voogd. 8 vols. Gainesville: University Press of Florida, 1978–2008.

———. *Letters of Laurence Sterne.* Edited by Lewis Perry Curtis. Oxford: Clarendon Press, 1935.

Stock, John Edmond. *Memoirs of the Life of Thomas Beddoes, M.D. with an Analytical Account of his Writings.* London, 1811.

Swift, Jonathan. *Gulliver's Travels.* Edited by David Womersley. Cambridge: Cambridge University Press, 2012.

Temple, William. *Memoirs of what Past in Christendom from the War Begun 1672 to the Peace Concluded 1679.* 2nd ed. London, 1692.

"To the Editor of the Covent-Garden Magazine." *Covent-Garden Magazine; or Amorous Repository* 3 (1774): 225–27.

Tyers, Thomas. *An Historical Essay on Mr. Addison.* London, 1783.

The University of Oxford. *Theatri Oxoniensis Encaenia, Sive Comita Philologica, Julli 7, anno 1693, Celebrata.* Oxford, 1693.

Varillas. *Anecdota Heterouiaka, or the Secret History of the House of Medicis, Written Originally by that Fam'd Historian, the Sieur de Vallas.* Translated by Ferrand Spence. London, 1686.

———. *Les Anecdotes de Florence; ou, l'Histoire Secrète de la Maison de Médicis.* La Haye: Moetjens, 1686.

Voltaire, François-Marie Arouet de. *Œuvres complètes de Voltaire,* edited by Theodore Besterman et al. Oxford: Voltaire Foundation, 1968–.

Warburton, William. *Remarks on Mr. David Hume's Essay on the Natural History of Religion; Addressed to the Rev. Dr. Warburton.* London, 1757.

W.H.R. "Anecdotes and Bons Mots." *Attic Miscellany* 9 (1790): 344–45.

Wordsworth, William. *The Fenwick Notes of William Wordsworth.* Edited by Jared Curtis. Rev. ed. Tirril [England]: Humanities-Ebooks, 2007.

———. *Lyrical Ballads, and Other Poems, 1797–1800.* Edited by James Butler and Karen Green. Ithaca, NY: Cornell University Press, 1992.

———. *The Prelude, 1798–99.* Edited by Samuel Parrish. Ithaca, NY: Cornell University Press, 1977.

————. *The Prose Works of William Wordsworth*. Edited by W. J. B. Owen and Jane Worthington Smyser. 2nd ed. 3 vols. Oxford: Clarendon Press, 1974.

Wordsworth, William, and Samuel Taylor Coleridge. *Lyrical Ballads, with a few other Poems*. Bristol, 1798.

————., *Lyrical Ballads, with other Poems in Two Volumes*. 2nd ed. 2 vols. London, 1800.

Wordsworth, William, and Dorothy Wordsworth. *The Letters of William and Dorothy Wordsworth: The Early Years, 1787–1805*. Edited by Ernest de Selincourt. 2nd ed. Revised by Chester L. Shaver. Oxford: Clarendon Press, 1969.

Wotton, William. *Reflections upon Ancient and Modern Learning*. London, 1694.

SECONDARY SOURCES

Agamben, Giorgio. *Homo Sacer: Sovereign Power and Bare Life*. Translated by Daniel Heller-Roazen. Stanford, CA: Stanford University Press, 1998.

Anstey, Peter R. *John Locke and Natural Philosophy*. Oxford: Oxford University Press, 2011.

Auerbach, Erich. *Mimesis: The Representation of Reality in Western Literature*. Translated by Willard R. Trask. Princeton, NJ: Princeton University Press, 2003.

Badiou, Alain. *Being and Event*. Translated by Oliver Feltham. London: Continuum, 2006.

Baier, Annette C. *A Progress of Sentiments: Reflections on Hume's* Treatise. Cambridge, MA: Harvard University Press, 1991.

Bannet, Eve Taylor. "Haywood's Spectator and the Female World." In *Fair Philosopher: Eliza Haywood and* The Female Spectator, edited by Donald J. Newman and Lynn Marie Wright, 82–103. Lewisburg, PA: Bucknell University Press, 2006.

————. *Transatlantic Stories and the History of Reading, 1720–1810: Migrant Fictions*. Cambridge: Cambridge University Press, 2011.

Baucom, Ian. *Specters of the Atlantic: Finance Capital, Slavery, and the Philosophy of History*. Durham, NC: Duke University Press, 2005.

Bender, John. *Ends of Enlightenment*. Stanford, CA: Stanford University Press, 2012.

Bennett, Andrew. "Wordsworth's Poetic Ignorance." In *Wordsworth's Poetic Theory: Knowledge, Language, Experience*, edited by Andrew Regier and Stefan H. Uhlig, 19–35. Basingstoke: Palgrave Macmillan, 2010.

Bent, S. Arthur. "The Illuminating Power of Anecdote." *North American Review* 155, no. 430 (1892): 347–54.

Bewell, Alan. *Wordsworth and the Enlightenment: Nature, Man, and Society in the Experimental Poetry*. New Haven, CT: Yale University Press, 1989.

Black, Scott. *Of Essays and Reading in Early Modern Britain*. Basingstroke: Palgrave Macmillan, 2006.

Bialotosky, Don. H. "Coleridge's Interpretation of Wordsworth's Preface to *Lyrical Ballads*," *PMLA* 93, no. 5 (1978): 912–24.

———. "Genres from Life in Wordsworth's Art: *Lyrical Ballads* 1798." In *Romanticism, History, and the Possibilities of Genre: Re-forming Literature*, edited by Tilottama Rajan and Julia M. Wright, 109–21. Cambridge: Cambridge University Press, 1998.

———. *Making Tales: The Poetics of Wordsworth's Narrative Experiments*. Chicago: University of Chicago Press, 1984.

Bishop, Jonathan. "Wordsworth and the 'Spots of Time.'" *English Literary History* 26, no. 1 (1959): 45–65.

Bitzer, Lloyd F. "The 'Indian Prince' in Miracle Arguments of Hume and His Predecessors and Early Critics." *Philosophy and Rhetoric* 31, no. 3 (1998): 175–230.

Blackwell, Mark. "Preposterous Hume." In *Theory and Practice in the Eighteenth Century*, edited by Alexander Dick and Christina Lupton, 87–108. London: Pickering & Chatto, 2008.

Blanchard, Rae. "Richard Steele's West Indian Plantation." *Modern Philology* 39, no. 3 (1942): 281–85.

Boyson, Rowan. *Wordsworth and the Enlightenment Idea of Pleasure*. Cambridge: Cambridge University Press, 2012.

Brown, Homer Obed. *Institutions of the English Novel: From Defoe to Scott*. Philadelphia: University of Pennsylvania Press, 1997.

Brown, Laura. *Fables of Modernity: Literature and Culture in the English Eighteenth Century*. Ithaca, NY: Cornell University Press, 2001.

———. *Homeless Dogs and Melancholy Apes: Humans and Other Animals in the Modern Literary Imagination*. Ithaca, NY: Cornell University Press, 2010.

Brown, Michael. *The Irish Enlightenment*. Cambridge, MA: Harvard University Press, 2015.

Bullard, Rebecca. *The Politics of Disclosure, 1674–1725: Secret History Narratives*. London: Pickering & Chatto, 2009.

Butler, James. A. "Wordsworth, Cottle, and the *Lyrical Ballads*: Five Letters, 1797–1800." *Journal of English and Germanic Philology* 75, no. 1 (1976): 137–53.

Carey, Brycchan. "'Accounts of Savage Nations': The Spectator and the Americas." In *Uncommon Reflections: Emerging Discourses in* The Spectator, edited by Don J. Newman, 129–49. Newark: University of Delaware Press, 2005.

Carey, Daniel. *Locke, Shaftesbury, and Hutcheson: Contesting Diversity in the Enlightenment and Beyond*. Cambridge: Cambridge University Press, 2005.

Cassirer, Ernst. *The Philosophy of the Enlightenment*. Princeton, NJ: Princeton University Press,

Chandler, James. *England in 1819: The Politics of Literary Culture and the Case of Romantic Historicism*. Chicago: University of Chicago Press, 1998.

Chase, Cynthia. "'Anecdote for Fathers': The Scene of Interpretation in Freud and Wordsworth." In *Textual Analysis: Some Readers Reading*, edited by Mary Ann Caws, 182–206. New York: MLA, 1986.

Cheek, Pamela. *Sexual Antipodes: Enlightenment Globalization and the Placing of Sex.* Stanford, CA: Stanford University Press, 2003.

Chico, Tita. *The Experimental Imagination: Literary Knowledge and Science in the British Enlightenment.* Stanford, CA: Stanford University Press, 2018.

Christensen, Jerome. *Practicing Enlightenment: Hume and the Formation of a Literary Career.* Madison: University of Wisconsin Press, 1987.

Clayton, Jay. *Romantic Vision and the Novel.* Cambridge: Cambridge University Press, 1987.

Coe, Richard N. "The Anecdote and the Novel: A Brief into the Origins of Stendhal's Narrative Technique." *Australian Journal of French Studies* 22, no. 1 (1985): 3–25.

Cohen, I. Bernard. *Science and the Founding Fathers: Science in the Political Thought of Thomas Jefferson, Benjamin Franklin, John Adams, and James Madison.* New York: W. W. Norton, 1995.

Connell, Phillip. "Bibliomania: Book Collecting, Cultural Politics, and the Rise of Literary Heritage in Romantic Britain." *Representations* 71 (2000): 24–47.

Cowan, Brian. "The Curious Mr. Spectator: Virtuoso Culture and the Man of Taste in the Works of Addison and Steele." *Media History* 14, no. 3 (2008): 275–92.

Coventry, Angela, and Emilio Mazza. "Humeaneyes ('one particular shade of blue')." In *Cogent Arts and Humanities* 3 (2016): 1–20. https://doi.org/10.1080/23311983.2015.1128628.

Croce, Benedetto. *History as the Story of Liberty.* Translated by Sylvia Sprigge. London: George Allen and Unwin, 1941.

Culler, Jonathan. *Theory of the Lyric.* Cambridge, MA: Harvard University Press, 2015.

Darnton, Robert. *The Devil in the Holy Water, or the Art of Slander from Louis XIV to Napoleon.* Philadelphia: University of Pennsylvania Press, 2011.

Daston, Lorraine. "Description by Omission: Nature Enlightened and Obscured." In *Regimes of Description: In the Archive of the Eighteenth Century,* edited by John Bender and Michael Marrinan, 11–24. Stanford, CA: Stanford University Press, 2005.

Davidson, Donald. *Essays on Actions and Events.* 2nd ed. Oxford: Oxford University Press, 2001.

Davidson, Jenny. *Breeding: A Partial History of the Eighteenth Century.* New York: Columbia University Press, 2009.

Dear, Peter. *Discipline and Experience: The Mathematical Way in the Scientific Revolution.* Chicago: University of Chicago Press, 1995.

———. "Narratives, Anecdotes, and Experiments: Turning Experience into Science in the Seventeenth Century." In *The Literary Structure of Scientific Argument: Historical Studies,* edited by Peter Dear, 135–63. Philadelphia: University of Pennsylvania Press, 1991.

De Bolla, Peter. *The Architecture of Concepts: The Historical Foundation of Human Rights*. New York: Fordham University Press, 2013.

Degenaar, Marjolein. *Molyneux's Problem: Three Centuries of Discussion on the Perception of Forms*. Translated by Michael J. Collins. Dordrecht: Kluwer Academic, 1996.

Deleuze, Gilles. "He Stuttered." Translated by Constantin V. Boundas. In *Gilles Deleuze and the Theater of Philosophy*, edited by Constantin V. Boundas and Dorothea Olkowski, 23–29. New York: Routledge, 1994.

Deleuze, Gilles, and Félix Guattari. *What Is Philosophy?* Translated by Hugh Tomlinson and Graham Burchell. New York: Columbia University Press, 1994.

Deleuze, Gilles, and Claire Parnet. *Dialogues II*. Translated by Hugh Tomlinson and Barbara Habberjam. Rev. ed. London: Continuum, 2002.

Dening, Greg. *Mr Bligh's Bad Language: Passion, Power and Theatre on the Bounty*. Cambridge: University of Cambridge Press, 1992.

Derrida, Jacques. "Before the Law." Translated by Avital Ronell and Christine Roulston. In *Acts of Literature*, edited by Derek Attridge, 181–220. New York: Routledge, 1992.

———. "Signature Event Context." Translated by Samuel Weber and Jeffrey Mehlman. In *Limited Inc*, edited by Gerald Graff, 1–24. Evanston, IL: Northwestern University Press, 1988.

Deutsch, Helen. *Loving Dr. Johnson*. Chicago: University of Chicago Press, 2005.

Deutsch, Helen, and Felicity Nussbaum, eds. *Defects: Engendering the Modern Body*. Ann Arbor: University of Michigan Press, 2000.

Dickie, Simon. *Cruelty and Laughter: Forgotten Comic Literature and the Unsentimental Eighteenth Century*. Chicago: University of Chicago Press, 2011.

Duff, David. "The Retuning of the Sky: Romanticism and the Lyric." In *The Lyric Poem: Formations and Transformations*, edited by Marion Thain, 135–55. Cambridge: Cambridge University Press, 2013.

Duncan, Ian. *Scott's Shadow: The Novel in Romantic Edinburgh*. Princeton, NJ: Princeton University Press, 2007.

Edelstein, Dan. *The Enlightenment: A Genealogy*. Chicago: University of Chicago Press, 2010.

Felsenstein, Frank, ed. *English Trader, Indian Maid: Representing Gender, Race, and Slavery in the New World. An Inkle and Yarico Reader*. Baltimore: Johns Hopkins University Press, 1999.

Ferris, Ina. "Antiquarian Authorship: D'Israeli's Miscellany of Literary Curiosity and the Question of Secondary Genres." *Studies in Romanticism* 45, no. 4 (2006): 523–42.

Fineman, Joel. "The History of the Anecdote: Fiction and Fiction." In *The New Historicism*, edited by H. Aram Veeser, 49–76. New York: Routledge, 1989.

Fleming, Paul. "The Perfect Story: Anecdote and Exemplarity in Linnaeus and Blumenberg." *Thesis Eleven* 104, no. 11 (2011): 72–86.

Fludernik, Monika. *Towards a "Natural" Narratology.* Oxon: Routledge, 1996.

Forbes, Duncan. *Hume's Philosophical Politics.* Cambridge: Cambridge University Press, 1975.

Forde, Steven. *Locke, Science, and Politics.* Cambridge: Cambridge University Press, 2013.

Frasca-Spada, Marina. "The Science and Conversation of Human Nature." In *The Sciences in Enlightened Europe,* edited by William Clark, Jan Golinski, and Simon Schaffer, 218–45. Chicago: University of Chicago Press, 1999.

Freer, Alexander. "Wordsworth's Poetics of Disappointment." *Textual Practice* 36, no. 6 (2014): 1123–44.

Fulford, Tim, Debbie Lee, and Peter J. Kitson. *Literature, Science and Exploration in the Romantic Era: Bodies of Knowledge.* Cambridge: Cambridge University Press, 2004.

Gallagher, Catherine. "The Rise of Fictionality." In *The Novel,* vol. 1, *History, Geography, and Culture,* edited by Franco Moretti, 336–63. Princeton, NJ: Princeton University Press, 2006.

Gallagher, Catherine, and Stephen Greenblatt. *Practicing New Historicism.* Chicago: University of Chicago Press, 2001.

Gallop, Jane. *Anecdotal Theory.* Durham, NC: Duke University Press, 2002.

Garrett, Matthew. *Episodic Poetics: Politics and Literary Form after the Constitution.* Oxford: Oxford University Press, 2014.

Gascoigne, John. *Joseph Banks and the English Enlightenment: Useful Knowledge and Polite Culture.* Cambridge: Cambridge University Press, 1994.

———. *Science in the Service of Empire: Joseph Banks, the British State and the Uses of Science in the Age of Revolution.* Cambridge: Cambridge University Press, 1998.

Gee, Sophie. *Making Waste: Leftovers and the Eighteenth-Century Imagination.* Princeton, NJ: Princeton University Press, 2010.

Gelley, Alexander, ed. *Unruly Examples: On the Rhetoric of Exemplarity.* Stanford, CA: Stanford University Press, 1995.

Gendler, Tamar Szabó. *Thought Experiment: On the Powers and Limits of Imaginary Cases.* New York: Routledge, 2000.

Genette, Gérard. *Narrative Discourse: An Essay in Method.* Translated by Jane E. Lewin. Ithaca, NY: Cornell University Press, 1980.

Gigante, Denise. *Taste: A Literary History.* New Haven, CT: Yale University Press, 2005.

Gikandi, Simon. *Slavery and the Culture of Taste.* Princeton, NJ: Princeton University Press, 2011.

Ginsburg, Michal Peled, and Lorri G. Nandrea. "The Prose of the World." In *The Novel,* vol. 2, *Forms and Themes,* edited by Franco Moretti, 244–73. Princeton, NJ: Princeton University Press, 2006.

Girten, Kristin M. "Unsexed Souls: Natural Philosophy as Transformation in Eliza Haywood's Female Spectator." Eighteenth-Century Studies 43, no. 1 (2009): 55–74.

Goldberg, Brian. *The Lake Poets and Professional Identity*. Cambridge: Cambridge University Press, 2007.

Goodman, Kevis. *Georgic Modernity and British Romanticism: Poetry and the Mediation of History*. Cambridge: Cambridge University Press, 2004.

Gossman, Lionel. "Anecdote and History." *History and Theory* 42, no. 2 (2003): 151–55.

Greek-English Lexicon: With a Revised Supplement. Edited by Henry George Liddell and Robert Scott. Revised by Henry Stuart Jones with Roderick MacKenzie et al. Oxford: Clarendon Press, 1996.

Greene, Roland. "Island Logic." In *"The Tempest" and Its Travels,* edited by Peter Hulme and William H. Sherman, 138–45. Philadelphia: University of Pennsylvania Press, 2000.

Gummere, Francis B. *The Popular Ballad*. Boston: Houghton Mifflin, 1907.

Habermas, Jürgen. *The Structural Transformation of the Public Sphere: An Inquiry into a Category of Bourgeois Society*. Translated by Thomas Burger. Cambridge, MA: MIT Press, 1989.

Hall, Max. *Benjamin Franklin and Polly Baker: The History of a Literary Deception*. Chapel Hill: University of North Carolina Press, 1960.

Hampton, Timothy. *Writing from History: The Rhetoric of Exemplarity in Renaissance Literature*. Ithaca, NY: Cornell University Press, 1990.

Hamilton, Ross. *Accident: A Philosophical and Literary History*. Chicago: University of Chicago Press, 2007.

Harker, David. *Fakesong: The Manufacture of British Folksong from 1700 to the Present Day*. Milton Keynes, UK: Open University Press, 1985.

Hartman, Geoffrey H. *Wordsworth's Poetry, 1787–1814*. New Haven, CT: Yale University Press, 1964.

Hawley, Judith. "*Tristram Shandy,* Learned Wit, and Enlightenment Knowledge," In *The Cambridge Companion to Laurence Sterne,* edited by Thomas Keymer, 34–48. Cambridge: Cambridge University Press, 2009.

Hayot, Eric. *The Hypothetical Mandarin: Sympathy, Modernity, and Chinese Pain*. Oxford: Oxford University Press, 2009.

Heilbron, J. L. "A Mathematician's Mutiny, with Morals." In *World Changes: Thomas Kuhn and the Nature of Science,* edited by Paul Horwich, 81–129. Cambridge, MA: MIT Press, 1993.

Henare, Amiria J. M. *Museums, Anthropology and Imperial Exchange*. Cambridge: Cambridge University Press, 2005.

Horejsi, Nicole. "'A Counterpart to the Ephesian Matron': Steele's 'Inkle and Yarico' and a Feminist Critique of the Classics." *Eighteenth-Century Studies* 39, no. 2 (2006): 201–26.

Hudson, Nicholas. "From 'Nation' to 'Race': The Origin of Racial Classification in Eighteenth-Century Thought." *Eighteenth-Century Studies* 29, no. 3 (1996): 247–64.

Hühn, Peter. "The Problem of Fictionality and Factuality in Lyric Poetry." *Narrative* 22, no. 2 (2014): 155–68.

Hulme, Peter. *Colonial Encounters: Europe and the Native Caribbean, 1492–1797.* London: Methuen, 1986.

Hutner, Heidi. *Colonial Women: Race and Culture in Stuart Drama.* Oxford: Oxford University Press, 2001.

Jackson, Noel. *Science and Sensation in Romantic Poetry.* Cambridge: Cambridge University Press, 2008.

Jakobson, Roman. "Two Types of Language and Two Types of Aphastic Disturbances." In *Language in Literature,* edited by Krystyna Pomorska and Stephen Rudy. Cambridge, MA: Harvard University Press, 1987.

Jay, Mike. *The Atmosphere of Heaven: The Unnatural Experiments of Dr Beddoes and His Sons of Genius.* New Haven, CT: Yale University Press, 2009.

Jayne, Allen. *Jefferson's Declaration of Independence: Origins, Philosophy, and Theology.* Lexington: University Press of Kentucky, 1998.

Jolles, André. *Simple Forms.* Translated by Peter J. Schwartz. London: Verso, 2017.

Jost, Jacob Sider. *Prose Immortality, 1711–1819.* Charlottesville: University of Virginia Press, 2015.

Junod, Karen. *"Writing the Lives of Painters": Biography and Artistic Identity in Britain, 1760–1810.* Oxford: Oxford University Press, 2011.

Kareem, Sarah Tindal. *Eighteenth-Century Fiction and the Reinvention of Wonder.* Oxford: Oxford University Press, 2014.

———. "Enlightenment Bubbles, Romantic Worlds." *Eighteenth-Century: Theory and Interpretation* 56, no. 1 (2014): 85–104.

Kaufmann, Paul. *Borrowings from the Bristol Library, 1773–1784: A Unique Record of Reading Vogues.* Charlottesville: Bibliographical Society of the University of Virginia, 1960.

Keenleyside, Heather. *Animals and Other People: Literary Forms and Living Beings in the Long Eighteenth Century.* Philadelphia: University of Pennsylvania Press, 2016.

Kerr, Donald. *Census of Alexander Shaw's Catalogue of the Different Specimens of Cloth Collected in the Three Voyages of Captain Cook to the Southern Hemisphere, 1787.* Dunedin, NZ: University of Otago, 2015.

King-Hele, Desmond. *Erasmus Darwin and the Romantic Poets.* Houndmills, UK: Macmillan, 1986.

Knight, Charles A. "Bibliography and the Shape of the Literary Periodical in the Early Eighteenth Century." *Library* 8, no. 3 (1986): 232–48.

Kramnick, Jonathan Brody. *Actions and Objects from Hobbes to Richardson.* Stanford, CA: Stanford University Press, 2010.

———. "Locke's Desire." In *Theory and Practice in the Eighteenth Century: Writing between Philosophy and Literature,* edited by Alexander Dick and Christina Lupton. 31–50. London: Routledge, 2008.

Kramnick, Jonathan Brody, and Anahid Nersessian. "Form and Explanation." *Critical Inquiry* 43, no. 3 (2017): 650–69.

Krause, Sharon. "Despotism in *The Spirit of the Laws.*" In *Montesquieu's Science of Politics: Essays on "The Spirit of Laws,"* edited by David W. Carrithers, Michael A. Mosher, and Paul A. Rahe, 231–72. Lanham, MD: Rowman & Littlefield 2001.

Labov, William. "Speech Actions and Reactions in Personal Narrative." In *Analyzing Discourse: Text and Talk,* edited by Deborah Tannen, 219–47. Washington, DC: Georgetown University Press, 1982.

Lamb, Jonathan. "Minute Particulars and the Representation of South Pacific Discovery." *Eighteenth-Century Studies* 28, no. 3 (1995): 281–94.

———. *Preserving the Self in the South Seas, 1680–1840.* Chicago: University of Chicago Press, 2001.

Latour, Bruno. *Science in Action: How to Follow Scientists and Engineers through Society.* Cambridge, MA: Harvard University Press, 1987.

Liu, Alan. *Local Transcendence: Essays on Postmodern Historicism and the Database.* Chicago: University of Chicago Press, 2008.

Livingston, Donald W. *Hume's Philosophy of Common Life.* Chicago: University of Chicago Press, 1984.

———. *Philosophical Melancholy and Delirium: Hume's Pathology of Philosophy.* Chicago: University of Chicago Press, 1998.

London, April. *Literary History Writing, 1770–1820.* Basingstoke, UK: Palgrave Macmillan, 2010.

———. "Secret History and Anecdote." In *The Secret History in Literature, 1660–1820,* edited by Rebecca Bullard and Rachel Carnell, 174–87. Cambridge: Cambridge University Press, 2017.

Lupton, Christina. *Knowing Books: The Consciousness of Mediation in Eighteenth-Century Britain.* Philadelphia: University of Pennsylvania Press, 2012.

Lyons, John D. *Exemplum: The Rhetoric of Example in Early Modern France and Italy.* Princeton, NJ: Princeton University Press, 1989.

Mackie, Erin. *Market à la Mode: Fashion, Commodity, and Gender in* The Tatler *and* The Spectator. Baltimore: Johns Hopkins University Press, 1997.

Mallipeddi, Ramesh. *Spectacular Suffering: Witnessing Slavery in the Eighteenth-Century British Atlantic.* Charlottesville: University of Virginia Press, 2016.

Martínez, Alberto A. *Science Secrets: The Truth about Darwin's Finches, Einstein's Wife, and Other Myths.* Pittsburgh: University of Pittsburg Press, 2011.

Maurer, Shawn Lisa. *Proposing Men: Dialectics of Gender and Class in the Eighteenth-Century English Periodical.* Stanford, CA: Stanford University Press, 1998.

McGann, Jerome J. "The Meaning of the Ancient Mariner." *Critical Inquiry* 8, no. 1 (1981): 35–67.

McGrath, Brian. *The Poetics of Unremembered Acts: Reading, Lyric, Pedagogy.* Evanston, IL: Northwestern University Press, 2013.

McLane, Maureen. *Balladeering, Minstrelsy, and the Making of British Romantic Poetry.* Cambridge: Cambridge University Press, 2008.

———. *Romanticism and the Human Sciences: Poetry, Population, and the Discourse of the Species.* Cambridge: Cambridge University Press, 2000.

McKeon, Michael. *The Secret History of Domesticity: Public, Private, and the Division of Knowledge.* Baltimore: Johns Hopkins University Press, 2005.

Mee, John. *Conversable Worlds: Literature, Contention, and Community, 1762 to 1830.* Oxford: Oxford University Press, 2011.

Miller, David Philip. "Joseph Banks, Empire, and 'Centers of Calculation' in Late Hanoverian Britain." In *Visions of Empire: Voyages, Botany, and Representations of Nature,* edited by David Philip Miller and Peter Hanns Reill, 21–37. Cambridge: Cambridge University Press, 1996.

Molesworth, Jesse. *Chance and the Eighteenth-Century Novel: Realism, Probability, Magic.* Cambridge: Cambridge University Press, 2010.

Moss, Ann. *Printed Commonplace Books and the Structuring of Renaissance Thought.* Oxford: Oxford University Press, 1996.

Mossner, Ernest Campbell. *The Life of David Hume.* Oxford: Oxford University Press, 1980.

Nash, Richard. *Wild Enlightenment: The Borders of Human Identity in the Eighteenth Century.* Charlottesville: University of Virginia Press, 2003.

Newlyn, Lucy. *William and Dorothy Wordsworth: "All in Each Other."* Oxford: Oxford University Press, 2013.

Newman, Steve. *Ballad Collection, Lyric, and the Canon: The Call of the Popular from the Restoration to the New Criticism.* Philadelphia: University of Pennsylvania Press, 2007.

Newman, William R. *Atoms and Alchemy: Chymistry and the Experimental Origins of the Scientific Revolution.* Chicago: University of Chicago Press, 2006.

Noggle, James. "Literary Taste as Counter-Enlightenment in Hume's *History of England.*" *SEL: Studies in English Literature, 1500–1900* 44, no. 3 (2004): 617–38.

Nussbaum, Felicity A. *The Limits of the Human: Fictions of Anomaly, Race, and Gender in the Long Eighteenth Century.* Cambridge: Cambridge University Press, 2003.

Obeyeskere, Gananath. *Cannibal Talk: The Man-Eating Myth and Human Sacrifice in the South Seas.* Berkeley: University of California Press, 2005.

O'Brien, Karen. "Johnson's View of the Scottish Enlightenment in *A Journey to the Western Islands of Scotland.*" *Age of Johnson* 4 (1991): 59–82.

O'Donnell, Brennan. *The Passion of Meter: A Study of Wordsworth's Metrical Art.* Kent, OH: Kent State University Press, 1995.

Orr, Leah. *Novel Ventures: Fiction and Print Culture in England, 1690–1730.* Charlottesville: University of Virginia Press, 2017.

Outram, Dorinda. *The Enlightenment.* 2nd ed. Cambridge: Cambridge University Press, 2005.

The Oxford English Dictionary Online. Oxford: Oxford University Press. www.oed.com.

Pasanek, Brad. *Metaphors of Mind: An Eighteenth-Century Dictionary.* Baltimore: Johns Hopkins University Press, 2015.

Patterson, Annabel. *Early Modern Liberalism.* Cambridge: Cambridge University Press, 1997.

Paxman, David. "'Distance Getting Close': Gesture, Language, and Space in the Pacific," *Eighteenth-Century Life* 26, no. 3 (2002): 78–97.

Pfau, Thomas. *Wordsworth's Profession: Form, Class, and the Logic of Early Romantic Cultural Production.* Stanford, CA: Stanford University Press, 1997.

Phillips, Mark Salber. *Society and Sentiment: Genres of Historical Writing in Britain, 1740–1820.* Princeton, NJ: Princeton University Press, 2000.

Phillips, Natalie M. *Distraction: Problems of Attention in Eighteenth-Century Literature.* Baltimore: Johns Hopkins University Press, 2016.

Picciotto, Joanna. *Labors of Innocence in Early Modern England.* Cambridge, MA: Harvard University Press, 2010.

Pinch, Adela. *Strange Fits of Passion: Epistemologies of Emotion, Hume to Austen.* Stanford, CA: Stanford University Press, 1996.

Pocock, J. G. A. *Barbarism and Religion.* Vol. 1, *The Enlightenments of Edward Gibbon, 1737–1764.* Cambridge: Cambridge University Press, 1999.

———. *Barbarism and Religion.* Vol. 2, *Narratives of Civil Government.* Cambridge: Cambridge University Press, 1999.

Pollock, Anthony. *Gender and the Fictions of the Public Sphere, 1690–1755.* New York: Routledge, 2009.

Poovey, Mary. *A History of the Modern Fact: Problems of Knowledge in the Sciences of Wealth and Society.* Chicago: University of Chicago Press, 1998.

Porter, Roy. *Doctor of Society: Thomas Beddoes and the Sick Trade in Late-Enlightenment England.* London: Routledge, 1992.

———. *Enlightenment: Britain and the Creation of the Modern World.* London: Penguin, 2001.

Porter, Roy, and Mikuláš Teich, eds. *The Enlightenment in National Context.* Cambridge: Cambridge University Press, 1981.

Potkay, Adam. *The Fate of Eloquence in the Age of Hume.* Ithaca, NY: Cornell University Press, 1994.

Powell, Manushag N. *Performing Authorship in Eighteenth-Century English Periodicals.* Lewisburg, PA: Bucknell University Press, 2012.

Pratt, Mary Louise. *Imperial Eyes: Travel Writing and Transculturation.* 2nd. ed. London: Routledge, 2007.

Rennie, Neil. "The Point Venus 'Scene,' Tahiti, 14 May 1769." In *The Global Eighteenth Century,* edited by Felicity A. Nussbaum, 239–50. Baltimore: Johns Hopkins University Press, 2003.

Richardson, Alan. *British Romanticism and the Science of the Mind.* Cambridge: Cambridge University Press, 2001.

Richetti, John J. *Philosophical Writing: Locke, Berkeley, Hume.* Cambridge, MA: Harvard University Press, 1983.

Riskin, Jessica. *Science in the Age of Sensibility: The Sentimental Empiricists of the French Enlightenment.* Chicago: University of Chicago Press, 2002.

Rogers, Pat. *Johnson and Boswell: The Transit of Caledonia.* Oxford: Oxford University Press, 1995.

Russell, Corinna. "A Defence of Tautology: Repetition and Difference in Wordsworth's Note to 'The Thorn.'" *Paragraph* 28, no. 2 (2005): 103–18.

Russell, Gillian. "An 'Entertainment of Oddities': Fashionable Sociability and the Pacific in the 1770s." In *A New Imperial History: Culture, Identity, and Modernity in Britain and the Empire, 1660–1840,* edited by Kathleen Wilson, 48–70. Cambridge: Cambridge University Press, 2004.

Ruston, Sharon. *Creating Romanticism: Case Studies in the Literature, Science and Medicine of the 1790s.* Basingstoke, UK: Palgrave Macmillan, 2013.

Salmond, Anne. *Aphrodite's Island: The European Discovery of Tahiti.* Berkeley: University of California Press, 2009.

Schaffer, Simon. "'On Seeing Me Write': Inscription Devices in the South Seas." *Representations* 97, no. 1 (2007): 90–122.

Scott, Virginia. *Women on the Stage in Early Modern France, 1540–1750.* Cambridge: Cambridge University Press, 2010.

Shapin, Steven. *A Social History of Truth: Civility and Science in Seventeenth-Century England.* Chicago: University of Chicago Press, 1994.

Shapin, Steven, and Simon Schaffer. *Leviathan and the Air-Pump: Hobbes, Boyle, and the Experimental Life.* Princeton, NJ: Princeton University Press, 1985.

Shell, Marc. *Stutter.* Cambridge, MA: Harvard University Press, 2005.

Shevelow, Kathryn. *Women and Print Culture: The Construction of Femininity in the Early Periodical.* London: Routledge, 1989.

Shklovsky, Viktor. *Theory of Prose.* Translated by Benjamin Sher. Champaign, IL: Dalkey Archive, 1991.

Silver, Sean R. *The Mind Is a Collection: Case Studies in Eighteenth-Century Thought.* Philadelphia: University of Pennsylvania Press, 2015.

Simpson, David. *The Academic Postmodern and the Rule of Literature: A Report on Half-Knowledge.* Chicago: University of Chicago Press, 1995.

———. *Irony and Authority in Romantic Poetry.* London: Macmillan, 1979.

———. "Public Virtues, Private Vices: Reading between the Lines of Wordsworth's 'Anecdote for Fathers.'" In *Subject to History: Ideology, Class, Gender,* edited by David Simpson, 163–90. Ithaca, NY: Cornell University Press, 1991.

Siskin, Clifford. *System: The Shaping of Modern Knowledge.* Cambridge, MA: MIT Press, 2016.

Siskin, Clifford, and William Warner. "This Is Enlightenment: An Invitation in the Form of an Argument." In *This Is Enlightenment*, edited by Clifford Siskin and William Warner, 1–33. Chicago: University of Chicago Press, 2009.

Smith, Justin E. H. *Nature, Human Nature, and Human Difference: Race in Early Modern Philosophy*. Princeton, NJ: Princeton University Press, 2015.

Smith, Roger. "The Language of Human Nature." In *Inventing Human Science: Eighteenth-Century Domains*, edited by Christopher Fox, Roy Porter, and Robert Wokler, 88–111. Berkeley: University of California Press, 1995.

Smith, Vanessa. *Intimate Strangers: Friendship, Exchange and Pacific Encounters*. Cambridge: Cambridge University Press, 2010.

Sorkin, David Jan. *The Religious Enlightenment: Protestants, Jews, and Catholics from London to Vienna*. Princeton, NJ: Princeton University Press, 2008.

Stansfield, Dorothy A. *Thomas Beddoes, M.D., 1760–1808: Chemist, Physician, Democrat*. Dordrecht: D. Reidel, 1984.

Starr, G. Gabrielle. *Lyric Generations: Poetry and the Novel in the Long Eighteenth Century*. Baltimore: Johns Hopkins University Press, 2004.

Stewart, Larry. *The Rise of Public Science: Rhetoric, Technology, and Natural Philosophy in Newtonian Britain, 1660–1750*. Cambridge: Cambridge University Press, 1992.

Stewart, Susan. *Crimes of Writing: Problems in the Containment of Representation*. Oxford: Oxford University Press, 1991.

Stillinger, Jack. "Wordsworth, Coleridge, and the Shaggy Dog: The Novelty of *Lyrical Ballads* (1798)." In *Romantic Complexity: Keats, Coleridge, and Wordsworth*, 183–97. Urbana: University of Illinois Press, 2009.

Strawson, Galen. *The Secret Connexion: Causation, Realism, and David Hume*. Oxford: Clarendon Press, 1989.

Sullivan, Vickie. B. *Montesquieu & the Despotic Ideas of Europe: An Interpretation of The Spirit of the Laws*. Chicago: University of Chicago Press, 2017.

Sypher, Wylie. *Guinea's Captive Kings: British Anti-Slavery Literature of the Eighteenth Century*. New York: Octagon Books, 1969.

Temple, Kathryn. "'Manly Composition': Hume and the *History of England*." In *Feminist Interpretations of David Hume*, edited by Anne Jaap Jacobson, 263–82. University Park: Pennsylvania State University Press, 2000.

Thomas, Nicholas. *Discoveries: The Voyages of Captain Cook*. London: Allen Lane, 2003.

———. "Licensed Curiosity: Cook's Pacific Voyages," In *The Cultures of Collecting*, edited by John Elsner and Roger Cardinal, 116–36. London: Reaktion Books, 1994.

Tierney-Hynes, Rebecca. "Hume, Romance, and the Unruly Imagination." *SEL: Studies in English Literature, 1500–1900* 47, no. 3 (2007): 641–58.

Todorov, Tzvetan. *In Defense of the Enlightenment*. Translated by Gila Walker. London: Atlantic Books, 2009.

Tunstall, Kate E. *Blindness and Enlightenment: An Essay.* New York: Continuum, 2011.

Valenza, Robin. "Editing the Self: David Hume's Narrative Theory." *Eighteenth Century: Theory and Interpretation* 43, no. 2 (2002): 137–60.

———. *Literature, Language, and the Rise of the Intellectual Disciplines in Britain, 1680–1820.* Cambridge: Cambridge University Press, 2009.

Vickers, Neil. *Coleridge and the Doctors, 1795–1806.* Oxford: Oxford University Press, 2004.

Walmsley, Peter. *Locke's* Essay *and the Rhetoric of Science.* Lewisburg, PA: Bucknell University Press, 2003.

Wheeler, Roxann. *The Complexion of Race: Categories of Difference in Eighteenth-Century British Culture.* Philadelphia: University of Pennsylvania Press, 2000.

Williamson, R. W. *The Social and Political Systems of Central Polynesia.* 3 vols. Cambridge: Cambridge University Press, 1933.

Withers, Charles W. J. *Placing the Enlightenment: Thinking Geographically about the Age of Reason.* Chicago: University of Chicago Press, 2007.

Wolfson, Susan J. *The Questioning Presence: Wordsworth, Keats, and the Interrogative Mode in Romantic Poetry.* Ithaca, NY: Cornell University Press, 1986.

———. *Romantic Interactions: Social Being and the Turns of Literary Action.* Baltimore: Johns Hopkins University Press, 2010.

Wood, James Robert. "Periodicals and the Problem of Women's Learning." In *Women's Periodicals and Print Culture in Britain, 1690–1820s: The Long Eighteenth Century,* edited by Jennie Batchelor and Manushag N. Powell, 25–39. Edinburgh: Edinburgh University Press, 2018.

———. "*Peter Bell*'s Founding Anecdote," *Notes and Queries* 64, no. 1 (2017): 97–99.

———. "William Molyneux and the Politics of Friendship." *Eighteenth-Century Ireland* 30 (2015): 9–35.

Wu, Duncan. "*Lyrical Ballads* (1798): The Beddoes Copy." *Library* 15, no. 4 (1993): 332–35.

Yousef, Nancy. *Isolated Cases: Anxieties of Autonomy in Enlightenment Philosophy and Romantic Literature.* Ithaca, NY: Cornell University Press, 2004.

Zachs, William. *David Hume, 1711–1776: Man of Letters, Scientist of Man.* Edinburgh: Lady Stair's Close, 2011.

Zaretsky, Robert, and John T. Scott. *The Philosophers' Quarrel: Rousseau, Hume, and the Limits of Human Understanding.* New Haven, CT: Yale University Press, 2009.

Index

Index

Davidson, Donald, 178
Davidson, Jenny, 23–24, 190n23
Davy, Humphry, 154
Deane, Silas, 2–3. *See also* Baker, Polly
Dear, Peter, 36
de Bolla, Peter, 193n73
deformity, 20–21, 49, 73–75
Degenaar, Marjolein, 196n20
Deleuze, Gilles, 78, 200n27; anecdote of Immanuel Kant's use of a complicated mechanism to hold his stockings up, 23; on "vital anecdotes," 22–23
Dening, Greg, 121
De Quincey, Thomas, "Last Days of Immanuel Kant," anecdote of Immanuel Kant's use of a complicated mechanism to hold his stockings up, 23
Derrida, Jacques, 5, 194n93
Deutsch, Helen, 29, 189n3, 194n87, 197n43
Dictionnaire de l'Académie française, 14–15
Diderot, Denis, 189n9; *Supplément au voyage de Bougainville*, 2
Dido and Aeneas story, 59, 197n47
disability, 117, 205n9. *See also* blindness; deformity; stammering and stuttering
D'Israeli, Issac, *A Dissertation on Anecdotes*, 8, 12, 19, 33
Dunbar, James, *Essays on the History of Mankind*, 127
Duncan, Ian, 75
Dyce, Alexander (clergyman and friend of William Wordsworth), 168

Eccentric Biography, 2. *See also* Baker, Polly
Edelstein, Dan, 191n39
Edgeworth, Maria, 18, 19; *Castle Rackrent*, 18
Edinburgh Magazine and Review, 118
Edinburgh Magazine or Literary Miscellany, "Interesting Reflections on the Life of Miss Polly Baker," 4–5, 7
education, 61, 65, 143, 186
Elliot, Gilbert, 16
Elizabeth I, queen of England, 86–88

emotion. *See* feelings
empire, 31–32, 124
empirical evidence, 21, 38, 42–43, 62, 78, 96, 157
empiricism, Gilles Deleuze on, 78, 200n27
energia, 84–85, 201n36
English Review, 123
Enlightenment, the: and anecdotes, 3, 5, 8–13, 21–25, 27–29, 34, 36, 41, 96, 105, 131, 138, 143, 178–79, 180, 183, 186; British, 3, 34; current approaches to, 8–9; intellectual and institutional approaches to, 8–10; as less than rational, 10, 31, 180–88; religious Enlightenments, 8; Scottish, 68–98, 127–36; shift toward naturalistic conceptions of the human in, 8–9, 21–22, 24
Ephesian Matron, anecdote of, 58–60, 197n43
Erskine, Thomas, sixth Earl of Kellie, 99–100
essays, 9, 34–35
Eve, 4
events: in "Anecdote for Fathers," 142; anecdotes and, 6, 173, 190n22, 194n93; Alain Badiou on, 194n85; David Hume on, 83
examples, 26–27
exceptions, 26–27
exempla, 27, 34, 59, 62
experiments, 36, 38–39, 96; at the Bristol Pneumatic Institution, 154; difficulty of performing on human beings, 58, 66; *experimentum crucis*, 118; and failure, 55; self-experiments, 56. *See also* alchemy; thought experiment

factuality, 2–3, 5–6, 52, 105, 108, 120, 128, 140–41, 163–65, 169–70, 205n5
failure, 53, 55; Samuel Taylor Coleridge and, 168, 171–72
feelings, 138, 144–46, 149, 153. *See also* pain; pleasure
Felsenstein, Frank, 60
Fenwick, Isabella, 141–42, 168–69, 176

Pocahontas, 59, 197n47

Pocock, J. G. A., 8, 86

poetry: about the *Endeavour* voyage, 119–21; David Hume on, 79–82; *Lyrical Ballads* and, 136–80; relationship to prose, 166–68, 172. *See also* verse, etymology of

Pollock, Anthony, 198n62

Poovey, Mary, 134

Porlock, person from, 171–72

Potkay, Adam, 84

Powell, Manushag N., 199n63

Pratt, Mary Louise, 111

preposterous, the (figure of speech), 91–92

Priestley, Joseph, 133

Procopius: *Anekdota seu Arcana Historia*, 13–14, 17; *Of the Buildings of Justinian*, 13; *Wars of Justinian*, 13

prose: Georg Wilhelm Friedrich Hegel on, 167–68; relationship to poetry, 166–68, 172

Proust, Marcel, 190n25

public sphere, 9, 31

Purea (highborn Tahitian woman), 119–21

Puttenham, George, *Art of English Poesy*, 88

"Queen Oberea." *See* Purea (highborn Tahitian woman)

Rabelais, 35

race: and the anecdote of the talking parrot, 50–51; Enlightenment ideas of, 204n55; John Hawkesworth on, 117; human nature as divided by, 22–23; Lord Kames on, 129; Justin Smith on, 22–23; and the *Spectator* anecdote of a tragic love triangle between slaves, 61

Ramsay, Allan (painter), 200n16

Ramsay, Michael (friend of David Hume), 85

Ray, Martha (Basil Caroline Montagu's grandmother), 142

Ray, Martha (figure in Wordsworth's "The Thorn"), 142, 150

Raynal, Guillaume-Thomas-François, 2–3, 189n9, 198n54; *Histoire philosophique et politique*, 1–2. *See also* Baker, Polly

religion: and the Enlightenment, 8; David Hume on, 92–94; in New Zealand, 115–16; in Tahiti, 110–11; the Trinity explained to Tahitians, 133

Rennie, Neil, 112, 118

repetition, 6–7, 139, 173, 190n25; in "Goody Blake and Harry Gill," 160–61; in "The Thorn," 148–51

rhetoric, 84, 88, 91, 175. *See also* apostrophe (figure of speech); preposterous, the (figure of speech)

Richardson, Samuel, *Pamela*, 76, 120

Richetti, John, 68, 84

Riskin, Jessica, 43

Robertson, William (historian), 100, 134

Roebuck, John, 16–17

Rousseau, Jean-Jacques, 74–75, 143

Rowlandson, Thomas, "The Fish Dinner," 122–23, *123*, 125

Royal Society, 36, 41, 63, 65, 101, 115–16, 121–23, 125–26, 196n16

Russell, Corrina, 149

Russell, John, 16–17

Saint Christopher Island, 60–61

St. Clair, Lieutenant General James (soldier who commissioned David Hume to be his secretary), 71

St. Kitts. *See* Saint Christopher Island

Salmond, Anne, 128, 202n20, 203–4n52

Sanctorius (physician), *Medicina Statica*, 56; frontispiece, *57*

Schaffer, Simon, 196n11, 202n8

science of human nature. *See* human nature

science of man. *See* human nature

secret history, 13–19, 38, 120

Seneca, 33

senses, the. *See* perception

sexuality: in the Polly Baker anecdote, 1–5, 7; Joseph Banks and, 120–21, 123–24; in Laurence Sterne's journal to Elizabeth Draper, 187: in Tahiti,